John Benthall

Songs of the Hebrew Poets in English Verse

John Benthall

Songs of the Hebrew Poets in English Verse

ISBN/EAN: 9783337317430

Printed in Europe, USA, Canada, Australia, Japan

Cover: Foto ©Thomas Meinert / pixelio.de

More available books at **www.hansebooks.com**

Songs

OF

The Hebrew Poets

IN ENGLISH VERSE.

BY

THE REV. JOHN BENTHALL, M.A.

VICAR OF WILLEN, BUCKS,

FORMERLY AN ASSISTANT MASTER IN WESTMINSTER SCHOOL.

SONGS ILLUSTRATING

THE LIFE OF DAVID.

The man who was raised up on high,
The anointed of the God of Jacob,
And the sweet Psalmist of Israel, said,
The Spirit of the Lord spake by me.

2 SAMUEL xxiii. 1, 2.

London:

SAMPSON LOW, MARSTON, SEARLE, & RIVINGTON,

CROWN BUILDINGS, 188, FLEET STREET.

1879.

INTRODUCTION.

THE greater number of the Songs of the Hebrews, which have been preserved, are collected in the Psalter, or Book of Psalms, which forms a large portion of the services of the Christian Church, as it once did of those of the Jewish Temple. They have evidently been arranged in Holy Scripture with a view rather to spiritual edification than to enlightenment in matters of history; but the events to which they refer, and the circumstances under which their authors poured forth their joys and sorrows before God, must be a very interesting and profitable subject of study. It has occurred to me that an attempt to arrange these and other Songs contained in the Old Testament in something like historical order may not be an unacceptable work; for it may be beyond the power of the general reader to peruse the writings of the many learned Commentators, from whose various conjectures as to the dates at which these Songs were respectively composed I have selected those which appear to me to be the most probable. I have also endeavoured to supply what I have long felt to be much wanted, viz., a literal rendering of these magnificent poems, which should retain the special characteristic of Hebrew verse, and yet satisfy the ear accustomed in poetry to the musical effect of metre and rhyme.

The peculiar feature of Hebrew verse is that in two consecutive clauses there is such a resemblance that the latter clause seems to follow from, or to be an answer to, the former. Doubtless this style of poetry arose from the early custom of a company of singers rejoicing and praising God to the sound of music, when a sentence chanted by a leader of the band would be taken up and answered by the rest. The following are a few examples, selected from Songs composed at long intervals in a period ranging from the time of Moses until after the Babylonish captivity :—

THE SONG OF MOSES.—EXODUS XV.

v. 3. Jehovah is a man of war :
Jehovah is his Name.

v. 4. Pharaoh's chariots and his host hath He
cast into the sea :
His chosen captains also are drowned in the Red Sea.

v. 5. The depths have covered them :
They sank into the bottom as a stone.

The Song of Deborah.—Judges v.

v. 3. Hear, O ye kings:
Give ear, O ye princes:
I, even I, will sing unto Jehovah:
I will sing praise to Jehovah, God of Israel.

The Song of the Women after David's Victory.—I Sam. xviii.

v. 7. Saul hath slain his thousands,
And David his ten thousands.

Isaiah i.

v. 3. The ox knoweth his owner,
And the ass his master's crib:
But Israel doth not know,
My people doth not consider.

After the Return from Babylon.—Psalm cxiv.

v. 3. The sea saw it, and fled:
Jordan was driven back.
v. 4. The mountains skipped like rams,
And the little hills like lambs.

The trammels of metre and rhyme, from which the Hebrew poetry is entirely free, must often have a weakening effect; but I have endeavoured to avoid, as much as possible, both omission and enlargement, preferring a close adherence to the text of the English Bible to a more natural and graceful flow of language, which might have been attainable in a freer translation. Where, however, the English Bible fails to interpret accurately the original meaning, I have attempted to give a more literal rendering; and I hope that I have thus sometimes succeeded in unveiling a beautiful Hebrew figure or expression, not easy to be recognized in the authorized translations, and that a verse, which in them appears wanting in meaning and poetry, may be shown to contain some striking simile. I have had the advantage of being able to consult not only the works of Bishops Lowth, Horne, and Horsley, and those of Scott, Hartwell Horne, and others, but also the more recent writings of Bishop Wordsworth, Dean Stanley, Canon Perowne, Professors Murphy and Delitzsch, Neale and Littledale, &c., besides many interesting articles in books of reference, such as Smith's Dictionary of the Bible. To all the authors mentioned above, as well as to others whom I have consulted, I am under great obligations, although I have seldom given references to their works.

It cannot be doubted that most, if not all, of the Songs of the Hebrews were handed down to the great body of the people by oral tradition, written documents being extremely rare and costly. A large proportion of them relate to the life of David, and on that account are selected to form this volume.

Among these Songs we often meet with *Part*

Songs or *Dialogues,* which may generally be discovered to be such by changes in the use of the
personal pronouns. For instance, we sometimes
find, as in Psalm civ., one singer addressing the
Almighty in the second person, while another
speaks of Him in the third. Many Psalms again,
composed in order to recall to memory past events
(e.g. Psalms xx. and xxi.), seem to partake of a
dramatic character, and to be likewise intended
for more than one voice; and in some of the
Psalms the Almighty Himself is represented as
one of the speakers. In this case I have thought
it more reverent to put the words into the mouth
of an inspired priest or prophet, who is supposed
to utter them in God's name.

The Psalter was divided by the Hebrews into
five Books, or Collections of Psalms, made at
different periods of time. The first Book contains
a Preface (Psalm i.) and forty other Psalms (viz.
ii. to xli.); the second Book contains thirty-one
Psalms (viz. xlii. to lxxii.); the third Book seventeen
(viz. lxxiii. to lxxxix.); the fourth Book also
seventeen (viz. xc. to cvi.); and the fifth Book the
remaining forty-four (viz. cvii. to cl.). There is a
great diversity of opinion with regard to the
authors of the Psalms and the dates of the several
Collections. The following conjecture appears to
me the most probable, viz. that Solomon wrote the

first Psalm as an introduction to a Collection, made during his reign, of the poems of his father; that the second and third Books contain Songs of David and of other poets, recovered or written after the death of Solomon, but not collected into Books until the reign of Hezekiah; and that the two last Books were compiled after the return from Babylon. It is important to bear in mind that, if this supposition be correct, no Psalm can have been composed by an author who lived at a later period than that of the Book in which we find it placed, although an old Song, unknown to the Compiler of an early Book, may have been discovered afterwards, and inserted in a later Book either with or without alterations.

Poems preserved by oral tradition must always be liable to many changes, and we cannot be surprised at finding that some of the Psalms appear to have received additions, and others to have been divided into two or more parts. Sometimes a Song, or a fragment of a Song, composed for one occasion, seems by these means to have been subsequently adapted to another, so that, in the same poem, we may find one part suitable to the age of David and another to that of a later period.

Again, there must often have been different versions of the same Song; for instance, Psalm liii. is the same as Psalm xiv. (Bible Version), with a slight variation, while St. Paul seems to have been

acquainted with a third version (Romans iii. vv. 10
—18), which is the one given in our Prayer Book
as Psalm xiv.

In these various ways the Psalms were altered
and collected together until the Psalter was completed and finally arranged in its present form.

My attention has been particularly drawn to
thirty-nine Psalms in which the word *Selah* is
found.   It occurs twice in the middle of a verse,
sixty-five times between two verses, and four times
at the end of a Psalm.   Of these thirty-nine
Psalms, nine are placed in the first, and two in the
fifth Book of the Psalter, and all these are ascribed
to David by their Hebrew titles.   Of the remaining
twenty-eight, seventeen are contained in the second
Book, and eleven in the third.   These two Books
(as has been already said) were probably compiled
in the reign of Hezekiah, who " commanded the
Levites to sing praise unto the Lord with the words
of David and of Asaph the seer" (2 Chron. xxix.
30).   Now it is remarkable that in the second Book,
although more than half the Psalms contained in
it are assigned to David, only one is entitled " A
Psalm of Asaph," while in the third Book these
proportions are exactly reversed.   This would lead
to the conclusion that in Hezekiah's time two
separate Collections were added to the Psalter—the
first, of Songs chiefly composed by, or having

reference to, David ; and the other, of Songs supposed to contain chiefly the words of Asaph. On further examination it seemed to me that this conjecture, especially in reference to the second Book, was in a great measure correct, although I found a difficulty in regard to some of the Psalms in it, e.g. Psalms xlvi. and lxxvi., parts of which bear internal evidence of being of later date than the time of David and Asaph. On the other hand I observed that these parts were quite distinct from the others and were divided from them by the word *Selah*.

This naturally led me to inquire into the meaning attached to this word by the various Commentators. They entertain different opinions as to its exact signification, but they all agree in thinking that it is a musical notice of some kind. The greater number suppose it to signify that particular attention is to be paid wherever it occurs, and that a pause, made for meditation, will be filled up by a musical symphony. In many cases this opinion is supported by the fact that *Selah* not only comes at the end of an emphatic passage, but that it marks the commencement of a new train of thought. Professor Murphy often draws attention to this, and I may mention Psalm xxiv. as an instance. Indeed the change here is so marked that a Commentator of no less authority than Ewald looks on the remainder of the Psalm as a separate Song.

In other cases, however, *Selah* occurs in the

middle of a connected sentence, as in Psalm lxvii. 1, which verse, although itself a paraphrase of the blessing in Numbers vi. 24—26, is so connected with the verse which follows it that a pause would weaken the effect.

Again in Psalm lv., where *Selah* is found at the end of v. 7, the sentence indeed is complete, and the figure of the Psalmist desiring to fly far away from danger like a frightened bird is complete also, for the next verse, although expressing the same desire to escape, does not carry on the figure, inasmuch as a bird, when overtaken by a storm, instead of flying far away, would seek refuge in the nearest covert. But in this instance, as in Psalm lxvii., it is apparent that, although the sentence is complete in itself, yet the same train of thought is continued in the following verse, and a lengthened pause would be quite out of place.

Hence, after a careful examination of all the Psalms in which the word *Selah* is found, the conclusion is forced upon me that the theory mentioned above, viz. that a pause was to be made where this word occurs, cannot be sustained.

Is there no other explanation which would be applicable to every instance?

After much consideration I have been led to believe that *the thirty-nine Selah Psalms are all composite poems, made up of short Songs or fragments of Songs, and that, as entire Psalms, they were generally applied to occasions different from those for which the several component parts were originally written.* The word *Selah* would then be introduced at the point where the junction occurs, but would not denote (as in many cases it certainly does not denote) that the particular place especially calls for serious attention.

My reasons for this conclusion will be best explained by an examination of a few *Selah* passages selected by way of illustration.

Let us take first those instances to which reference has already been made.

It has been mentioned that in *Psalm xxiv. v.* 6, the change of subject is so complete that Professor Ewald looks on the remainder of the Psalm *as a separate Song.*

In the cases of *Psalms lxvii.* and *lv.,* where it has been pointed out that the same train of thought is continued after the *Selah* (although the simile in the latter case is not kept up), this would be a natural result on the supposition that two separate Songs, or fragments of Songs, distinct from each other but cognate in subject, were joined together.

Take next *Psalm lxviii.* This Psalm has generally been supposed to be one entire Song, relating to the removal of the Ark to Mount Zion ; but it appears to me to consist of several distinct Songs, or fragments of Songs, sung at various stages of the procession. The word *Selah* seems, by a clerical error, to have been placed in the middle of a sentence at the end of v. 7, instead of at the end of v. 6. If this mistake were corrected, the Psalm would consist of four Songs divided from each other by the musical notice, viz. vv. 1—6, 7—19, 20—32, and 33—35.

The first portion (1—6) commences with the words used when the Ark set forward in the wilderness (Numbers x. 35), and then goes on in words which, literally translated, would call upon the procession to prepare a highway for Jehovah. All this portion would probably have been sung at starting.

The next portion (7—19) begins with the opening of the Song of Deborah (Judges v. 4), and appears to have been sung as the procession marched up the hill of Zion.

The third portion (20—32) would be extremely applicable to the return down the hill, after the Ark had been placed in the Tabernacle. It relates the order of the march, and alludes to the doings in the Sanctuary.

The beginning and conclusion of these two parts (7—19 and 20—32) afford internal evidence of their being distinct, although corresponding, Songs.

The last portion of the Psalm (33—35) contains an expression very similar to that in the last portion of the first division, (viz. 4—6) ; but, although in our Bible version the words in v. 4. "that rideth upon the heavens" are almost identical with those in v. 33, "that rideth upon the heavens of heavens," the meaning of the two passages is so different in the original that they are probably fragments of separate poems. For in the Hebrew v. 4 represents the Almighty as riding along the sandy steppes of the desert, while His people are called on to cast up a highway for Him (a simile which is also employed in Isaiah xl 3 and lvii. 14 and which is very suitable to the setting out of the Ark), whereas in v. 33 God is represented as enthroned in the Heavens.

Psalm lxviii. is generally admitted to be very difficult to be explained, but if my view—that it is composed of several distinct Songs—is adopted, the meaning becomes much less obscure.

Let us now turn to *Psalm lxxxviii.* This Psalm is so unvarying in its tone of misery, and so full of repetitions of the same cries of woe, that at first sight it might appear to be one continuous poem. A closer examination, however, leads me to a different conclusion. Many of its most pathetic expressions, or very similar ones, are found in other Psalms (e. g. in Psalms vi., xxviii., and xxxi.) ; but in all these the author, however mournfully he may commence, seems to gather consolation from communion with God, and concludes in a more hopeful strain. Psalm lxxxviii., on the contrary, contains nothing but despair, and is one unbroken wail of misery.

Now how can this be accounted for? If my theory in regard to the word *Selah* is correct, the explanation would be that, whereas the other Psalms (in which no *Selah* is found) are continuous and complete Songs, Psalm lxxxviii. is composed of three fragments of separate poems, joined together where the *Selah* mark occurs. One at least of these fragments seems to have been composed by Heman, and they were probably combined in order to frame a Psalm suitable to some well-known period of sickness or other calamity, coming directly from the hand of God, which I have imagined to be the pestilence recorded in 2 Sam. xxiv. and 1 Chron. xxi.

Here again it may be observed that the *Selahs* are found at places to which there seems to be no particular reason for calling special attention, and where there is no change of sentiment. On the contrary, in v. 11 the substance of the previous verse is repeated, although in a different form.

My theory in regard to the word *Selah* seems to be still further corroborated by *Psalms lvii.* and *lx.*, each of which contains a portion of Psalm cviii.

This last-mentioned Psalm has no *Selah* in it, and is, therefore, probably one continuous and complete Song. It is, however, remarkable that, although it is assigned to David and is generally supposed to have commemorated his victory in the Valley of Salt recorded in 2 Sam. viii., and

although separate portions of it appear in the
second Book of the Psalter as parts of Psalms lvii.
and lx., yet it is not placed earlier than in the
fourth Book as an entire Song. Its omission from
the second Book as a continuous Song shows that,
although it may have been composed by David in
that form, it was not known to be a complete
Psalm by the Compiler in the reign of Hezekiah,
but was one of those recovered after the return
from Babylon and collected in the fourth Book.
The two parts of which it is composed appear to
have been known in Hezekiah's time as two distinct Songs, or fragments of Songs, and as such to
have been added, respectively, to the earlier portions of Psalms lvii. and lx., the *Selah* mark being
placed to denote the additions.

Independently, however, of the fact that Psalms
lvii. and lx. contain the very words found in another
Psalm, there is in each of them internal evidence of
its being a composite Song.

Take first *Psalm lvii.* Bishop Horsley describes
it as follows :—" It begins in a plaintive strain, im-
ploring aid and expressing deep distress and ex-
treme danger ; when suddenly in v. 7, in the sure
prospect of the Divine assistance, the stanza is
changed to notes of praise and triumph as over an
enemy already fallen."

So sudden a revulsion of feeling in a continuous
short poem appears very unnatural, and incon-

sistent with the title, which assigns it to "David when he fled from Saul in the cave." It is true, as Canon Perowne remarks, that sudden transitions from despondency to triumph are very common in the Psalms, but they may almost always be explained by a careful examination of the passages in which they occur. In the *Selah* Psalms such changes would be accounted for by the composite character of those poems. Thus Psalm lvii., which we are now considering, is, according to my view, composed of three distinct fragments, linked together by the Compiler in order to form a consecutive history of the various feelings which must have been aroused in David's heart by his adventure in the cave. The first of these fragments expresses his alarm at the approach of Saul's army ; the second describes his hopes on perceiving the king coming without any attendants towards the cavern in which he and his companions are concealed ; while the last is a Song of praise suitable to the morning which followed the escape of the party, after David had cut off the skirt of the royal garment.

Psalm lx. also appears to be a composite Song, for if the *Selah* notice had been intended to call particular attention to the passage in which it occurs, or to point to the introduction of a new sentiment only, it would surely have been found, not at the end of verse 4, but at that of verse 5,

before the words "God hath spoken in His holiness;" but if, as has been already explained, the
second part of the Psalm is a fragment of Psalm
cviii. and *Selah* marks its commencement, the
musical notice is in its right place.

The Psalm also bears other internal evidence of
being made up of separate Songs. It is assigned
by the Hebrew title to the victory of Joab over
Edom in the Valley of Salt. Now the only
accounts of a victory during the reign of David
over the Edomites and their allies in the Valley of
Salt are found in 2 Sam. viii. 13 and 1 Chron. xviii.
12. These two passages, though differing in some
important particulars, are supposed to refer to the
same event, but neither of them agrees with the
title of the Psalm.

Two other victories in the Valley of Salt over
the same allied armies are recorded as having
taken place at later periods, the first in the reign
of Jehoshaphat (2 Chron. xx.), and the other in
the reign of Amaziah (2 Chron. xxv.). Now we
learn from 2 Chron. xx. that there was a great
panic in the kingdom of Judah when the news
arrived of the advance of the confederate army,
and the first part of Psalm lx. seems very suitable
to the prayer of Jehoshaphat in his distress.
Bishop Horsley indeed supposes that the whole
Psalm, although assigned to the reign of David,
refers to this later invasion; but to me it seems

more probable, that, although very appropriate to
the alarm felt in the time of Jehoshaphat, the first
part was really composed in reference to the invasion in David's reign (2 Sam. viii. 5), and that
afterwards, in the reign of Hezekiah, the latter
part of Psalm cviii. was added to it, with the *Selah*
mark and the present doubtful title, in order to
form a hymn for the Temple service.

I have already mentioned that there are four
Psalms (viz. *iii.*, *ix.*, *xxiv.*, and *xlvi.*) in which the
word *Selah* is found at the end of the last verse.
This might at first sight appear to militate against
my theory that *Selah* is always intended to denote
the place where two distinct Songs or fragments
are joined together.   On further examination,
however, it will, I think, prove a strong argument
in its favour.   I had already observed that Psalm iii.
was probably the commencement of the devotions
of the Hebrews both in public and private, and
that Psalms xxiv. and xlvi. were processional
hymns, when I found the following note on
Psalm iii. v. 4 in Bishop Wordsworth's Commen-
tary.   Alluding to the word *Selah* (here first
introduced in the Psalms) he says,—"It never
occurs at the end of a Psalm, except in Psalms
which are coupled to the following ones, as
Psalms iii., xxiv., and xlvi., which were festival
hymns succeeded by others."   In regard to
Psalm ix.—in the Septuagint, the Vulgate, and

some other versions, Psalms ix. and x. are linked together so as to form one poem. Thus in all these cases we may suppose that *Selah* was the mark of transition placed between two distinct Songs which were used continuously in the same service.

My view of the meaning of this mysterious word will also often reconcile the conflicting opinions of Commentators of high standing in regard to the probable dates of the various Psalms (especially of those contained in the second and third Books of the Psalter). For example, Psalm xlvi. is assigned by

Professor Murphy	to the age of	David,
„ Delitzsch	„	Jehoshaphat,
Bishop Wordsworth	„	Hezekiah,
Canon Perowne	„	Hezekiah.

But if this Psalm consists of three distinct and separate Songs, I should agree with Murphy so far as to assign the first and last Songs to the time of David, with Delitzsch so far as to think that these two Songs were united and sung as one in the reign of Jehoshaphat, and with Wordsworth and Perowne in supposing that the middle part was inserted and that the Psalm was sung as a whole in the time of Hezekiah, after the defeat of Sennacherib.

It has already been mentioned that all the *Selah* Psalms in the first and fifth Books of the Psalter,

as well as many of those in the other Books, are
by their Hebrew titles ascribed to David. The
rule in regard to the ascriptions seems to have
been as follows :—When all the component parts
of a *Selah* Psalm were *believed* by the Compiler
(whether rightly or wrongly) to have been written
by David, or Asaph, or any other poet, the Psalm
was ascribed to its supposed author (e. g. Psalms l.,
lii., liv., lx., lxxxviii., &c.); but if part of a *Selah*
Psalm was *believed* to have been composed by one
person and part by another, no name was prefixed
to indicate the writer (e. g. Psalms xlvi., xlvii.,
xlviii.).

The *Selah* Psalms thus unascribed in the second
and third Books are all addressed to "the Chief
Musician," or "the sons of Korah," or "the Chief
Musician for the sons of Korah;" and, as it
appears to have been a common practice of David
so to address his Psalms, it seems fair to presume
that parts of these unascribed *Selah* Songs were
composed by him.

By detaching the various portions of the *Selah*
Psalms and restoring to them the distinct form
which (if my view be correct) they originally pos-
sessed, the number of Scriptural Songs is greatly
enlarged ; and by comparing them carefully with
the history of David, as related in the Books of
Samuel, 1 Chronicles, and 1 Kings, I find that to

almost every recorded event in his chequered career some poem, either complete or fragmentary, appears to be more or less appropriate.

I have assumed that all the Psalms ascribed by their Biblical prefixes to David were written by him, and I have placed those of which the particular occasions are mentioned according to their Hebrew titles. I have also assumed that, with few exceptions, some portion at least of each *Selah* Psalm was probably composed in David's time, and these detached portions are applied to the events with reference to which they may be supposed to have been written. These events are not generally the same as those to illustrate which the Compiler at a later period combined their component parts.

In order to avoid repetition a *Selah* portion has always been rendered by me in a different metre from that of the complete Psalm.

The fifteen Psalms entitled in our Bible "Songs of degrees" are generally supposed to be ancient poems sung, either in their original form or in one somewhat altered, after the return from Babylon, by the pilgrims to the yearly festivals at Jerusalem. I have, therefore, made use of such as seemed to me to be applicable to the history of David.

It would be most presumptuous in me to say that all, or even any, of these Songs were actually composed for the occasions to which I have taken

upon myself to assign them ; but, in attempting to
connect the Psalms with events recorded in the
historical portions of Scripture, I have only followed
the example of the most pious and learned Commentators, and indeed in most cases have been
guided by their conjectures.

It is remarkable that in the first, fourth, and fifth
Books of the Psalter, which include many Psalms
of David, the Almighty is almost invariably designated as " Jehovah," whereas in the second and
third Books, which, although compiled by the
Levites in the reign of Hezekiah, consist chiefly
of Psalms assigned to David and Asaph (see *ante*,
page ix), He is seldom spoken of otherwise than
as " God."   It seems not unreasonable to suppose
that the Levites changed the word " Jehovah " into
" God " (a Name more commonly used in their
time), as we know they did in the case of Psalm
liii., which was a later version of Psalm xiv.
However this may have been, it is not generally
considered that the date at which a Psalm was
composed can be determined with any certainty
from the use in it of either the one or the other of
these appellations.   Still I have thought it best to
follow the Hebrew text in regard to the employ-
ment of the words "Lord," "God," and "Jehovah,"
which last is the "LORD" of the English Bible.

It has not been my province in this collection of Songs to point out how far many of them are prophetical, nor indeed to assume the duties of a Commentator. My object has been to show that these Songs may be so arranged as to illustrate the life of David from his anointing by Samuel to his death, and that they give a faithful picture of his character. That character was very far from perfect. David was unrivalled as a poet, but, living in a barbarous age, he sometimes uses language which to us appears painful and difficult to be understood. Yet there is throughout all his Songs such a spirit of ardent piety, such an unwavering dependence on the loving care of the Almighty, that, whether he invokes blessings on his friends or curses on his enemies, we still feel that God is in all his thoughts. It is this which is the great charm of his writings ; it is this which enables us to read these glorious Songs with delight in the time of joy and with comfort in the hour of sorrow, and which never fails to increase their value the more that they are studied.

CONTENTS.

—————◆—————

NOTE.—For *Lord* read *LORD*, in pages 1, 6, 28, 36, 81, 83, 95.

ERRATUM.

The reference to the Introduction in the Prefaces to the Songs must be carried two pages forward in every instance.

THE LIFE OF DAVID.

THE asterisk (*) before a line in the songs signifies some noticeable departure from the sense of the Bible or Prayer-book version, in order to give a more literal rendering. It is not generally affixed at merely slight deviations from the authorized translations, such as changes of person, number, tense, &c., although, with a few unavoidable exceptions, such changes are not made without the authority of modern translators and commentators of high standing.

I SAMUEL XVI.

Song i.

" The Spirit of the Lord came upon David from that day forward."—v. 13.

THE history of David commences with the visit of Samuel to Bethlehem, to anoint one of Jesse's sons to be the future king of Israel. The ostensible reason of the prophet's coming was to preside at an annual sacrificial feast, at which it appears that Jesse, as the greatest man of the place, with his family, usually took the lead (v. 5; also chap. xx. 6).

It is not clear to what extent Samuel explained his object in desiring Jesse to present to him in turn his seven tall and goodly sons, for we learn from verse 2 that, for the safety of Samuel, and probably of David himself,

B

the transaction was to be kept secret. Possibly, even when the anointing oil was poured forth, those most deeply interested did not yet understand its full meaning. It was plain, however, that the simple lad, to whom were allotted the humblest duties, and whom no one had even thought of summoning to the sacrifice, was henceforth the chosen of the Almighty to some high and holy office.

No feeling of pride appears to have entered the young shepherd's heart. He returned to his peaceful occupation, sweetened as it was by his wonderful talent for music and poetry. But from this time his songs were to assume a new character. Filled with joy and reverential awe by the consciousness of the Divine influence within him, he would sing the praises of Jehovah in such strains as those of Psalm viii., which may have been composed on some bright cloudless night, with his father's sheep around him.

In verse 2, alluding to his recent call, the youth seems lost in admiration of the ways of God, who had " founded " (or stablished) strength from a source which he compares in its weakness to an infant's wail.

Gazing on the glories of the visible heavens, he rejoices that their Creator is the God of Israel, to whom He has revealed Himself by His own most holy Name, and with adoring rapture the song begins and ends : " How excellent is Thy Name, Jehovah *our* Lord ! "

PSALM VIII.

JEHOVAH, Thou our Lord, Thy Name
How excellent ! how high !
Thou Who in earth hast set Thy fame,
In Heaven Thy majesty.

2 Strength is from infants' mouths ordained
  *And stablished by Thy will,
That the avenger be restrained,
  That Thou the foe may'st still.

3 Jehovah, when Thy heavens I see,
  Created by Thine hand,
The moon and stars ordained by Thee
  To shine on every land :

4 Oh ! what is man that in Thy mind
  He should obtain a place ?
Or son of man, that he should find
  With Thee such wondrous grace ?

5 Than angels little lower made,
  With glory crowned by Thee,
6 Thou at his feet Thy works hast laid,
  Beneath his rule to be,—

7 Beasts of the field, the flocks of sheep,
8   Oxen, the fowls of air,
Fishes that dwell within the deep,
  Whatever moveth there.

9 Jehovah, Israel's God and Lord,
  How excellent Thy Name !
In all the earth Thou art adored,
  Thy praise Thy works proclaim.

Song ii.

Psalm viii., being apparently a midnight composition, is naturally succeeded by the first part of Psalm xix., which may have been suggested to David's mind by the splendour of a morning sky. When, however, the sun arises to illuminate the whole world, the Psalmist no longer uses the name by which Jehovah had specially revealed Himself to His peculiar people, but that title by which the great Creator is universally worshipped.

May not David thus unconsciously allude to that Sun of Righteousness who was to arise with healing in His wings, and to be not only the glory of Israel, but a light to the Gentiles also? (Mal. iv. 2; Isa. xlix. 6.) It is remarkable that, in the *second* part of this Psalm, which is written in praise of the law of Moses, as Israel's law, David no longer uses the general name of God, but returns to the more limited title of Jehovah. This leads to the conclusion that the second part was a later composition, joined to the other by David himself.

PSALM XIX. 1—6.

THE heavens declare God's boundless praise,
    The firmament His work displays;
2 Day unto day doth utter speech,
  And night to night doth knowledge teach;
3 No sound is there, no uttered word,
  No language in their voice is heard;

4 Yet hath their line reached earth's far end,
  And through the world their words extend.
  From his pavilion there the sun
  Sets forth at morn his course to run,
5 Joyful as bridegroom from his bride,
  Or racer in his strength and pride.
6 He goeth forth from heaven's far bound ;
  From end to end his path is found ;
  To all his circuit is revealed,
  Nor from his heat is aught concealed.

Song iii.

" Prudent in matters . . . . and the Lord is with him."—v. 18.

The word "prudent" is generally employed in the
Bible in a higher sense than that in which we are accustomed to use it ; and we may look on Psalm cxxxix. as a
specimen of those communings with God and his own
heart on the lonely plains of Bethlehem which, aided by
the Holy Spirit's influence, filled the shepherd-lad with
wisdom far beyond his years.

This Divine song possesses a depth and spirituality
more in harmony with a solitary life than with the stirring
events of a court or camp, traces of which we find in
most of David's later compositions.   Perhaps the latter
part of the Psalm may have been added after the conquest of Goliath, verses 19—22 referring to David's
indignation at the blasphemous language of the giant,
and verses 23 and 24 to his conscious integrity when
reproached by his brother Eliab for pride and naughtiness
of heart.

PSALM CXXXIX.

JEHOVAH, Thou hast searchèd me ;
    2 When down I sit, when up I rise,
    All that I do is known to Thee ;
       Thine eye my thoughts far off descries.
  3 Thou dost my path and bed surround,
    And all my ways to Thee are clear ;
  4 For on my tongue no word is found
    But Thou, Jehovah, dost it hear.

5 Behind, before me Thou art nigh,
   And hast upon me laid Thine hand ;
6 Such knowledge is for me too high ;
   Such things I cannot understand.

7 From Thee O whither shall I go ?
   Where from Thy Spirit shall I hide ?
 What place doth not Thy Presence know
   Where doth Jehovah not abide ?
8 If up to heaven my flight I take,
   The heavens Thy Presence always share ;
 And if in hell my bed I make,
   Thou still art with me—Thou art there.
9 If I should seek the utmost sea,
   Borne on the wings of dawning day,
10 E'en there Thine hand my guide shall be,
   Thy right hand hold shall on me lay.
11 "In darkness I will take my flight,"
   (Thus peradventure I may say),
 "I shall be covered by the night,"
   Then shall my night be turned to day.
12 Yea, darkness hideth not from Thee ;
   It shineth clearly as the sun ;
 The night to Thee as day shall be ;
   Darkness and light to Thee are one.

13 My reins are Thine, are Thine alone ;
   When in my mother's womb I slept
 To Thee were all my members known ;
   By Thee I was in safety kept.
14 Thee, O Jehovah, I will praise ;
   For I am wonderfully made ;
 That wondrous are Thy works and ways
   Is clearly to my soul displayed.

15 My bones were not concealed from Thee,
    Beneath the earth though they were framed;
16 Thou didst mine unformed substance see;
    My members in Thy book were named;
    Yea, surely they were written there;
    Fashioned by Thee was every one,
    (And daily grew beneath Thy care,)
    E'en while as yet of them was none.
17 O God, when on Thy thoughts I dwell,
    How precious are those thoughts to me!
18 The sand in number they excel;
    I wake, and I am still with Thee.

19 Surely the wicked shall be slain!
    Ye bloodthirsty, from me away.
20 * Thy foes against Thee rise in vain;
    * In vain they plots against Thee lay.
21 Hate I not them who hate Thee dare?
    And grieve when they against Thee rise?
22 To them I perfect hatred bear,
    I count them as mine enemies.
23 Search me, O God, and know my heart;
    Try me; my thoughts before Thee lay;
24 See if my feet to sin depart,
    And lead me in the living way.

Song ib.

"It came to pass when the evil spirit from God was upon Saul, that David took an harp and played with his hand; so Saul was refreshed, and was well, and the evil spirit departed from him."—v. 23.

Beneath the Divine displeasure Saul was afflicted with a mental malady, described in Scripture as an evil spirit from the Lord. Music being found beneficial during the paroxysms, his servants suggested that an accomplished player on the harp should be found, to be in attendance on the king. David was proposed, as tradition says, by Doeg, who, having the superintendence of the royal herds, may have met with him when making his rounds. Although no mention is made of song, we cannot doubt that the king delighted in the additional charm of the young minstrel's voice, and no words could have been better suited to the required object than those of Psalm ciii., which have been a solace to the distressed, both in mind and body, in every subsequent age.

· The Syriac Psalter refers this psalm to David's last illness, and the fervent gratitude and piety which breathes in every line render it very probable that it was repeated by him on his death-bed.

PSALM CIII.

THOU, my soul, Jehovah bless,
　　My soul, and all that dwells in me ;
2 Think of His mercies numberless,
Forget not all He doth for thee.

3 Who doth forgive thee all thy sin ;
   By Whom thy sicknesses are healed ;
4 Who from the grave thy life doth win ;
   His tender love thy crown and shield.
5 Thy mouth with blessings ever new
   Whose gracious hand doth satisfy ;
   Thy youth with strength Who doth endue,
   Yea, with the eagle's strength supply.

6 Jehovah righteousness displays ;
   The oppressed by Him upheld have been ;
7 To Moses He made known His ways ;
   By Israel's sons His acts were seen.
8 Great mercy doth Jehovah show ;
   He gracious is, of tender love,
   Of suffering long, to anger slow,
   Plenteous in mercy from above.
9 He will not us for ever chide,
   Nor alway His displeasure keep ;
10 He oft His wrath hath turned aside,
   Nor let our sins due vengeance reap.

11 For as the heaven o'er earth is high,
   To them who fear Him is His love ;
12 Far as the east from west doth lie,
   He doth our sins from us remove.
13 To them that fear Him greater far
   Than father's pitying love is His ;
14 Jehovah knows that dust we are,
   Well known to Him our frailty is.
15 The days of man are as the grass,
   Himself a flower that decks the plain ;
16 Gone as the wind doth onward pass,
   Its place shall know it not again.

17 But yet Jehovah's loving grace
    To endless ages doth endure ;
To all who fear Him, and their race,
    His mercy still remaineth sure.
18 To such as on Him humbly wait,
    Nor dare from His commandments stray,
Who on His statutes meditate,
    And love His precepts to obey.
19 Jehovah hath in Heaven His throne,
    And there His seat hath ready made ;
His is the kingdom, His alone ;
    By all His rule shall be obeyed.

20 Bless ye Jehovah, ye who dwell
    With Him, and hearken to His voice,
Ye who in strength and power excel,
    Ye to obey Him who rejoice.
21 Bless ye Jehovah, ye on high,
    His Hosts, who in His presence stand ;
Bless Him, His ministers who fly,
    With speed fulfilling His command.
22 Bless ye Jehovah, bless His Name,
    Where'er His laws the worlds control ;
Ye works of His, His praise proclaim ;
    Bless thou Jehovah, O my soul.

Song b.

" David went and returned from Saul to feed his father's sheep at Bethlehem."—v. 15.

Psalm civ. is one of those appointed for the Sabbath, and belongs to a series to which the word Hallelujah was attached. It seems to have been composed as a companion to the preceding Psalm. They begin and end with the same words; and while one dwells on the goodness of the Almighty Father, the other describes the wonders of the great Creator. In each, as he approaches the conclusion of his song, the poet's thoughts seem to wander from the subjects on which he has been dwelling to those which form the groundwork of the other Psalm. There is, however, a remarkable difference in their structure; for in Psalm civ. one singer always addresses God in the second person, while the other always speaks of Him in the third, an arrangement not followed in ciii. Psalm civ. has been assigned to the age of Moses, the reign of Solomon, and other periods; but its companion form points to the conclusion of those commentators who think that it was composed by David about the same time as ciii.; and its numerous allusions to country scenes appear in character with his return to shepherd life.

Psalm civ.

First Voice.

THOU, my soul, Jehovah bless.
   My God, Thou art in glory high ;
What tongue Thy greatness can express
   Whom honour clothes and majesty !
2 Who coverest Thyself with light
   Around Thee as a garment shed,
And Who the heavens in splendour bright
   Dost like a mighty curtain spread.

Second Voice.

3 A place Who in the waters finds
   Whereon His chambers' beams may lie ;
Who walks upon the wings of winds,
   His chariot makes the clouds that fly ;
4 *Who winds His messengers hath made,
   *His ministers of fiery flame ;
5 Who hath the earth's foundations laid,
   And fixed immovably its frame.

First Voice.

6 To cover it, the flowing tide
   A garment formed at Thy command ;
Thou mad'st its robe the ocean wide,
   The waters o'er the hills to stand.

7 They heard Thy thunder's voice and fled;
8   They rise above the mountains' crest;
  Then fall to their appointed bed,
    And in the valleys sink to rest.
9 Their settled bound from Thee they learn,
    Which never may their waves pass o'er;
  They are forbidden to return;
    Their floods shall cover earth no more.

Second Voice.

10 He sendeth in their courses springs,
    Whose waters from the mountains flow,
  And these He to the valleys brings,
    That run among the hills below.
11 Beasts of the field to drink are there;
    And there their thirst wild asses slake;
12 Beside them dwell the fowls of air,
    And in the boughs glad concert make.
13 He from His chambers in the sky
    Sends rain to water every hill;
  His works all creatures satisfy;
    Their fruits the earth with goodness fill.
14 Grass for the cattle in the field
    He makes abundantly to spring,
  And herb for man the ground to yield,
    That food He from the earth may bring.
15 Yea, plenteously it brings forth wine,
    Which gladness doth to man impart;
  And oil, that makes his face to shine;
    And bread, that strengtheneth his heart.

16 With sap the cedar-trees are filled
    On Lebanon, His handiwork;
17 In them the birds delight to build,
    And in the fir-trees dwells the stork.
18 The goats find refuge in the hills;
    The conies in the rocks abound;
19 The moon her monthly course fulfils;
    The sun performs his daily round.

First Voice.

20 Thou makest night succeed to day,
    When creep from out their dark retreat
21 Wild beasts, and, roaring for their prey,
    Young lions seek from God their meat.
22 The sun ariseth in his might
    With beams of day the morn to crown;
They haste together from his light,
    And in their dens they lay them down.
23 Man, going forth upon his way,
    The labour of his hands renews;
And, till the evening's fading ray,
    He his appointed work pursues.
24 Jehovah, O how manifold
    Are all Thy works, in wisdom made;
The riches of the earth untold
    Are Thine, and are by Thee displayed.
25 The ocean, great and wide, Thy care
    A home for countless creatures makes;
26 There go the stately ships; and there
    Leviathan his pastime takes.

27 These all upon Thee waiting rest,
    That Thou may'st give them timely food ;
28 And when Thine hand Thou openest,
    They all are satisfied with good.
29 Thy face Thou hidest, and dismay
    And troubles on them multiply ;
When Thou dost take their breath away,
    Returning to their dust, they die.
30 Again Thy quickening breath doth raise
    New life and freshness to the earth ;
Beauty again her face displays,
    Renewed, as by a second birth.

Second Voice.

31 Jehovah's glory fast shall stand ;
    To everlasting it shall be ;
The works of His almighty hand
    Jehovah shall rejoicing see.
32 The earth with dread His presence fills,
    Beneath His eye it trembling lies ;
And if He do but touch the hills,
    Thick clouds of smoke are seen to rise.

First Voice.

33 My song Jehovah's praise shall tell ;
    Long as I live shall rise my voice ;
34 Sweet shall it be on Him to dwell ;
    I in Jehovah will rejoice.
35 All those who walk in wickedness
    Shall perish in their evil ways ;
But Thou, my soul, Jehovah bless ;
    Ascribe ye to Jehovah praise.

Song bi.

" So David prevailed over the Philistine with a sling and with a stone."—v. 50.

It is uncertain how much time elapsed between David's departure from the Court and the outbreak of the war mentioned in this Chapter, when David was sent to carry provisions to his brothers in the camp near the valley of Elah.

Both Hebrews and Christians have been familiar from their childhood with the account of the combat between David and the giant which took place there, and some songs must surely have been written to celebrate the young shepherd's victory; yet there is no Psalm which is peculiarly appropriate to it.

Ewald and others have supposed that the song assigned to Hannah (1 Sam. ii.) was really composed by David in reference to this conquest; and its triumphant tone is certainly more in unison with the feelings of a youthful conqueror than with the overflowing gratitude of a gentle and much-enduring woman, while the allusion to the king, near the end, is unsuitable to the time of Hannah.

For these reasons I think that this song, by whomsoever written, may be introduced here as applicable to the history of David.

1 SAMUEL II. 1—10.

 IN Jehovah do rejoice ;
　　My horn in Him is lifted high ;
　In Thy salvation glad, my voice
　·· Doth glory o'er mine enemy :
2 Jehovah is the Holy One ;
　No rock like God ; beside Thee none.

3 No more your pride in boasting show ;
    No longer arrogance display ;
Jehovah every thought doth know ;
    Our God doth every action weigh.
4 The bows are broken of the strong ;
Now to the weak doth strength belong.

5 The rich are hungry and forlorn ;
    The poor for bread have ceased to moan ;
Now to the barren seven are born ;
    She that hath sons is feeble grown.
6 Jehovah slays, gives life again,
Brings to the grave, brings back the slain.

7 Jehovah poor and rich doth make ;
    He lifteth up, and low He lays ;
8 The poor from out the dust doth take,
    The beggar from the dunghill raise,
To make them among princes known,
And set them on a glorious throne.

The pillars of the earth are His,
    And He on them the world hath set ;
9 Guide of His saints Jehovah is ;
    To keep them He will ne'er forget :
In silent death shall sinners fail,
For by his strength shall none prevail.

10 Broken in pieces shall be those
    Who rise against Jehovah's might ;
He shall send thunder on His foes,
    In earth's far ends give judgment right,
With strength endue His chosen king,
To honour His anointed bring.

Song vii.

" And the men of Israel and of Judah arose, and shouted, and pursued the Philistines until thou come to the valley, and to the gates of Ekron."—v. 52.

The overthrow of their champion filled the army of the Philistines with dismay; the panic was complete, and the soldiers fled in the utmost disorder to seek for safety within the walls of their fortified towns. On the other hand, the courage of the Israelites was thoroughly restored, and they pursued their flying enemies to the very gates of Gath and Ekron. The following song may not improbably have been composed by David in remembrance of this glorious day.

PSALM XLIV. 1—8.

Soldiers.

GOD, Thy servants have been taught,
Our fathers in our ears have told,
The works which Thou for them hast
wrought,
Thy wonders in the days of old :

2 How Thou their foes didst dispossess,
Drive out the heathen with Thine hand,
Didst plant them in, their foes distress,
* That they might spread throughout the
land.

3 Their sword made not the nations yield,
    Nor theirs the might that victory gave ;
Vain was their strength on battle-field,
    Helpless their arm from death to save :

But Thy right hand, Thine arm of might,
    Their enemies did overthrow,
And of Thy countenance the light,
    Because Thou didst them favour show.

David.

4 Thou art my King, O God, command
    Deliverances for Jacob's race ;
5 Through Thee we conquerors shall stand ;
    Our feet we on the foe shall place :

6 For I confide not in my bow,
    My sword shall not the victory claim ;
7 Nay, Thou hast saved us from the foe,
    And put our enemies to shame.

David and Soldiers.

8 In God we boast ; a joyful song
    To God Who helpeth us we raise :
In God we triumph all day long ;
    .Thy Name, O God, we ever praise.

Song viii.

" David took the head of the Philistine, and brought it to Jerusalem."—v. 54.

Thus ends the history of David's conquest of Goliath, and, as we learn from Joshua xv. 63 and Judges i. 21 that (although the Jebusites still held the citadel) the town of Jerusalem was inhabited by portions of David's own tribe of Judah and of the royal tribe of Benjamin, it was a fitting place in which to deposit the head of the slain giant as a trophy. It is, however, possible that Jerusalem may here mean the neighbouring sanctuary of Nob.

This, being the termination of David's shepherd-life, is a suitable place in which to introduce the following song, though its style is totally unlike that of David. The Psalter is closed in the Septuagint version by a Psalm numbered cli., with the title:—"This is a Psalm of . David's own writing, and outside the number, when he fought the single combat with Goliath."

Psalm cli.

WITHIN my father's house the one
  Of least account, the youngest son,
  My lot it was my father's sheep
Upon the mountain-side to keep.
A harp my fingers fashioned there;
A psaltery did my hands prepare.

How shall it reach Jehovah's ear?
He is Jehovah; He doth hear.

Called by His messenger from toil,
I was anointed with His oil :
My brethren fair, of stature high,
Grace found not in Jehovah's eye.

'Twas mine undaunted forth to go
To meet the proud Philistine foe.
I met him on the battle-plain ;
He cursed me by his idols vain.

Lo, victor in the unequal fight,
My hand drew forth his sword of might ;
His head I severed.   On that day
I took our Israel's shame away.

I SAMUEL XVIII.

Song ix.

" The soul of Jonathan was knit with the soul of David, and Jonathan loved him as his own soul."—v. 1.

Saul was so delighted with the overthrow of the giant and the defeat of the Philistines that he insisted on retaining the conqueror at court, and placing him in immediate attendance on his own person. In this situation David rapidly acquired the esteem and affection of the king's eldest son, and their mutual love is one of the most pleasing incidents related in the Hebrew Scriptures. There must have been something peculiarly attractive in David to secure so immediately the affection of the heir of the throne—a valiant soldier, many years his superior in age. Psalm cxxxiii. is an exquisite little song, which is possibly a memorial of their friendship. It is the first that I have quoted of those fifteen Psalms called in our Bible "Songs of degrees," which were probably contained in some ancient book of hymns.

PSALM CXXXIII.

BEHOLD, how good it is and sweet,
　　Yea, full of pure delight !
In bonds of love when brethren meet,
　　In peace unite.

2 Sweet as the oil on Aaron's head,
    Whose streams of fragrance rare
Flowed down his beard to overspread,
    And garments fair.

3 On Hermon's top, on Zion's sides,
    As gently falls the dew,
There with Jehovah's love abides
    Life ever new.

Song x.

" It came to pass as they came, when David was returned from the slaughter of the Philistine, that the women came out of all cities of Israel, singing and dancing to meet king Saul."—v. 6.

Saul had no intention of allowing David to become a mere idler about the court. In order to make use of his military talents he gave him an appointment in the army, and sent him on various occasions against the enemy. In these expeditions David's fame became such, that he was regarded as a greater conqueror than the valiant king himself, as we learn from the following song of the women.

1 SAMUEL XVIII. 7.

Women.

SAUL hath, with uplifted spear,
    Stretched his thousands on the plain !

Women answering.

David's deeds let Israel hear,
    Tens of thousands he hath slain.

Song xi.

" Saul was very wroth."—v. 8.
" And Saul eyed David from that day and forward."—v. 9.

It is scarcely surprising that Saul's natural jealousy, increased by his constitutional malady, should have been aroused by comparisons, so unfavourable to himself, drawn between him and David. Envious courtiers seem to have plotted to increase this change of feeling in the king; and from that time David's peace of mind at the court was gone.

In Psalm lxiv. he implores the protection of the Almighty from Saul's murderous fits of rage (to which he seems to allude in verse 1) and from the slanders of the sycophants who combined to destroy his character.

PSALM LXIV.

GOD, my supplication hear;
 Preserve my life from deadly fear;
2 Hide me from those in council met
 In secret, on my ruin set;
3 From men who whet their tongues like swords,
 And shoot their arrows, bitter words;
4 Who with a sudden treacherous dart
 Fear not to wound the true of heart.
5 Each doth his fellow bolder make,
 As evil deeds they undertake;
 They commune, hidden snares to lay;
 And Who shall see them, now? they say.

6 The wickedness that they have sought
 *Is to perfection by them brought.
  The inward thoughts of all are deep ;
  These in their hearts they secret keep.

7 But God His bow shall quickly bend,
  And swift to wound an arrow send ;
8 Their tongues shall their own ruin be ;
  They who behold shall trembling flee ;
9 Yea, men shall fear, and pondering own
  The work of God, His work alone.
10 The just shall trust in Him, and raise
  The voice of joy, the song of praise.

Song xii.

" David behaved himself wisely in all his ways ; and the Lord was
with him."—v. 14.

We learn from the following Psalm the secret of
David's wisdom in circumstances of such extraordinary
difficulty ; he lived a life of prayer.   Ver. 11 especially
appears to be the petition to which the text quoted above
shows the abundant answer.

Psalm LXXXVI.

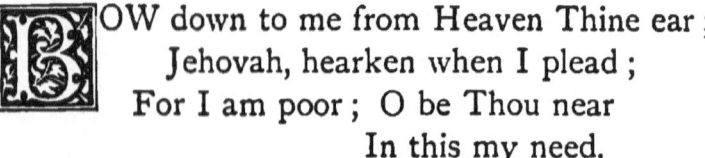OW down to me from Heaven Thine ear ;
  Jehovah, hearken when I plead ;
  For I am poor ; O be Thou near
    In this my need.

2 Preserve my soul ; for that my heart
  Is Thine, Thou, O my God, dost see.
  O to Thy servant help impart
    Who trusts in Thee.

3 Be now to me Thy mercy shown,
  Jehovah, day by day I cry ;
4 Rejoice my soul, which to Thy throne
    I lift on high.

5 For Thy forgiveness freely flows ;
  Jehovah, Thou art good to all ;
  Plenteous Thy mercy is to those
    Who on Thee call.

6 Give ear, Jehovah, to my prayer
  When at Thy footstool low I bend ;
  O to my supplications there
    Do Thou attend.

7 To Thee in sorrow I will cry ;
  To Thee in time of trouble flee ;
For Thou to hearken wilt be nigh,
                And answer me.

8 Surely among the gods is none,
  Jehovah, who is like to Thee ;
Of others' works with Thine not one
                Compared may be.
9 All nations whom Thou didst create
  Shall, worshipping, Thy praise proclaim ;
They all shall magnify Thy great,
                Thy glorious Name.
10 For Thou art great, O Thou Most High ;
   In wondrous things Thy might is shown ;
Thou, Who Thy Name dost magnify,
                Art God alone.

11 Teach me Thy way ; Thy truth impart ;
   My path to Thee shall then be near ;
Jehovah, knit to Thee my heart,
                Thy Name to fear.
12 O Lord my God, its song to raise
   My thankful heart to Thee shall soar ;
Thy glorious Name my lips shall praise
                For evermore.
13 Because Thy mercy I have seen
   Far greater than my tongue can tell ;
My soul by Thee hath rescued been
                From lowest hell.

14 O God, the proud against me rise ;
　　And wicked men, who scorn control
　And set not Thee before their eyes,
　　　　Have sought my soul.

15 But Thou, O Lord, art ever found
　　A gracious God, compassionate ;
　Thy mercies plenteously abound ;
　　　　Thy truth is great.

16 O turn Thee unto me and hear ;
　　Have mercy, lest I be undone ;
　Still let Thy saving strength be near
　　　　Thine handmaid's son.

17 Some gracious token to me show,
　　Which they that hate me shamed may see;
　For Thou dost help on me bestow,
　　　　And comfort me.

Song xiii.

*" Seemeth it to you a light thing to be a king's son-in-law, seeing that
I am a poor man, and lightly esteemed?"*—v. 23.

Finding that all Israel loved David, Saul decided that
it would be safer to expose him to the sword of the
Philistines than himself to destroy him. As a bribe to
go frequently into battle, he offered him first his elder
daughter, and then the younger, in marriage; but David,
with wise humility, hesitated to accept an honour not
suitable to his station and circumstances, the usual dowry
of a princess being far beyond his means.

Learning, however, that a deed of valour was all that
was needed, and (as is evident from his after-life) reci-
procating Michal's love, he at length acceded to the
proposal, and became the king's son-in-law.

Psalm cxxxi. seems very appropriate to this occasion.

PSALM CXXXI.

MEEK, O Jehovah, is my heart,
Not proud mine eye ;
Nor do I seek to take a part
In things too high.

2 Humble my spirit is, and mild ;
Meekly I go ;
My soul is as a weanèd child,
Quiet and low.

3 Let Israel trust Jehovah's grace,
And Him adore ;
Henceforth their hope upon Him place,
And evermore.

Song xib.

" Saul became David's enemy continually." — v. 29.

David's power of winning all hearts, except those which envy and malice had hardened against him, filled Saul with increasing fear and hate. David's life had now become one of constant anxiety and dread. The following song expresses his longing desire to escape to a humbler and more peaceful home, and may probably have been composed at this time.

PSALM LV. 1—7.

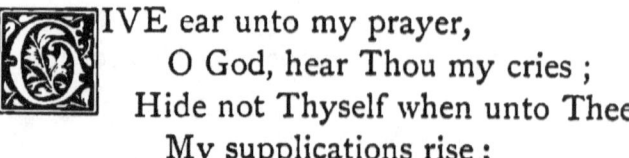

IVE ear unto my prayer,
  O God, hear Thou my cries ;
Hide not Thyself when unto Thee
  My supplications rise ;
2 Attend to me, and hear my moan ;
  I mourn in my complaint, and groan.

3 The foe doth evil speak ;
  The wicked me oppress ;
Anger and hate to me they bear,
  Imputing wickedness.
4 Anguish hath entered to my soul ;
  The fear of death doth o'er me roll.

5 Trembling hath o'er me come,
  And dread hath filled my breast ;
Yea, fearfulness hath on me seized,
  Horror my heart oppressed ;

Until at length, o'erwhelmed with grief,
My soul in words thus found relief.

6 " O that I had the wings
    " That bear the dove on high !
  " Then would I fly and shelter seek
    " Where I at rest might lie ;
7 " Lo, I would wander far away,
  " And in the wilderness would stay."

I Samuel XIX.

Song xv.

"Saul spake to Jonathan his son, and to all his servants, that they should kill David."—v. I.

Saul's enmity, hitherto confined to secret stratagems, at length burst through all restraint. It is conjectured that he instituted a legal process against David, and, by corrupting the assembly of the elders, obtained an iniquitous sentence of treason against him.

Psalm LVIII.

YE great assembly, do ye then
        Speak righteousness?
    And do ye, O ye sons of men,
        The wronged redress?

2   Nay, in your hearts ye go astray,
        Devising sin;
    The violence of your hands ye weigh
        The land within.

3   Sin is of wicked men the guide
        Strange paths to seek;
    E'en from their birth they go aside,
        And lies they speak.

4   Like serpent's poison causing pain
        Doth theirs appear;
    Like the deaf adder they remain,
        That stops her ear;

5 Which to the charmer doth refuse
　　To give due heed,
Charms though he ne'er so wisely use,
　　Her will to lead.

6 Break Thou the lions' teeth, O God ;
　　Destroy their might ;
Let the young lions' teeth Thy rod
　　In anger smite.

7 To melt away as waters flow,
　　Such be their lot ;
To be destroyed when from His bow
　　His darts are shot.

8 O let them like a snail be worn,
　　And melt away ;
And, like a child untimely born,
　　Not see the day.

9 Before your pots the thorns have felt,
　　*Burning and green,
They shall by wrath upon them dealt
　　Swept off be seen.

10 The righteous shall rejoice to know
　　This vengeance meet ;
While sinners' blood in streams shall flow,
　　To wash his feet.

11 So that " The righteous," men shall say,
　　" Rewards shall bless ;
" He is a God that doth repay
　　" In righteousness."

' Saul sware, As the Lord liveth, he shall not be slain."—v. 6.
" And Jonathan brought David to Saul."—v. 7.

Jonathan, whose dutiful conduct appears to the last to have preserved his influence over his father, contrived for a time to restore Saul to a better frame of mind. Warning David of a plan to murder him in the night, he told him to hide near the spot where the king was accustomed to take his morning walk, that he might hear what passed; there joining his father, he with the arguments of truth and justice so effectually pleaded the cause of his friend as to obtain the solemn assurance of his safety quoted above. We may imagine the following short and joyful song to be David's thanksgiving for his restoration to favour.

PSALM III. 3, 4.

JEHOVAH, Thou dost near me stand,
My Shield to be;
Thou art my Glory, Thy right hand
Uplifteth me.

4 I to Jehovah raised my cry,
He lent His ear;
And from His holy hill my sigh
Vouchsafed to hear.

Song xvii.

" And he was in his presence, as in times past."—v. 7.

Although David was for a time restored to his position at court, it is evident from what follows that the gleam of prosperity was soon clouded over. " Deadly enemies " seem to have encompassed the man whose valour and genius had made him the popular favourite. Saul's heart was again hardened against him, and in such circumstances David may in the following psalm have appealed to the Searcher of hearts, the Righteous Judge, the Refuge of the oppressed.

PSALM XVII.

HEAR Thou the right, incline Thine ear,
    Jehovah, to my cries;
My fervent prayer, my pleadings hear,
    From no false lips that rise.

2 O let the sentence passed on me
    From out Thy Presence spring;
*Because Thine eyes look down and see
    The fair and equal thing.

3 Thou in the watches of the night
    Hast tried mine inmost soul,
And found it guiltless in Thy sight,
    For I my words control.

4 In all men's doings, lest I stray,
    Thy word hath been my guide;
So, shunning the destroyer's way,
    I have not turned aside.

5 O make me in Thy paths to go,
    And safely there abide;
 Uphold me; Thy support bestow;
    Nor let my footsteps slide.

6 To Thee did my petition rise,
    For Thou, O God, dost hear;
 O hearken to Thy servant's cries,
    Incline to me Thine ear.

7 Thy wondrous loving-kindness show,
    O Thou that savest those,
 Who Thee their only refuge know,
    From all assailing foes.

8, 9 Keep, as the apple of the eye,
     Him to Thine arm who clings;
  From deadly foes who hover nigh
     O hide me with Thy wings.

10 Puffed up with wealth and earthly fame,
    With haughty steps they stride;
 Their greatness their own mouths proclaim;
    Their words are full of pride.

11 Whithersoe'er our steps are bent,
    Our goings they surround;
 Their eyes are set with fixed intent
    *To cast us to the ground;

12 E'en as a lion for his prey
    Doth wait with greedy eyes;
 As lion's whelp beside the way
    In secret lair that lies.

13 Arise, Jehovah, in Thy might, .
    *And forth to meet him go :
*Thy sword shall save me in the fight,
    And lay the wicked low.

14 *Thine hand of men of worldly mind
    Shall disappoint the will,
Their portion who in this life find,
    Whom Thou with wealth dost fill.

They wish for children and receive
    Their wishes at Thine hand ;
Sons they beget to whom they leave
    Their substance in the land.

15 But as for me, in righteousness
    Thy Face mine eyes shall see ;
Thy likeness shall me waking bless ;
    I satisfied shall be.

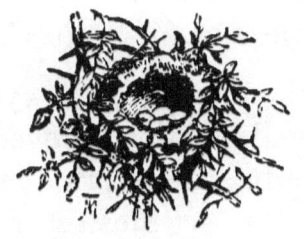

Song xviii.

" There was war again : and David went out, and fought with the Philistines, and slew them with a great slaughter ; and they fled from him."—v. 8.

It seems that during their short reconciliation Saul reinstated David in his command in the army.

The second part of Psalm lxvi. is a song of triumph which may be referred to the victory described above, although the psalm is not specially assigned to David.

PSALM LXVI. 5—7.

COME, the works of God behold ;
Terrible His deeds have been ;
Yea, the sons of men have seen
God His wondrous might unfold.

6 Through the flood on foot they trod,
When the sea He made dry land ;
There, delivered by His hand,
We were joyful in our God.

7 On the nations is His eye ;
By His power He ever reigns;
He the rebels' pride restrains,
Lest they set themselves on high.

Song xix.

"Saul sought to smite David even to the wall with the javelin."—v. 10.

Though quieted for a time by the good offices of Jonathan, Saul's jealousy broke out afresh in consequence of his son-in-law's new triumph over the Philistines.

David, however, was still ready with his harp to soothe the diseased mind of the king, until this second attack with the ever-present spear made immediate escape imperative.

The Syriac Psalter assigns Ps. cxl. to this occasion. Probably it was compiled with reference to it, some parts alluding to Saul, and others to the malicious sycophants who surrounded him, while v. 7, may relate to the recent battle.

PSALM CXL.

SAVE me, Jehovah, keep my life
    From men on violence intent,
2 Who mischief plot ; on war and strife
    Whose hearts are bent.

3 Sharp like the serpent's they have made
    Their tongues, to hurt me that delight ;
Poison beneath their lips is laid,
    Like adder's bite.

4 Be Thou, Jehovah, my Defence ;
    Let not the wicked lay me low ;
Nor let the man of violence
    My steps o'erthrow.

5 The proud a trap and cords have set
   To take me passing unawares;
Beside the way have spread a net,
            And laid their snares.

6 Thus to Jehovah did I say,
   "Thou art my God, O bend Thine ear,
 "Before Thee when my prayer I lay,
            "My voice to hear."

7 O God the Lord, on battle-field
   Whose strength hath my salvation wrought,
Thou o'er my head hast held Thy shield
            Where foemen fought.

8 Grant not the wicked man's desire,
   And further not his schemes of sin,
Lest prosperous days should pride inspire
            His heart within.

9 As for the head of those who seek
   With ruin to encompass me,
O let the mischief which they speak
            Their covering be.

10 Let fall on them the fiery blast,
    Hot burning coals upon them rain;
*Into the floods let them be cast,
            Nor rise again.

11 Prosperity shall ne'er attend
    The steps of him who evil speaks;
Evil shall hunt him to the end
            Who mischief seeks.

12 Jehovah will, I surely know,
  The cause of the afflicted plead,
 Will justice mete, and help bestow
     On those in need.

13 The righteous shall give thanks to Thee,
  And ever in Thy Name delight ;
 Their safe abiding-place shall be
     Within Thy sight.

Song xx.

" Saul also sent messengers unto David's house, to watch him, and to slay him in the morning. — v. 11.

Saul, finding that his own murderous attack on David had failed, employed others to accomplish his deadly purpose. Michal, who doubtless had friends among the royal household, obtained secret intelligence of the instructions to seize him given to a band of men, who appear to have paraded the streets at night, and to have intimidated the citizens lest they should rise to defend or avenge their hero.

Aided by his wife, David effected his escape, while the murderous band continued their round, little thinking that their victim had eluded them, and David could exultingly exclaim, "Let them return at evening, let them grudge if they be not satisfied!"

Even without the Hebrew title there could be no question about assigning Ps. lix. to this occasion. It is apparently composed of three distinct songs illustrating the different stages of the proceeding;—the first expressing anxiety at the evidently hostile preparations; the second perhaps showing the hope inspired by Michal's suggestion; the third mingling mockery of the baffled foe with thanksgiving to the God Whose mercy had brought deliverance.

Psalm lix. 1—5.

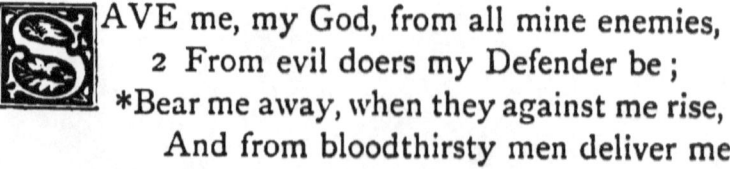

AVE me, my God, from all mine enemies,
   2 From evil doers my Defender be;
  *Bear me away, when they against me rise,
    And from bloodthirsty men deliver me.

3 For lo, to take my life they lie in wait,
  The mighty are against me gathered round ;
It is not for my sin they bear me hate ;
  No fault in me, Jehovah, have they found.

4 They run, and make them ready to begin,
  Although I have in no way done them wrong :
Look down, Jehovah, and behold their sin ;
  Awake, and let Thy succour make me strong.

5 O Thou, Jehovah, God of Hosts, awake ;
  O God of Israel, Thy wrath prepare ;
On all the heathen speedy vengeance take,
  Nor let Thy mercy the transgressor spare.

Song xxi.

*" Michal, David's wife, told him, saying, If thou save not thy life to-night, to-morrow thou shalt be slain."—*v. 11.

PSALM LIX. 6—13.

T evening they return, aloud they cry,
   Like howling dogs around the walls they
      go ;

7 Swords are within their lips, for "Who is nigh ?"
   They say, " Who doth us hear ? Yea, who
      shall know ?"

8 By Thee, Jehovah, they shall laughed at be ;
   Thou wilt the heathen's vain attempts deride.

9 *O Thou my Strength, I ever wait on Thee,
   For God my Fortress is wherein to hide.

10 My God, to me Who loving-kindness shows,
    Shall go before, and lead me on the way ;
   Yea, He shall grant my heart's desire on those
    *In ceaseless watch who waiting for me stay.

11 Destroy them not ; my people may forget ;
    But scatter them ; be thus Thy power re-
       vealed ;
   Bring down all those whose hearts on sin are set ;
    Yea, bring them down to dust, O Lord, our
       Shield.

12 Let them be even taken in their pride,
    For wickedness is ever in their talk,
   For bitter curses on their lips abide,
    And in the crooked path of lies they walk.

13 Consume them, on their heads destruction
   bring,
   Consume them in Thy wrath, no more to be,
And let them know that God is Jacob's King,
   And earth's far ends are ruled by His decree.

Song xxii.

"And when the messengers were come in, behold, there was an image in the bed."—v. 16.

PSALM LIX. 14—17.

LET them return at evening ; let their cries,
　　As those of dogs, be heard on every side ;
15 And as they wander, let their voices rise
　　Like hungry dogs with meat unsatisfied.

16 But I will sing aloud to praise Thy power ;
　　Yea, in the morning I Thy Name will bless ;
For Thou hast been to me a saving Tower,
　　My Refuge in the day of my distress.

17 O Thou my Strength, to Thee shall rise my song,
　　*To Thee I with the harp my voice will raise ;
For God is my Defence, my Fortress strong,
　　My God of loving-kindness Whom I praise.

Song xxiii.

" So David fled, and escaped."—v. 18.

This plaintive song seems to express the feelings, which must have filled the heart of the fugitive, both towards Him who had set him at liberty and towards the slanderers who had " turned his glory into shame."

PSALM IV. 1, 2.

GOD, God of my righteousness,
 To this my call give ear ;
Thou hast enlarged me in distress ;
 My prayer in mercy hear.

2 Ye sons of men, how long will ye
 My glory turn to shame ?
How long shall lies your pleasure be,
 And vanity your aim ?

Song xxiv.

" David . . . . came to Samuel to Ramah, and told him all that Saul had done to him."—v. 18.

Although there is no mention of any meeting of David with Samuel, between the anointing at Bethlehem and this time, we cannot doubt that the prophet took a deep interest in the welfare of the youth chosen through his instrumentality to rule over Israel. Ramah was only a few miles distant from the court of Saul at Gibeah, and it was very natural that David should seek the powerful protection of Samuel from the violence of the king and the malice of the courtiers. The following psalm is generally referred to the time of Saul's persecution, and many expressions in it are suggestive of this hasty flight. "Stop the way against them that persecute me," "let their way be darkness and slipperiness," refer to actual pursuers, while all the latter part vividly describes the calumnies, insults, and persecutions from which the Psalmist is escaping. The two last verses may express his joy at finding himself among friends at Ramah.

Psalm XXXV.

STRIVE Thou, Jehovah, strive with those
　　Who rise to strive with me ;
And in the warfare with my foes
　　On my side be.
2 Lay hold on buckler, take the shield,
　　Stand up, and help bestow ;
3 Draw out the spear, the good sword wield,
　　And stop the foe.

Yea, stop the persecutors' way,
   Their speed, their power control ;
" I thy Salvation am," O say
         Thou to my soul.
4 Confound them, cover them with shame
   Who thus my hurt devise ;
And turn them back from whence they came
         Who 'gainst me rise.

5 As chaff before the driving blast,
   So let them scattered be ;
Forth by Jehovah's angel cast,
         O let them flee.
6*Their pathway darkness let them find,
   Let pitfalls them o'erthrow,
Jehovah's angel press behind
         As on they go.

7 For privily my life to take
   Their hands a net did lay,
Without a cause a pit did make
         My soul to slay.

8 O let destruction unawares
   Fall swiftly on his head ;
Let him be taken in the snares
         Himself hath spread.

9 Then, in Jehovah's Name, its voice
   My thankful soul shall raise ;
In His salvation shall rejoice,
         And sing His praise.

E 2

10 Jehovah, all my bones shall cry,
    "O who is like to Thee,
  "Who to the poor oppressed art nigh
            "To set him free;
  "And Who the helpless dost defend
  "From him that is too strong;
  "Aid to the needy Who dost send
          "That suffer wrong ? "

11 False witnesses against me laid
    Things that I ne'er conceived ;
12 My good with evil is repaid,
        *My soul bereaved.
13 When they were sick, in sackcloth clad
    I fasted, worn with care ;
  And to my bosom, grieved and sad,
        Returned my prayer.
14 As for a friend, or brother dear,
    With grief my head was bent ;
  As one beside his mother's bier,
        I mourning went.

15 But in my fall they did rejoice,
    And thronged their joy to vaunt ;
  *E'en unknown abjects raised their voice
        With ceaseless taunt.
16 Base flatterers who know not shame,
    And hypocrites drew near ;
  Gnashing their teeth they round me came
        With scoff and jeer.

17 How long, O Lord, this wilt Thou see?
    Deliverance to me send ;
My darling save, and rescue me,
        Lest lions rend.

18 I in the great assembled throng
    Thy goodness will proclaim ;
And where the people meet, my song
        Shall praise Thy Name.

19 O let not those mine enemies
    Be joyful o'er my fate ;
Nor let them scoff whose mocking eyes
        Reveal their hate.
20 For peaceful words they do not speak,
    But they deceit have planned
Against the quiet and the meek
        Within the land.
21 Yea, they with open mouth draw nigh,
    And, with exulting mien,
"Aha ! aha !" they loudly cry,
        "Our eye hath seen."

22 This, O Jehovah, Thou didst see ;
    No more Thy tongue restrain ;
O Lord, be Thou not far from me ;
        Return again.
23 Stand up in my defence, awake,
    For judgment stretch Thy rod ;
Arise, my cause to undertake,
        My Lord and God.

24 According to Thy righteousness,
    Jehovah, judge Thou me ;
  And let them not in my distress
         Triumphant be.
25 Forbid them in their hearts to say,
    " This our desire hath been ;
  " We have devoured him for our prey,
       " His ruin seen."
26 Brought to confusion let them lie
    Who at my hurt are glad,
  And all themselves who magnify,
       With shame be clad.

27 Let them in shouts uplift their voice,
    Their gladness thus display,
  *Who in my righteousness rejoice,
       Yea, alway say,
  " Jehovah's Name exalted be,
    " Jehovah's praise forth tell,
  " Whom prosperous His own to see
       " It pleaseth well."

28 Thy righteousness shall be my song ;
    And I my voice will raise
  To magnify Thee all day long,
       And sing Thy praise.

Song xxb.

"Saul sent messengers to take David."—v. 20.

Shortly after David came to Ramah he accompanied Samuel to Naioth, a neighbouring school of the prophets over which Samuel presided. The arrival of Saul's messengers must have caused the fugitive great alarm ; and Psalm xxxvii. may express David's recollections of the words of encouragement given to him by Samuel. In v. 25 the prophet is represented as speaking of his long experience of God's faithfulness and care for the righteous, and indeed the substance of the whole psalm is contained in the words "Wait on Jehovah," a lesson which left a deep impression on David's mind, as is shown in this and many of his psalms.

PSALM XXXVII.

LET not displeasure fret thine heart
    Because the wicked prosperous be;
Let envy from thy breast depart
    When thou their high estate dost see;
2 Cut down like grass they shall decay,
Like the green herb they pass away.

3 Thou in Jehovah's Name confide ;
    Cease not the path of good to tread ;
So in the land thou shalt abide,
    And verily thou shalt be fed.
4 Let joy in Him thy soul inspire,
And He will grant thy heart's desire

5 Trust to Jehovah's care thy way,
    And He will all thy doings bless ;
Thy hope upon His mercy stay,
    And He will give thee great success;
6 He clear shall make thy truth as light,
Thy judgment as the noonday bright.

7 Upon Jehovah firmly rest,
    And patiently upon Him wait ;
Let no disquiet vex thy breast
    Because of sinners' prosperous state ;
Fret not, although each scheme and deed
Of men ungodly doth succeed.

8 From anger cease, thy wrath restrain,
    No envy keep thy heart within ;
Nor let displeasure there remain,
    Lest thou at length be moved to sin.
9 Destruction waits the wicked band,
While patient saints shall hold the land.

10 For yet a little, of the race
    Of godless men thou none shalt see ;
Yea, though thou seek their dwelling-place
    With careful search, it shall not be.
11 Yet shall the meek the earth possess,
And plenteous peace their souls shall bless.

12 The wicked man doth lie in wait,
    And counsel seek against the just ;
Gnashing his teeth with rage and hate
    He plots to lay him in the dust.
13 Jehovah sees his end is nigh,
And laughs to scorn his jealousy.

14 The godless men have bent their bow,
    Their outdrawn sword-blades they display,
To lay the poor and needy low,
    And those of upright life to slay;
15 Broken shall be the bow and dart,
Their sword shall enter their own heart.

16 A little that the righteous hath
    Is better than much sinners' gain;
17 Jehovah guards him in his path
    And breaks the ungodly's arms in twain.
He on His foes His wrath unfolds,
But all the righteous He upholds.

18 Jehovah watcheth o'er the pure,
    He knows their days, doth them sustain;
Their heritage shall still endure,
    And ever in the land remain;
19 Through danger they shall safe be led,
And in the days of famine fed.

20 But wicked men shall pass away,
    *As doth the pasture's glory fade;
Jehovah shall His wrath display,
    And low His enemies be laid;
Yea, in His fire shall they consume
And vanish as of smoke the fume.

21 The sinner borrows of his friend,
    And ne'er the borrowed goods repays;
But righteous men are free to lend,
    And merciful in all their ways;
22 These He within the land will bless,
But whom He curseth dispossess.

23 Jehovah doth a good man guide;
    His way is pleasing in His eye;
24 He never shall be cast aside,
    For though he falleth help is nigh;
Though oft he falleth, he shall stand
Upholden by Jehovah's hand.

25 I have been young, and now am old,
    Yet saw I ne'er the righteous left,
Nor e'er his seed in want and cold
    Imploring bread, of friends bereft;
26 The righteous helpeth the distressed,
And surely shall his seed be blessed.

27 Depart from evil, do the right,
    And in the land for ever dwell;
28 For judgment is our God's delight,
    And they in virtue who excel
Shall alway find Jehovah nigh,   .
And on His care in peace rely.

But wrath awaits the godless band,
    Whose seed shall perish for their sin;
29 The righteous shall possess the land,
    And gain a heritage therein;
There shall they dwell in rest and peace,
And ever prosper and increase.

30 His mouth in wisdom doth excel,
    Who in the righteous path doth walk;
His tongue of judgment loves to tell,
    And justice is in all his talk;
31 The statutes of his God abide
Within his heart; he shall not slide.

32 The wicked watch and counsel take,
　　Intent the righteous man to slay;
33 Jehovah will not him forsake,
　　Nor let his soul become their prey;
He will not leave him in their hands
When at the judgment-seat he stands.

34 Wait on Jehovah, keep His way,
　　And He thy soul shall surely bless,
Shall greater honour on thee lay,
　　Until thou dost the land possess;
When godless sinners are brought low
Thou shalt behold their overthrow.

35 In strength and glory I have seen
　　The wicked, like a bay-tree fair;
36 He passed from where his power had been;
　　I sought him, but he was not there.
37 Mark well the perfect man, nor cease
To watch the just; his end is peace.

38 As for transgressors, they shall die;
　　Destruction doth on sinners wait;
They shall be rooted out, and lie
　　O'erwhelmed in one untimely fate;
39 But from Jehovah, Whom they trust,
Is the salvation of the just.

He is their Strength in time of woe;
40 　　He at their side to save shall stand;
Yea His right arm shall help bestow,
　　And save them from the ungodly's hand:
Their foes shall all be overthrown,
Because they trust in Him alone.

I SAMUEL XX.

Song xxvi.

" Thou . . . . shalt remain by the stone Ezel."—v. 19.
" So David hid himself in the field."—v. 24.

Although attempts to seize David had been hitherto frustrated by the Holy Spirit, it was evident that, his place of retreat being known to Saul, the shelter of Naioth must be abandoned. But before going farther away he ventured back to ascertain from Jonathan whether any possibility of reconciliation remained. This seemed not wholly out of the question, for, between his paroxysms of rage, Saul still looked on David as one of his family, whom he expected to gather round his table, according to the religious custom, at the feast of the new moon, and it was agreed between the brothers-in-law that the conduct of the king, on missing David from his place, would indicate his real feelings towards the fugitive.

Meanwhile David was to remain concealed beside a well-known stone or cairn (the literal rendering being "heap of stones"), until the third day, and we may imagine the following to have been his evening prayer, in his solitary hiding-place, for support, protection, and guidance.

PSALM CXLIII. 7—12.

HASTE, Jehovah, hear my cry ;
My heart doth fail ;
No more Thy Presence veil,
Lest I be like to them that die.

8 Let me Thy loving-kindness hear
    When dawns the day ;
    Cause me to know Thy way,
For Thee I trust, for Thee I fear.

9 I lift my longing soul to Thee ;
    Thy succour send,
    And me from foes defend ;
To hide me unto Thee I flee.

10 Thy will O teach me to obey,
    My God Thou art ;
    Thy Spirit good impart,
*And lead me in an even way.

11 Me with Thy quickening Spirit bless
    For Thy Name's sake ;
    My soul from trouble take,
Jehovah, in Thy righteousness.

12 And of Thy mercy put to shame
    And slay all those
    My proud oppressive foes ;
For I Thy servant fear Thy Name.

Song xxbii.

" The Lord be with thee, as He hath been with my father."—v. 13.
" Go in peace."—v. 42.

Jonathan's endeavour to appease his father's wrath at David's absence resulted in a frenzied attempt on his own life, and he returned to his brother-in-law's hiding-place, only for a long farewell embrace, and for renewed vows of unchanging kindness.

This simple and beautiful song may perhaps have been written by David in memory of the parting words of himself and the friend who " loved him as his own soul."

PSALM CXXI.

David.

 TO to the mountains high
        Will lift mine eyes ;
    *From whence shall help be nigh ?
        From whence arise ?

2 E'en from Jehovah's love
        Doth come mine aid,
    Whose hand the heavens above,
        And earth hath made.

Jonathan.

3 He will thy foot sustain,
        Nor let it slide ;
    He watchful will remain,
        Thy Guard and Guide.

4 Lo! He that Israel leads,
    And doth him keep,
To slumber never needs ;
    He will not sleep.

5 Jehovah keepeth thee,
    By thee doth stand ;
Thy spreading shade is He
    On thy right hand.

6 Thy head the sun by day
    Shall never smite ;
Nor shall the moon's pale ray
    Hurt thee by night.

7 Jehovah from all harm
    Shall keep thee free ;
Preserved by His right arm
    Thy soul shall be.

8 He shall preserve thy way
    And go before,
To guard thee night and day
    For evermore.

I SAMUEL XXI.

Song xxviii.

" And David arose, and fled that day for fear of Saul, and went
to Achish, the king of Gath.
" And the servants of Achish said unto him, Is not this David,
the king of the land? Did they not sing one to another of him in
dances, saying, Saul hath slain his thousands and David his ten
thousands ? "—vv. 10—11.

There being no safety for David in the dominions of
Saul, he resolved on the desperate step of seeking refuge
with the bitterest enemy of his country. Before doing so,
however, he paid that unfortunate visit to Nob, which,
through the instrumentality of the informer Doeg, was
the cause of Saul's massacre of its inhabitants.

Possibly by means of the sword of Goliath, which
David had brought from thence, the nobles of Philistia
recognized in the guest of Achish the slayer of their
champion, and tried to poison the mind of the king
against him. A rumour of David's high destiny appears,
moreover, to have reached as far as Gath, and fear and
hate were no doubt mingled with triumph in the insulting laugh with which they beheld their dreaded enemy,
the expectant king of Israel, now an outcast, dependent
on the compassion of their sovereign.

Ps. lxx., which seems to be a fragment of Ps. xl.,
may have been the prayer of David " to bring to remembrance " of his God his misery in this heathen land.

PSALM LXX.

MAKE haste, Jehovah, to mine aid ;
    O God, make haste to set me free ;
2 Confusion on their heads be laid
    Whose hearts are set my fall to see ;
3 Let those be backward turned in shame
Who cry "aha," and mock my name.

4 Let all who seek Thy Name rejoice ;
    And all who in Thy love abide
Say alway, with exulting voice,
    "Let God our God be magnified."
5 But I am poor ; to help be near ;
    O tarry not ; Jehovah, hear.

Song xxix.

"And David laid up these words in his heart, and was sore afraid."—v. 12.

Suspected by all around him, David must have been oppressed with the necessity of weighing every word before uttering it, lest he should endanger himself, or dishonour his God.   The change between his position as a member of the royal family and the idol of the nation, while residing at the Court of Saul, to that of an exile must have impressed deeply on his mind the lesson with which he concludes the following sad strain.

PSALM XXXIX. 1—5.

 SAID, I will take heed
  Whereto my ways may tend,
 Lest they should lead my lips to sin,
  And lest my tongue offend.

 As with a bridle strong
  My mouth I will restrain ;
 Whilst wicked men before me stand
  From speech I will refrain.

2 I spake not with my tongue,
  And as one dumb I stood ;
 I held my peace, and silence kept,
  Yea, silence e'en from good.

3 Grief was within me stirred,
    My heart then hotly burned ;
The fire was kindled as I mused,
    And speech at length returned.

4 Make me to know mine end,
    My length of days reveal ;
Jehovah, teach me what it is,
    My frailty let me feel.

5 Lo, Thou hast made my days
    No longer than a span ;
Mine age is nothing before Thee,
    Nought is the age of man.

Though greatness he attain,
    Man, I have surely known,
*At best estate is but a breath,
    A fleeting breath alone.

Song xxx.

" And he changed his behaviour before them, and feigned himself mad in their hands."—v. 13.

The Hebrew title of Ps. lvi. implies that the Rabbins believed David to have been imprisoned in Gath, and the above-described expedient, to which he resorted, supports this view.

The Psalm itself seems to have been written before he was taken, but while he was fully aware of the machinations of his enemies. It declares his sure confidence in God, Who has already delivered him from death, and Who will enable him to render in the sanctuary the praises vowed in a heathen land.

PSALM LVI.

GOD, be merciful to me,
   For man would my devourer be ;
   Yea, to oppress me he doth fight ;
   For blood he thirsteth day and night.
2 Mine adversaries day by day
   Seek to obtain me for their prey ;
   For they be many in the strife
 *That proudly rise to take my life ;
3 And yet what time I am afraid
   My trust on Thee is firmly stayed ;
4 In God His word I magnify,
   Upon my God do I rely ;
   I trust in Him, I will not fear ;
 *What can flesh do ? my God is near.

5 They all day long my words pervert,
  Their thoughts are all to do me hurt ;
6 They meet together, mark my way,
  And lie in wait my soul to slay.
7 Shall they through sin unpunished be ?
  Let peoples fall 'neath wrath from Thee !
8 Thou hast my wanderings numberèd,
  Thy bottle holds the tears I shed,
  Thou dost upon my sorrows look,
  Are they not written in Thy book ?
9 Whene'er I cry my foes shall flee,
  For this I know, God fights for me.
10 In God His word I magnify,
   I on Jehovah's word rely ;
11 In God I trust, I will not fear ;
  *What can man do ; my God is near.

12 I by my vows to Thee am bound ;
   O God, Thy praises I will sound,
13 For Thou hast kept me from the grave ;
  *My feet Thou dost from falling save,
   That I may walk in God's own sight,
   And with the living see the light.

I Samuel XXII.

Song xxxi.

" David therefore departed thence, and escaped."—v. 1.

The Hebrew title of Ps. xxxiv. assigns it to the time
of David's departure from Gath, and the holy joy with
which it overflows could only have been expressed by
one who in his troubles had cried to the Lord in such
words as those of the preceding psalms.

A note in Stanley's "History of the Jewish Church"
mentions the escape of an Arab Chief from the Governor
of Acre by a stratagem similar to that of David.

Psalm XXXIV.

EHOVAH'S praise my mouth shall tell ;
　　It ever on my lips shall dwell :
　2 My soul shall boast in Him ; the sad
　　　Shall hear it, and their hearts be glad.
　3 With me Jehovah magnify,
　　With me exalt His Name on high ;
　4 I sought Him ; He an answer gave,
　　And from my terrors did me save.
　5 They looked to Him ; their hearts were light ;
　　He put their shame and fear to flight.

6 Jehovah heard the afflicted cry,
  And saved him from his misery;
7 Jehovah's Angel campeth near,
  To save all them His Name who fear.

8 O taste and see Jehovah's grace,
  How blest in Him their trust who place!
9 Jehovah fear, ye saints of His;
  No want to them that fear Him is.
10 Though hungry lions lack their prey,
  They nought shall want who Him obey.
11 O come to me, ye children, hear,
  *Learn ye from me Jehovah's fear.
12 Dost thou desire long life to see,
  And prosperous all thy days to be?
13 Thy tongue from evil words refrain,
  Thy lips from all deceit restrain.
14 Do good; from ways of evil cease,
  Love gentleness, and follow peace.
15 Beneath Jehovah's watchful eye
  The righteous dwell; He hears their cry:
16 Against the wicked is His face;
  He blots from out the earth their trace.
17 The righteous cry; He hears their prayer,
  And saves them out of all their care.
18 Jehovah contrite hearts will seek,
  And bring salvation to the meek.
19 Though great the woes the just doth see,
  Jehovah will his Saviour be.
20 He keepeth all his bones that none
  Shall e'er be broken, no not one.

21 But evil shall the godless slay,
　　Them shall misfortune bear away;
　　And they who persecute the just
　　Shall lie forsaken in the dust.
22 Jehovah doth His servants save,
　　Yea, He redeems them from the grave;
　　No ills on them who trust Him'wait,
　　Nor shall their house be desolate.

Song xxxii.

" The cave Adullam."—v. 1.

The cave of Adullam is believed to be identical with an extensive cavern near the city of that name in the lowlands of Judah. This retreat would be easily reached from the Philistine border, and still more so from Bethlehem, whence ere long David's family joined him, as did many others, until his little band swelled to the number of four hundred.

Ps. cxlii., which is entitled "A Prayer when he was in the cave," may have been composed in the earlier part of his abode there, after the first joyful sensation of freedom had given place to that of depressing loneliness, before the arrival of his friends and followers.

PSALM CXLII.

TO Jehovah raised my prayer,
　　To Him my supplication made;
2 Before Him I poured out my care,
　　My trouble laid.

3 *When I am overwhelmed with woe,
　My path Thou knowest; Thou art there;
Hid in the way wherein I go
　　They lay a snare.

4 Lo, on my right hand there is none
    To know me, nor to help supply,
None for my soul to care, not one ;
        No refuge nigh.

5 Jehovah, I have cried to Thee,
    Thou Who in life my portion art,
The Refuge whereunto may flee
        In grief my heart.

6 Incline Thine ear unto my cry,
    Low in the dust behold me laid ;
My foes are stronger far than I ;
        O send Thine aid.

7 My soul from prison set Thou free,
    That I to Thee may praise address ;
Then shall the just resort to me,
        Whom Thou shalt bless.

Song xxxiii.

*"And the prophet Gad said unto David, Abide not in the hold;
depart, and get thee into the land of Judah."*—v. 5.

David seems to have gone from Adullam to Mizpeh
of Moab, and, after placing his parents under the care of
the king of that country, to have removed to a stronghold
on the borders of the Dead Sea, afterwards spoken of as
the Cave of Engedi. Here he remained until enjoined
by the prophet to depart. This is the first mention of
Gad, who appears henceforth to have been David's faithful counsellor through all his varied fortunes. The suggestion of Ewald that he was of the school of Samuel is
pleasing and natural. We can well imagine the attach-
ment being formed at Naioth, whence the young prophet
would take this first opportunity of rejoining his friend.

In the following song (which may probably come next
in historical order, as it does in the Bible arrangement)
David seems to liken the gloom of his abode at Engedi
to the darkness of the grave, and to appeal to God in sad
and longing accents for deliverance.

PSALM CXLIII. 1—6.

JEHOVAH, my petitions hear,
To mine entreaties lend Thine ear ;
In faithfulness an answer send,
And in Thy righteousness attend.

2 Thy servant's sins from memory blot ;
  O into judgment enter not ;
  For in Thy sight, when he is tried,
  No living man is justified.

3 My life the persecuting foe
  Down to the ground hath smitten low,
  And made me dwell in darkness dread,
  As those long numbered with the dead.

4 My spirit therefore is oppressed,
  And overwhelmed within my breast ;
  And, mourning o'er my sad estate,
  My heart within is desolate.

5 I call to mind the olden days ;
  I meditate on all Thy ways ;
  I muse, and strive to understand
  The works of Thine almighty hand.

6 To Thee, in all mine anxious care,
  I stretch my longing hands in prayer ;
  I thirst for Thee—my soul doth cry—
  As thirsts a land in summer dry.

Song xxxii.

" Then answered Doeg the Edomite, which was set over the servants of Saul, and said, I saw the son of Jesse coming to Nob, to Ahimelech the son of Ahitub."—v. 9.

In obedience to the words of Gad, David had removed to the forest of Hareth in the land of Judah. On hearing this, Saul in a paroxysm of rage falsely accused Jonathan of stirring up David to rebellion. Doeg, who was present, then informed him of the assistance given to David at Nob by Ahimelech.

The title of Ps. lii. refers it to this occasion, without explaining whether the "mighty man," against whom David's righteous indignation is so strongly aroused, is Saul or Doeg. It appears to me that the three portions of which the Psalm is composed are, separately, more applicable to Ahithophel than to either of these, although the compiler may probably have had this occasion in view when combining them into the following song.

PSALM LII.

MIGHTY man, in pride secure,
    Why boast each evil plot ?
God's loving-kindnesses endure,
    His goodness faileth not.

2 Thy tongue doth wickedness devise,
    And cut like razor keen :
3 To righteousness preferring lies,
    Thy choice hath evil been.

4 Devouring words to thee belong,
   Thou lov'st of sin to speak ;
Deceitful tongue, to bring forth wrong
   And mischief thou dost seek.

5 God also with His upraised hand
   Shall bring thee to the ground,
Shall seize, and pluck thee from the land
   Where living men are found.

6 The righteous this shall see and fear,
   His judgments they shall praise ;
Triumph shall in their laugh appear
   While thus their voice they raise—

7 "Lo ! this the man who turned aside
   " From God, nor sought His aid ;
" But on his heaped-up wealth relied,
   " Who sin his strength hath made."

8 But I am like an olive tree
   In God's own House that grows ;
My trust in Him shall ever be
   To me Who mercy shows.

9 For this I will proclaim Thee great,
   And magnify Thy might,
And ever on Thy Name will wait,
   Which is Thy saints' delight.

Song xxxb.

" And the king said to Doeg, Turn thou, and fall upon the priests.
And Doeg the Edomite turned, and he fell upon the priests, and
slew on that day fourscore and five persons that did wear a linen
ephod."—v. 18.

The actual object of his hatred being beyond his
reach, Saul gave vent to his insane fury by slaughtering
the priests who had befriended David.

Not one of his servants could be found to commit
this impious deed except Doeg, against whom, even
more than against his cruel and sacrilegious master, the
following petition was probably offered.

PSALM CXL. I—3.

JEHOVAH, from the evil man
　　Deliver me ;
From him who violence doth plan
　　My Saviour be ;

2 Who in their wicked hearts deceit
　　And mischief seek ;
Who day by day together meet
　　Of war to speak.

3 With tongues like serpents' sharp they deal
　　Mischief and woe ;
The adder's poison they conceal
　　Their lips below.

Song xxxvi.

" He that seeketh my life."—v. 23.

Abiathar, a son of Ahimelech, the sole survivor of the
priest at Nob, fled to David, and received the assurance
of his protection.   The particulars he brought of the
horrible massacre must have increased David's sense of
his own danger.   The intense hatred, which had prompted
such dreadful vengeance on those who had rendered him
a trifling service, would surely pursue him with every
device that craft or violence could suggest.   The following is a short prayer for protection in such circumstances.

PSALM CXL. 4, 5.

KEEP me, Jehovah, let Thine arm
  Preserve Thy servant safe from harm,
   Safe from the wicked foe ;
  Guard me from men of blood and strife,
  Whose purpose is to take my life,
   My steps to overthrow.

5 The proud have laid a snare for me
  And cords, my cause of fall to be,
   Yea, they have spread a net ;
  They cruelly beset my way,
  Seeking to gain me for their prey ;
   Their traps are round me set.

1 SAMUEL XXIII.

Song xxxvii.

" Then they told David, saying, Behold, the Philistines fight against Keilah, and they rob the threshingfloors. Therefore David enquired of the Lord, saying, Shall I go and smite these Philistines?"—vv. 1, 2.

The city of Keilah was situated in the lowlands of Judah, and in dangerous proximity to the Philistine border. David, always eager to do battle in defence of his countrymen, on hearing of its distress, applied to the Lord for permission to smite these marauders.

His followers, wearied and dispirited, hung back with fear, and in the following words David seems to encourage them with the assurance that God will execute vengeance on the heathen. Then, lifting the prayer of faith to God, Who has promised success to his arms, he implores Him to strike terror into the hearts of His foes.

PSALM IX. 17—20.

THE wicked shall be turnèd into hell,
　　With nations that from God have dared
　　　to stray ;
18 The needy in His mind shall ever dwell,
　　Nor shall their expectation pass away.

19 Arise, Jehovah, let not man prevail,
　　O let the heathen now Thy judgments know ;
20 Put fear within their hearts, yea, make them
　　quail,
　　　That they to be but men themselves may know.

G

Song xxxviii.

" And it was told Saul that David was come to Keilah. And Saul said, God hath delivered him into mine hand."—v. 7.

David had been shielded in the battle at Keilah by his God, Whose will he had inquired with earnest prayer before entering on the expedition. In the following song he prays for the defeat of the wicked devices of his ungrateful king, to whose subjects he had just rendered such signal service.

PSALM CXL. 6—8.

 SAID unto Jehovah,
　　My God, my God Thou art ;
Jehovah, hear my pleading,
　　The crying of my heart.

7 *Thou, O my Lord Jehovah,
　　Hast in the battle spread,
Thou Strength of my salvation,
　　A covering on my head.

8 Let sinners' vain devices
　　Their purpose never win,
Lest they, by pride exalted,
　　Be strengthened in their sin.

Song xxxix.

" Then said David, Will the men of Keilah deliver me and my men into the hand of Saul? And the Lord said, They will deliver thee up."—v. 12.

Abiathar having brought the ephod with him, David had now the privilege of obtaining from God Himself, through His priest, guidance in all cases of doubt and difficulty.

Doubtless the men of Keilah were profuse in their expressions of praise and flattery to their deliverer, but there must have been something suspicious in their behaviour, which induced David to inquire of the Lord whether they were worthy of trust. On receiving the answer, he might well exclaim, "Help, Lord; for the godly man ceaseth; for the faithful fail." Then, turning his thoughts from the traitors within the city to Saul's approach with such men as Doeg for his advisers, he would cry, "The wicked walk on every side, when the vilest men are exalted."

PSALM XII.

David.

JEHOVAH, help ; the godly race
    Have now become a feeble band ;
The faithful few who sought Thy Face
    Have well-nigh perished from the land.
2 To speak of idle vanity,
    His neighbour every one doth seek ;
With false and flattering lips they lie,
    While with a double heart they speak.

Abiathar.

3 The flattering lips, the tongue of pride,
    Jehovah's wrath shall take away,
4 "Our tongues shall rule" who loud have cried,
    "'Tis ours to speak, we none obey."
5 "Now for the poor and needy's sake,"
    Jehovah saith, "I will arise,
  "For him a refuge I will make,
    * "And grant the rest for which he sighs."

David.

6 Behold, Jehovah's words are pure
    As silver in the furnace tried,
  Which seven times doth the fire endure,
    And thus from dross is purified.
7 Thou, O Jehovah, shalt provide
    A safeguard from this evil race;
  The wicked walk on every side,
    When vilest men are high in place.

Song xl.

" Then David and his men, which were about six hundred, arose and departed out of Keilah, and went whithersoever they could go."—v. 13.

The last words of this verse touchingly express the fear and desolation of the unhappy wanderers, and Psalm xiii. is singularly in unison with the description. Yet, though pleading with God for relief from his distress, David does not forget His late mercy in warning him of his danger in Keilah. He had inquired of Jehovah with sure trust, and now rejoices in the salvation which has been granted to him.

PSALM XIII.

HOW long wilt Thou forgetful be,
    And far from me abide?
Wilt Thou for ever turn from me?
    Thy Face for ever hide?

2 How long shall I within my breast
    Each day sad counsel take?
How long shall I be sore oppressed
    By foes who boasting make?

3 Jehovah, hearken to my cries,
    Consider when I weep;
My God, O lighten Thou mine eyes,
    Lest in the grave I sleep,

4 And lest mine enemy should say
    "I o'er him have prevailed;"
And they that trouble on me lay
    Rejoice that I have failed.

5 But as for me, my trust hath been
　　Upon Thy mercy stayed ;
On Thy salvation while I lean,
　　My heart shall glad be made.

6 Now to Jehovah I will sing,
　　And all His praise make known ;
Yea, I will praise my God and King,
　　Who plenteous love hath shown.

Song xli.

" And David abode in the wilderness in strong holds, and remained in a mountain in the wilderness of Ziph."—v. 14.

If Psalm xiii. was the first outburst of feeling of the escaped fugitive, Psalm xxxi. is a longer prayer, which appears to have been composed when he had found a resting-place.

To David's mind, ever ready to soar upwards, the mountainous fortresses of Ziph would be emblems of the Great Rock, the Place of Defence to which he might always flee.

Saul had thought to find him "shut in" in Keilah (see v. 7 of chapter), but God, by warning him of his danger had "shown him His marvellous kindness in a strong city," and had "set his feet in a large room." Might not this allude to some spacious cavern capable of containing himself and his followers?

In verses 11 and 13, David seems to refer to the fear shown by the Keilites of continuing to entertain one whose friendship would bring down on them the wrath of the king.

Dean Stanley considers this Psalm to have been composed in Keilah, to which strong fortress it is undoubtedly full of allusions, but all these are in the past tense, and v. 8 could hardly have been written before the escape had been effected.

The varying tones of mournful pleading, brightening hope, and at length of sure and joyful confidence presented by this beautiful Psalm make it peculiarly precious to the afflicted soul.

PSALM XXXI.

JEHOVAH, all my trust
   Is firmly fixed on Thee ;
    Save me from shame ; in righteousness
    Do Thou deliver me.
2 Bow down to me Thine ear ;
   Deliver me with speed ;
    Be Thou my House of sure Defence,
    My Rock in time of need.

3 Thou art my Fortress strong,
   The Rock where I abide ;
    Then for Thy Name's sake lead me on,
    And ever be my Guide.
4 O draw me from the net
   They privily have laid ;
    For Thou alone art all my Strength ;
    On Thee my hope is stayed.

5 Jehovah, I commend
   My spirit unto Thee ;
    For it is Thine, O God of truth ;
    Thou hast redeemèd me.
6 I hate all those who love
   Deceitful vanities ;
    But on Jehovah's strength my trust
    Unshaken ever lies.

7 In Thee I will rejoice,
   Made by Thy mercy glad ;
    For Thou hast thought on my distress,
    And known my soul when sad.

8 Thou hast not shut me up
    With those who plots devise ;
  Large is the room Thou giv'st my feet,
    Safe from mine enemies.

9 Jehovah, pity me,
    For troublous times return ;
  My soul and body waste with care,
    Mine eyes with weeping burn.
10 My life is spent with grief,
    My years with sighs decay ;
  My strength doth fail me through my sin,
    My bones consume away.

11 My neighbours and my foes
    Reproaches on me laid ;
  E'en mine acquaintance from me fled,
    To look on me afraid.
12 Forgotten, out of mind,
    Like one of life bereft,
  A broken vessel I am deemed,
    To scorn and ruin left.

13 I heard their slanderous tongues ;
    Fear was on every side,
  While they to take away my life
    With secret counsel tried.
14 Still did I trust in Thee,
    On Thee did I rely ;
  "Thou art my God ; Thou art my God,"
    This ever was my cry.

15 My times are in Thine hand;
    Be Thou to succour nigh;
Save me from them who persecute,
    And from mine enemy.

16 Jehovah, make Thy Face
    Upon Thy servant shine;
And save me for Thy mercy's sake;
    O save me who am Thine.

17 Deliver me from shame,
    To Thee hath been my cry;
Confound the wicked in the grave,
    Let them in silence lie.

18 O let the lying lips
    Be silent in the dust,
Which, proudly and disdainfully,
    Speak evil of the just.

19 How great Thy goodness is,
    Laid up by Thee in store,
And wrought before the sons of men
    For them who Thee adore!

20 These, in Thy presence, Thou
    *From plots of men shalt hide;
In a pavilion they shall safe
    From strife of tongues abide.

21 Blest be Jehovah's Name!
    Praise be to Him alone!
Who in a city strong to me
    Hath wondrous kindness shown.

22 For in my haste I said,
　　" Thine eyes are turned aside ; "
　Yet thou didst hearken to my prayer
　　When unto Thee I cried.

23 Ye saints, Jehovah love ;
　　The faithful He defends,
　And on the proud who evil do
　　Their due reward He sends.

24 Be of good courage then ;
　　Strong shall your hearts be made,
　All ye that in Jehovah hope ;
　　Whose trust on Him is stayed.

Song xlii.

*" And Jonathan Saul's son arose, and went to David into the wood,
and strengthened his hand in God."*—v. 16.

Intercourse with a character like that of Jonathan,
pure and unworldly in the midst of a corrupt court,
gentle, brave, generous, and devoted in his duty to his
God, his father, and his friend, must indeed have
"strengthened David's hand in God."

It might surely have been after his covenant with
Jonathan that David sang of "the saints, the excellent, in
whom was all his delight."

To quote the words of Canon Perowne, Psalm xvi. is
"bright with a happiness which nothing earthly can
touch."

PSALM XVI.

 GOD, preserve me, for my heart
       In Thee doth trust ; my cry shall be,
2 My Lord Thou, O Jehovah, art,
       *I have no other good but Thee.
3 Those who are righteous in Thy sight,
     The saints upon the earth who dwell,
   In them is ever my delight,
     E'en those in virtue who excel.
4 Their sorrows shall be great who run
       Another for their god to claim ;
  Their offerings of blood I shun,
       Nor shall my lips pronounce their name.

5 Jehovah's Self my portion is ;
     Jehovah's Self my cup doth fill ;
  The hand that holdeth me is His ;
     Thou all my lot maintainest still.
6 In places fair, in pleasant ground,
     Behold the lines to me are cast ;
  There mine inheritance is found,
     There shall my days in peace be passed.
7 To bless Jehovah I will sing
     Who counsel gave me from on high ;
  My reins instruction to me bring
     When in the night I wakeful lie.

8 Jehovah I before mine eye
     Have alway set, my guide is He ;
  At my right hand He standeth nigh,
     And therefore I unmoved shall be.
9 For this my heart with gladness swells ;
     Filled with rejoicing is my breast ;
  Its joyfulness my glory tells ;
     My flesh in hope shall also rest.
10 Because my soul Thou wilt receive,
     *And from the world unseen wilt save
  Thine Holy One Thou wilt not leave
     To see corruption in the grave.

11 Thou wilt to life my footsteps guide,
     The pathway show and go before :
  Pleasures at Thy right hand abide,
     Fulness of joy for evermore.

Song xliii.

"Then came up the Ziphites to Saul to Gibeah, saying, Doth not David hide himself with us in strong holds in the wood?"—v. 19.

The title of Psalm liv. refers it to the treachery of the Ziphites, but, as it ends with a thanksgiving for deliverance from trouble, the second part is applicable only to the circumstances mentioned in the concluding verses of 1 Sam. xxiii., which relate that Saul was diverted from his pursuit of David by the invasion of the Philistines.

I think, however, that the latter portion is a totally distinct song composed for another occasion, for, although delivered from present danger, David had not beheld the punishment of his enemies, as is implied in v. 7.

I have therefore placed here the short and earnest petition in the first part which alone appears to me to have been written for this occasion.

PSALM LIV. 1—3.

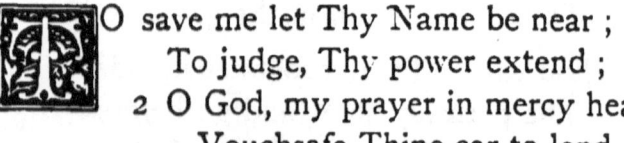

O save me let Thy Name be near ;
 To judge, Thy power extend ;
2 O God, my prayer in mercy hear,
 Vouchsafe Thine ear to lend.

3 For strangers up against me rise,
 Oppressors seek their prey ;
They set not God before their eyes,
 But strive my soul to slay.

Song xlib.

" And Saul said, Blessed be ye of the Lord."—v. 21.
*" See therefore, and take knowledge of all the lurking-places where he
  hideth himself. . . : If he be in the land, I will search him out
  throughout all the thousands of Judah."*—v. 23.

Psalm x. may represent an interview of David with
Abiathar, through whom he would doubtless seek counsel
from God in this new danger.   He seems to give a
detailed account of the conduct of Saul, describing him
in v. 3 as blessing "the covetous" (i. e. the Ziphites, who,
doubtless, expected a reward for their betrayal), and in
verses 8 and 9 as instituting a search corresponding
with the quotation given above. V. 15 is looked on
by Bishops Horne, Horsley, and others, as a prediction,
and appears to be an answer to the preceding prayers.
The reassured tone of the concluding verses is thus
naturally accounted for.

PSALM X.

David.

WHY, O Jehovah, dost Thou now
    So far away from me abide?
In time of trouble why dost Thou
    Thy Presence hide?
2 The wicked in his pride hath sought
    To gain the needy for his prey;
O let him in the snares be caught
    That he doth lay.

3 His boastings the desire express
 Which in his heart he meditates
The covetous whom he doth bless .
    Jehovah hates.
4 *The wicked in his scorn hath cried,
 "Will God to punish lift His rod?"
*This is the sum of all his pride—
   "There is no God."
5 *At all times prosperous are his ways;
 Thy judgments are above his sight;
As for his foemen he displays
   Scorn of their might.
6 "I shall by nought be moved," he cries
 Within his heart, "for I am he
"To whom there no adversities
   "Shall ever be."
7 His mouth in curses doth abound;
 Deceit and fraud within it lie;
Under his tongue is mischief found
   And vanity.
8 Hid in the villages he lies,
 Lurking to slay the innocent;
In secret 'gainst the poor his eyes
   Are alway bent.
9 He, like a lion in his lair,
 To carry off the weak hath sought,
Waiting until within his snare
   The poor are brought.
10 *He croucheth as prepared to spring
 On them he seeketh to devour,
*That he may thus the helpless bring
   Within his power.

11 He in his secret heart doth say
   "God hath forgotten ; surely He
   " Hath turned from this His Face away ;
        "He will not see."

Abiathar.

12 Lift up Thine Hand, Jehovah ; rise,
    O God; in mind the humble bear ;
13 Why should they say who God despise
        " Thou dost not care ?"
14 Lo, Thou hast seen it, for Thine eye
    Beholds iniquity and wrongs ;
Yea, to requite it speedily
        To Thee belongs.
In his affliction and distress
    The poor commits himself to Thee ;
Thou Helper of the fatherless
        Wilt ever be.
15 Break Thou the arm, the power repress
    Of him of dark and evil mind ;
Yea, seek Thou out his wickedness,
        Till none Thou find.
16 Jehovah reigns for evermore ;
    As for the heathen, where are they ?
Gone from the land, their day is o'er
        And passed away.

David.

17 Jehovah, Thou hast lent Thine ear,
    And heard the crying of the meek ;
Thou wilt prepare their heart, and hear
        When Thee they seek.

H

18 Thou to the poor wilt give their right,
  And ever judge the fatherless ;
That thus the earthly tyrant's might
      No more oppress.   .

Song xlb.

" And they arose, and went to Ziph before Saul : but David and his
men were in the wilderness of Maon, in the plain on the south of
Jeshimon."—v. 24.

David had descended from the hill of Hachilah when
he found himself betrayed by the Ziphites.

Psalm xi. may represent him, strong in faith and perhaps guided by his inspired counsellors, as endeavouring
to allay the fears of the more timid of his followers.
Possibly David's familiarity with the neighbourhood of
the Dead Sea may account for his frequent allusions to
the descent of fire and brimstone on the wicked.

Psalm XI.

David.

MY heart doth on Jehovah rest ;
How to my soul then do ye say
"Like birds that seek their mountain nest,
"Flee far away."

Followers.

2 Behold, the wicked bend their bows,
They on the string prepare the dart,
With secret aim to shoot at those
Of upright heart.

3 And if the pillars be o'erthrown,
　　What can the righteous man avail ?
　If crushed be the foundation stone
　　　　　His power must fail.

David.

4 Heaven is Jehovah's Throne on high ;
　　His Temple is His dwelling-place ;
　His eyes behold, His eyelids try
　　　　　All Adam's race.

5 He trieth in the furnace bright
　　The righteous who on Him do wait ;
　Those who in violence delight
　　　　　His soul doth hate.

6 Snares on the wicked He shall rain,
　　Brimstone, and fire, and storm shall send ;
　This is the cup that they shall drain ;
　　　　　Yea, this their end.

7 Jehovah righteous is ; and He
　　In righteousness hath great delight ;
　All those His countenance shall see
　　　　　Who walk aright.

Song xlvi.

" Saul and his men compassed David and his men round about to take them. But there came a messenger unto Saul, saying, Haste thee, and come; for the Philistines have invaded the land."—v. 26, 27.

Hunted, as David was, and almost caught by his implacable foe, his position seemed hopeless, when a signal and unexpected deliverance was provided for him and his followers by this summons to Saul.

Psalm liv., of which the title is "A Psalm of David, when the Ziphims came and said to Saul, Doth not David hide himself with us?" was evidently intended by the Compiler to refer to this occurrence.

PSALM LIV.

BY Thy Name my Saviour be;
*And by Thy strength uphold Thou me.
2 Vouchsafe, O God, my prayer to hear;
And to my words incline Thine ear.

3 The men of violence and strife,
Oppressors, seek to take my life;
And strangers 'gainst my soul uprise,
Who set not God before their eyes.

4 Behold my God His help extends;
The Lord Himself is with my friends;
5 He shall with ill my foes requite:
O in Thy truth destroy their might.

6 A sacrifice, an offering free,
Jehovah, I will bring to Thee,
And to Thy Name a song will raise ;
For it is good.   I Thee will praise.

7 He hath delivered me from grief ;
And to my trouble brought relief ;
Yea, He hath granted to mine eyes
To triumph o'er mine enemies.

1 SAMUEL XXIV.

Song xlvii.

" And it came to pass, when Saul was returned from following the
Philistines, that it was told him, saying, Behold, David is in the
wilderness of Engedi.   Then Saul took three thousand chosen
men out of all Israel, and went to seek David and his men upon
the rocks of the wild goats."—v. 1, 2.

Psalm lvii., which by its Hebrew title is assigned to
" David when he fled from Saul in the cave," appears to
be composed of three distinct songs joined together by
the Compiler in order to form a sort of history of the
events related in this Chapter.   The first is a cry for help
such as David may have used on perceiving the approach
of Saul's army.

PSALM LVII. 1—3.

GOD, be merciful to me ;
    Plenteous let Thy mercy be ;
    For to Thee my spirit clings,
    Hid beneath Thy sheltering wings ;
    Let them shadow o'er me cast,
    Till these troublous times be past.

2 I will call on God Most High,
    Unto God my voice shall cry,
    God Who granteth me success,
    God Who doth my doings bless ;
3 When devouring foes upbraid
    God from Heaven shall send His aid.

Song xlviii.

" He came to the sheepcotes by the way, where was a cave; and Saul went in to cover his feet: and David and his men remained in the sides of the cave."—v. 3.

Such caverns as that here mentioned are by no means uncommon in Palestine. They may contain one or more chambers, but in either case a large band of men in the darkness of the interior would be entirely concealed from a person near the entrance, of whom, on the other hand, they would have a full view.

In the second portion of the Psalm, David, while anxiously watching the movements of the army, expresses his continued confidence in God's mercy, even though he espies his most inveterate enemies amongst the party surrounding the king.

Suddenly, on seeing Saul leave them and approach the cave alone, he bursts forth into a shout of triumph at the thought that the persecutor is fallen into the trap in which he had intended to enclose his victim.

PSALM LVII. 3—6.

GOD His mercy shall extend ;
    God His truth to me shall send.
4 With the lions I am cast—
    Men who breathe a fiery blast :
    Piercing arrows are their words,
    Spears their teeth, their tongues are swords.

5 God, be Thou exalted high,
  Set Thyself above the sky ;
  O'er the heavens exalt Thy Throne ;
  Be o'er earth Thy glory shown.
6 They had laid for me a snare ;
  They had bowed my soul with care ;
  With a pit my fall they sought,
  They themselves therein are caught.

Song xlix.

*" The men of David said unto him, Behold the day of which the Lord
said unto thee, Behold, I will deliver thine enemy into thine hand,
that thou mayest do to him as it shall seem good unto thee. Then
David arose, and cut off the skirt of Saul's robe privily."—v. 4.*

We gather from these words that God had in some
way promised to deliver Saul into David's power. The
narrative describes the generous forbearance with which
the exile used his opportunity, whilst prudently securing
ample proof of his loyalty.

The Compiler has concluded the Psalm with a song of
joy and gratitude such as David might have raised after
this remarkable occurrence, not being aware that it originally formed part of Ps. cviii. composed to celebrate the
defeat of the Syro-Ammonite confederacy—(See Introduction, page xv.).

PSALM LVII. 7—11.

GOD, to Thee my heart doth cling,
   *I with harp will praises sing ;

   8 Wake, my glory ; wake, my lute ;
Nor shalt thou, my harp, be mute ;
Harp and psaltery I will take,
*Dawn of morning to awake.

   9 *'Mid the people will I sing,
Praises 'mid the nations bring ;
   10 For Thy love to heaven ascends,
To the clouds Thy truth extends.

   11 God, be Thou exalted high,
Set Thyself above the sky ;
O'er the heavens exalt Thy Throne,
Be o'er earth Thy glory shown.

Song I.

"And David said to Saul, Wherefore hearest thou men's words, saying, Behold, David seeketh thy hurt?"—v. 9.
"The Lord judge between me and thee."—v. 12.

The remainder of the Chapter contains David's affecting expostulation with his father-in-law, which for a time overcame even the stony heart of Saul.

The first portion of Ps. vii. appears to be a recapitulation of this assertion of his innocence laid before the Searcher of hearts, to Whose justice he had appealed.

PSALM VII. 1—5.

MY God Jehovah, I on Thee rely;
   O save. my life from persecutors' power;
   2 Lest, like a lion, when no help is nigh,
He rend my soul, he tear me, and devour.

3 My God Jehovah, if I this have done,
   If these my hands in wickedness have shared,
4 If I have ill repaid the peaceful one,
   (Yea, I my causeless enemy have spared).

5 Then let my foe with snares my soul surround,
   With hate pursue, and take my life away;
Yea, in his fury tread it to the ground,
   And in the dust of earth mine honour lay.

Song li.

"Nabal is his name, and folly is with him."—v. 25.

The districts of Maon and Carmel (which latter must not be confounded with the distant mountain of that name) were situated to the south of Ziph, and again beyond these was the wilderness of Paran, whither David and his men had removed soon after the former's temporary reconciliation with Saul.

To this unappropriated pasture-land Nabal sent his flocks, a common custom, which, however, exposed them to considerable danger from attacks of wandering marauders.

The protection afforded by David and his well-disciplined band would, by one less churlish and perverse than Nabal, have been highly valued, and repaid by a handsome present ; and David was naturally indignant at the insulting reply called forth by his request for some recognition of their services.

Nabal, both in name and conduct, may, I think, have been represented by "the fool" denounced in Ps. xiv. In almost every one of the first six verses we may trace something applicable to him, such as the shaming "of the counsel of the poor," by which designation David usually speaks of himself and his needy fellow outcasts.

Nabal's utter meanness seems to David's excited mind the climax of human wickedness, of which he has had hateful experience in the bloodthirstiness of Saul, the ingratitude of the men of Keilah, and the treachery of the Ziphites, so that he exclaims in the bitterness of his heart, "There is none that doeth good, no, not one."

The last verse of this Psalm is generally considered to be a liturgical addition, and is therefore omitted, as inappropriate to the life of David.

PSALM XIV.

David.

"THERE is no God," within his heart
　　The fool hath whispered—"none."
They are corrupt in every part,
　　None doeth good—not one.

2 Jehovah out of Heaven above
　　Looked down on Adam's race,
To see if any truth did love,
　　If any sought His Face.

3 All are corrupt—all turned aside—
　　All vilest deeds have done;
None will in righteousness abide—
　　None doeth good—not one.

Abiathar, speaking in Jehovah's Name.

4 Have they no knowledge—all who meet
　　Their wicked plots to frame?
They who as bread My people eat,
　　Nor seek Jehovah's Name.

David.

5 There were they filled with dread and fear,
  Where cause of fear was not ;
  For God is to the righteous near,
  His watchful care their lot.

6 What though the counsel of the meek
  Ye thus have put to shame,
  With trust he doth Jehovah seek,
  His refuge is His Name.

Song lii.

" The man was very great."—v. 2.
" The Lord smote Nabal, that he died."—v. 38.

The following song is strikingly suitable to the circumstances of Nabal's life and death.

PSALM XLIX. 16—20.

EAR not, though one be wealthy made,
    In glory if his house increase ;
17 For, when he in the grave is laid,
    His glory and his pomp shall cease ;
In death he nought shall take away,
He leaves behind his vain display.

18 In life though blessings on him flow
    (Men praise thee if thou prosperous be),
19 Yet to his fathers he shall go,
    And light his eye shall never see.
20 The fool that is to honour brought,
    Like beasts that perish, is but nought.

Song liii.

" The Lord hath returned the wickedness of Nabal upon his own head."—v. 39.

This song, although not applying so entirely to Nabal as the preceding one (for there is no reason to suppose that he carried his meanness to the point of dishonesty), may yet very possibly have been composed with reference to him, the last clause especially being almost a reproduction of the verse above quoted.

PSALM LXII. 9—12.

SURELY men of low degree
  Lighter are than vanity ;
  Others are, of station high,
  In the balance weighed, a lie.
  Vain are men of every state,
  Less than vanity their weight.
10 In oppression put not trust,
  Boast not in your gains unjust.
  If increasing wealth ye get,
  Cease your heart on it to set.
11 God hath spoken once the word—
  Twice mine ears the voice have heard—
  " God is mighty, God is strong,
  " Power and might to God belong."
12 Yea, Jehovah, Thou art kind ;
  Man in Thee doth mercy find ;
  Each shall have reward from Thee,
  As Thine eye his work doth see.

Song liv.

"And the Ziphites came unto Saul to Gibeah, saying, Doth not David hide himself in the hill of Hachilah?"—v. I.

At the opening of this Chapter we find David again in the district of the Ziphites, and the object of their renewed treachery.

The fiery indignation expressed in this Song may probably have been aroused by such repeated perfidy.

PSALM CXL. 9—13.

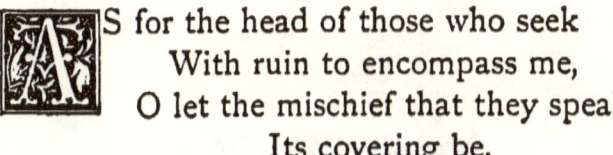S for the head of those who seek
  With ruin to encompass me,
O let the mischief that they speak
  Its covering be.

10 Let burning coals upon them fall,
  And fire descending from the skies,
The yawning pit devour them all,
  No more to rise.

11 None shall on earth established see
  The man by words of evil known ;
The violent shall surely be
  By ill o'erthrown.

12 The cause of him that suffers wrong
  I know Jehovah will maintain ;
From Him protection from the strong
    The poor shall gain.

13 Those who in righteousness delight
  Their thanks unto Thy Name shall give,
And all the upright in Thy sight
    Shall ever live.

Song lb.

" Then Saul arose, and went down to the wilderness of Ziph, having three thousand chosen men of Israel with him."—v. 2.

Again surrounded by foes, and probably vexed by the reproaches of despairing followers, David may have laid his troubles before God in this song.

PSALM III. 1—2.

EHOVAH, how mine enemies,
    And those against me who arise,
    In numbers grow before mine eyes!

2 They many are who raise the cry,
    " God surely is no longer nigh
    " To help him in his misery."

Song lvi.

" Destroy him not: for who can stretch forth his hand against the
Lord's anointed, and be guiltless ?"—v. 9.

We now come to a daring exploit of David, who,
accompanied by his nephew Abishai, went by night to
the enemy's camp and carried off the spear and cruse of
the sleeping king, as proofs that Saul's life had been a
second time at his mercy, and spared by him.

The following portion of Psalm iv. contains a rebuke
somewhat similar in character to that in which David
admonished his companion, whose impatience would
have led him into the sin of regicide.

PSALM IV. 3—4.

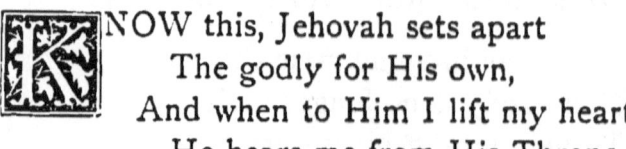

NOW this, Jehovah sets apart
    The godly for His own,
And when to Him I lift my heart
    He hears me from His Throne.

4 Then stand in awe, nor dare to sin,
    Let fear your bosom fill ;
Upon your bed, your heart within,
    O commune, and be still.

Song lvii.

" The Lord render to every man his righteousness and his faith-fulness."—v. 23.

The incident which we are now considering bears a remarkable resemblance to the previous occurrence in the cave of Engedi. A like opportunity naturally called forth a similar line of conduct in the generous, yet prudent, outlaw, and the mad and miserable king seems always to have been touched by the unexpected sound of the voice he had once loved to hear. David, however, would recognize in the momentary softening of the heart of Saul an express answer to his prayers, and in this song he speaks of such an answer as a proof of his innocence.

PSALM LXVI. 16—20.

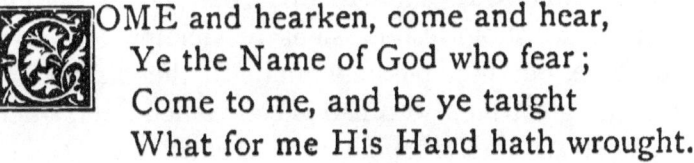OME and hearken, come and hear,
Ye the Name of God who fear;
Come to me, and be ye taught
What for me His Hand hath wrought.

17 I to Him my voice upraised,
With my tongue my God I praised.

18 If my heart had purposed sin,
I had failed His ear to win;

19 But my God my prayer hath heard,
He hath hearkened to my word.

20 Blessed be God Who, when I cried,
Hath not cast my prayer aside,
Hath not turned away His Face,
Nor withdrawn from me His grace.

I Samuel XXVII.

Song lviii.

" David dwelt with Achish at Gath, he and his men, every man with
his household."—v. 3.

Placing no confidence in the continuance of Saul's kindly
feeling, David again threw himself on the protection of
Achish, who appears never to have shared in the enmity
of his nobles when David was a solitary outcast in Gath.
In this second visit, however, with his numerous band
David undoubtedly led a very different life, and his
danger may have been of another kind. He may have
been expected to join in the idolatrous feasts of his hosts,
and in v. 4 of the following Psalm he seems to pray for
strength against such a temptation. Probably in v. 5
he entreats that Gad and Abiathar may prove faithful
monitors if he should show signs of yielding. V. 6 is
very obscure, but may possibly allude to the disappointment of the great men who had accompanied Saul, when
they perceived the reconciliation effected by David's
gentle remonstrance; and in v. 7 there may be an
allusion to the massacre at Nob.

Psalm CXLI.

WITH Thee, Jehovah, do I plead,
Make haste to help me in my need,
And when I cry vouchsafe to heed.

2 O let my prayer as incense rise,
My lifted hands before Thine eyes
Become an evening sacrifice.

3 Keep of my lips the door with care,
  Make me of idle words beware,
  Nor e'en to think of evil dare.

4 From paths of sin O keep my feet,
  Nor let me evil doers meet,
  And let me not their dainties eat.

5 Nay rather let a righteous friend
  In kindness chastisement extend,
  And give reproof when I offend.

  *This as a precious oil shall be,
  *It shall not be refused by me ;
  *I meet their wrongs by prayer to Thee.

6 All they who are as judges known
  *As from a rock are overthrown,
  *And they my words as welcome own.

7 Our bones beside the grave are found,
  Scattered abroad and spread around
  *As when one plougheth up the ground.

8 *Jehovah, Lord, I lift mine eyes
  To Thee on Whom my soul relies;
  Forsake me not, but hear my cries.

9 Keep me in safety from the net
  Of wicked men for mischief met,
  Who for my feet their traps have set.

10 Let sinners perish in the snare
   Which their own hands with craft prepare ;
   But let not me their ruin share.

Song lix.

" The time that David dwelt in the country of the Philistines was a full year and four months." — v. 7.

Probably to avoid the temptations alluded to in the foregoing Psalm, as well as fearing the renewed jealousy of the courtiers, David asked from Achish permission to retire to some country city. Ziklag was allotted to him, and we may imagine how long and dreary the period of his sojourn there must have appeared to the exile. From this place on the border-land he may have raised his cry to God in such words as the following.

PSALM LXI. 1—4.

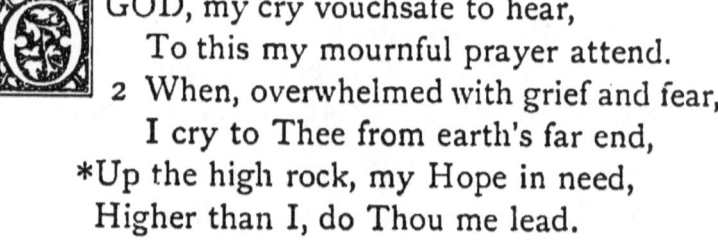 GOD, my cry vouchsafe to hear,
　　To this my mournful prayer attend.
　2 When, overwhelmed with grief and fear,
　　　I cry to Thee from earth's far end,
　*Up the high rock, my Hope in need,
　　Higher than I, do Thou me lead.

　3 For Thou hast ever been to me
　　　A Refuge in the time of woe ;
　　A Tower of Strength I found in Thee,
　　　In Thee a Refuge from the foe.
　4 Beneath Thy wings I will abide,
　　And in Thy tabernacle hide.

Song lx.

" Behold, it was burned with fire ; and their wives, and their sons, and their daughters, were taken captives."—v. 3.

The latter part of Chapter xxvii. gives an account of the bloody raids made by David and his followers on the Amalekites and on other old inhabitants of Canaan, friends of the Philistines.

David may have considered that, as the anointed of Jehovah, he was right in carrying out the command given to Saul (1 Samuel xv. 3), whose disobedience to it had been punished by the forfeiture of his crown. But the deception practised on Achish by one living under his protection cannot be justified.

The nobles of Gath were, with good reason, more suspicious of his conduct than the king, and, owing to their representations, David and his men were sent back from the Philistine army when on its march to meet Saul on the fatal field of Gilboa. The verse quoted above describes the state in which they found Ziklag on their return.

In the first agony of the discovery his followers laid all the blame on David (whose murderous attacks had been the cause of this retaliation), and they even "spake of stoning him."

The following mournful complaint expresses a bitterness of heart such as David must have felt in this moment of seemingly hopeless distress.

HOW long wilt Thou Thyself, Jehovah, hide?
    Shall I Thy wrath for ever burning find?
47 Short is the time that I may here abide ;
    O why hast Thou in vain made all
      mankind ?
48 What man who liveth shall escape the grave ?
Who from the hand of death his soul can save ?

Song lxi.

" When David was returned from the slaughter of the Amalekites, and
David had abode two days in Ziklag ; it came even to pass on the
third day, that, behold, a man came out of the camp from Saul
with his clothes rent, and earth upon his head."—v. 1, 2.
" And he answered, That the people are fled from the battle, and many
of the people also are fallen and dead ; and Saul and Jonathan
his son are dead also."—v. 4.

David's despair was quickly put to flight by the unfailing remedy.

He "enquired at the Lord, saying, Shall I pursue after
this troop ? . . . and He answered him, Pursue." The
result was the recovery of all that the Amalekites had
taken away.

The joy of the triumphant band was, however, of short
duration, for on the third day after their return to Ziklag
arrived the disastrous tidings from the field of Gilboa.

Ps. xliv. is not assigned to David, and may have been
formed by the Compiler with reference to these events
out of two poems believed to have been composed by
different authors.—(See Introduction, page xxi.) The
first part of the Psalm, which has already been introduced
(see page 19), is a song of praise, such as David and his
men may have been singing when their triumph was suddenly changed to a wail over the disgrace of their country
and the death of their king.

PSALM XLIV.

David and Soldiers.

GOD, our ears were early taught,
    Our forefathers have told,
What mighty works by Thee were wrought
        In time of old.

2 Nations were driven from the land,
    And they therein were led ;
The heathen perished by Thine Hand
        *That they might spread.

3 For not their weapon in the fight
    Possession did obtain,
Nor did their own strong arm and might
        The victory gain.

But Thy right Hand, Thine Arm alone,
    The light of Thine own Face ;
Because by Thee was favour shown
        To Israel's race.

David.

4 O God, O Thou Who art my King,
    My God, give Thy command ;
*To Jacob full salvation bring
        With Thy right Hand.

5 Cast down shall be our enemies,
    By Thee when we are led ;
Through Thee on those who 'gainst us rise
        Our feet shall tread.

6 No power to save my sword may claim,
    I trust not in my bow ;
7 Nay, Thou hast saved us, Thou to shame
        Hast put the foe.

David and Soldiers.

8 In God we glory all day long,
    And shouts of triumph raise ;
  And we Thy Name in joyful song
        Will ever praise.

Arrival of the Messenger from Gilboa.

9 But Thou hast cast us off, and made
    Confusion on us light ;
  Nor goest forth our hosts to aid
        To win the fight.

10 Thou makest us our backs to turn,
    And flee on battle plain ;
  And they whose hearts with hatred burn
        Our spoils obtain.

11 By Thee, as sheep for food, we are
    Delivered for a prey,
  Among the heathen scattered far,
        And cast away.

12 Thy people Thou dost sell for nought,
    Their price as nought is found ;
13 To be a scorn is Israel brought
        To those around.

14 A byword for our heathen foes
     By Thee is made our name,
   A shaking of the head to those
          Who seek our shame.

David.

15 Mine eyes confusion and disgrace
     Before me daily see ;
   Shame that is ever on my face
          Hath covered me ;

16 Because of him who blasphemy
     And foul reproaches speaks,
   Because the enemy is nigh
          And vengeance seeks.

David and Soldiers.

17 All this is come on us, and yet
     Our refuge Thee we make ;
   Nor do Thy covenant forget,
          Nor falsely break.

18 'Gainst Thee our heart doth not rebel,
     From Thee we have not strayed,
19 *That crushed we lie where dragons dwell
          In death's dark shade.

20 Our God forgetting had we sought
     A strange god ours to be,
21 Would God not search this out ? each thought
          His eye doth see.

22 Yea, we for Thy sake all the day
    Are numbered with the dead ;
  Like sheep to slaughter led away
            Our blood is shed.

23 Awake, O why dost Thou delay ?
    In sleep why close Thine eyes ?
  Cast us not utterly away ;
            O Lord, arise.

24 Why turnest Thou away Thy Face ?
    Thy wrath why dost Thou show,
  Forgetful of our sore distress,
            Our grievous woe ?

25 Our soul is bowed to earth with grief,
    In dust our body lies ;
26 O in Thy mercy send relief,
            To save arise.

Song lxii.

"And David lamented with this lamentation over Saul and over Jonathan his son."—v. 17.

The grief of David on receiving the melancholy tidings from Gilboa was expressed in the last song. It was, however, as an Israelite that he there lifted up his voice, with those around him, in the wail which contrasts so strikingly with the joyful commencement of Ps. xliv.

But David's own heart was wounded in its deepest and tenderest part, and from his country's woes he turned to pour forth his private grief. The lament over the early death of Jonathan is unrivalled in its earnestness and pathetic beauty. Scarcely less touching is the generosity which, forgetting the persecutor in the father and the king, will not separate in his heart and song those whom death has not divided.

II SAMUEL I. 19—27.

BEAUTY of our Israel,
　　Slain on thy mountains high,
　Fallen are the brave and mighty,
　　The great dishonoured lie!

20 Let Askelon not hear it,
　　In Gath lift not your voice,
　Lest base Philistia's daughters
　　O'er Israel's shame rejoice.

21 Ye mountains of Gilboa,
　　No more let fruitful field,
　Blest by soft dew and showers,
　　From you rich offerings yield.

The buckler of the valiant
  On you was cast away;
The shield of God's anointed
  Was made the heathen's prey.

22 In battle with the mighty,
  In warfare with the foe,
Saul's sword ne'er turnèd backward,
  Nor Jonathan's true bow.

23 These, in their lives so lovely,
  In death unparted lay;
More swift were they than eagles,
  More strong than lions they.

24 Weep, weep, O Israel's daughters,
  Weep over Saul the brave,
Who clothèd you in scarlet,
  Who gold and jewels gave.

25 How fallèn are the mighty
  In thickest of the fight!
O Jonathan, they slew thee
  Upon thy mountain's height.

26 I weep for thee, my brother;
  My joy hath been in thee;
Passing the love of women
  Hath been thy love to me.

27 How fallèn are the mighty!
  How lie the bravest low!
The sword and spear are perished,
  And broken is the bow.

K

Song lxiii.

" They dwelt in the cities of Hebron."—v. 3.

On the death of Saul David inquired of the Lord
whether he should go up to any of the cities of Judah
(his own tribe), and was directed to repair to Hebron,
the oldest city and the burial-place of the patriarchs.
He accordingly removed thither with his followers.

It seems almost superfluous to call attention to the
appropriateness to this occasion of the following thanksgiving of persecuted wanderers who have found a place
of rest.

PSALM LXVI. 8—15.

David.

 BLESS our God, ye people,
  To sing His praises meet ;
9 Our soul in life He holdeth,
  And maketh firm our feet.

People.

10 For Thou, O God, hast proved us,
  And hast as silver tried ;
11 Thou in the net hast placed us,
  In sorrow to abide.

12 Thou madest men o'erride us ;
　　We fire and water passed ;
But to a wealthy country
　　Thou broughtest us at last.

David.

13 Burnt offerings on Thine altar
　　I joyfully will lay ;
14 The vows I made in trouble
　　I now to Thee will pay.

15 The incense of burnt fatlings
　　And rams to Thee shall rise ;
Yea, bullocks I will offer
　　And goats in sacrifice.

Song lxiv.

"They anointed David king over the house of Judah."—v. 4.

Ps. cxxxviii. seems to express David's feelings on this occasion.

In his joyful exultation he does not forget Him Who "had respect to the lowly" shepherd, heard and answered the exile's cry, and, having "magnified His word" in bringing His anointed servant to the throne, will surely "perfect" His work (which is as yet incomplete, while only Judah acknowledges David's sway), so that kings of other lands may recognize the faithfulness and truth of Jehovah.

PSALM CXXXVIII.

MY heart a song of joy shall raise;
　　Before the gods my tongue shall sing;
2 Thy truth and mercy I will praise,
　　Toward Thy Temple worship bring:
For Thou Thy word dost set on high,
Thy Name o'er all dost magnify.

3 Thou to my cry didst lend Thine ear;
　　My soul with strength Thou did'st endue;
4 The kings of earth Thy word shall hear,
　　Their tongues Thy praises shall renew;
5 They in Jehovah's ways shall cry,
　"Great is Jehovah's majesty."

6 Although Jehovah dwells on high,
   Although He reigns in might above,
He to the meek is ever nigh,
   He to the lowly shows His love,
But bids the proud afar to stay,
His Face from them He turns away.

7 What though I walk 'midst grief and woe,
   Thou wilt my fainting heart sustain,
Thine Hand, outstretched upon the foe,
   His burning fury shall restrain ;
Yea, Thy right Hand shall safety send,
Thine Arm Thy servant shall defend.

8 Jehovah's tender care for me
   His work will perfect make and sure ;
Thy love, Jehovah, firm shall be,
   Thy mercy ever shall endure ;
Forsake me not, nor leave undone
The work by Thine own Hands begun.

Song lxv.

" And the king lamented over Abner, and said . . ."—v. 33.

The claim of David to the throne was not acknowledged by the tribes situated on the east of the Jordan.
All these adhered to the family of Saul, whose eldest
surviving son, Ish-bosheth, was (at the instigation of
Abner, the first cousin of Saul and captain of the host)
chosen for their king, the seat of government being fixed
at Mahanaim.

After some years, however, in consequence of a private
quarrel with Ish-bosheth, Abner offered his powerful
support to David, and held a friendly conference with him
at Hebron.   Everything being there arranged, Abner had
departed on a mission to bring all Israel to make a league
with David, when Joab returned victorious from battle, and
heard with rage and jealousy of the cordial reception which
had been granted to the slayer of his brother.   By a message sent without David's knowledge, he induced Abner
to turn back and then basely murdered him.

David took instant measures to express his heartfelt
indignation and sorrow.   Sternly commanding the mur-
derer to join with him and all the people in the funeral
rites, he himself delivered a lament so earnest and
solemn, so free from all affectation, that not a doubt
remained in any mind of the king's perfect innocence in
the matter.

2 SAMUEL III. 33—34.

A S dies a fool didst thou, O Abner, die ?
  34 Unshackled were thy hands,
     Free were thy feet from bands ;
As one by malice slain, so thou dost lie.

Song lxvi.

" All the elders of Israel came to the king to Hebron."—v. 3.

The death of Abner destroyed the last hope of the adherents of the house of Saul. Ish-bosheth was assassinated, and his murderers received the just punishment for their crime from David, whose favour they had hoped to win. The leaders of Israel then resolved to put an end to the civil war by acknowledging the king of Judah as sovereign of the united tribes, and came to Hebron (as related in the text above) to propose to anoint him in that capacity.

The following Psalm, so abounding in thankfulness, joy, and holy confidence, is admirably suited to the title affixed to it in the Septuagint version, "Before the Anointing."

PSALM XXVII.

JEHOVAH is my Life and Light ;
　　Whom shall I dread when He is near ?
Jehovah is my Strength and Might ;
　　Whom shall I fear ?

2 The wicked, e'en my cruel foes,
　　Whose hearts with rage did 'gainst me swell,
When to devour me they arose,
　　Stumbled and fell.

3 Though hosts encamped against me lie,
  Yet shall my heart be not afraid ;
Though loud arise the battle cry,
    I trust His aid.

4 One thing hath been my heart's desire—
  Jehovah's House my home to be,
That I may there His will inquire,
    His beauty see.

5 In His pavilion I will hide,
  Concealed by Him in time of woe ;
Yea, in His secret place abide,
    Safe from the foe.

6 Set on a rock, now lifted high
  Above the foes who round me came,
Glad gifts I bring and magnify
    Jehovah's Name.

7 Hear, O Jehovah, when I cry,
  In mercy to my voice attend,
And graciously to every sigh
    An answer send.

8 " Seek ye My Face " when Thou didst say,
  " Thee will I seek " my heart replied ;
Thy Face O turn not Thou away,
    Nor longer hide.

9 Cast me not off in anger ; Thou
  Didst help when trouble was my lot ;
O God of my salvation, now
    Forsake me not.

10 Father and mother may forsake ;
    Then will Jehovah all supply :
11 Teach me, and plain Thy pathway make,
    For foes are nigh.   .

12 Let not mine enemies prevail ;
    False witnesses against me rise,
And wrongfully my life assail
    With cruel lies.

13 Weary and faint my heart had been,
    But for my trust that by mine eye
Jehovah's goodness should be seen
    Before I die.

14 Wait on Jehovah ; wait thou still ;
    Be strong ; O be thy courage great ;
Jehovah's strength thy heart shall fill ;
    Still on Him wait.

Song lxvii.

" They anointed David king over Israel."—v. 3.

Amongst all the outpourings of adoration and gratitude
which swell the Book of Psalms, Psalm cxlv. is emphatically entitled "David's Psalm of praise." It is indeed
worthy of the "man after God's own heart," and we cannot imagine a more fitting moment for its inspiration than
this, when the prayer offered more than seven years
before (Psalm cxxxviii. 8 : page 133) was thus fulfilled.
Jehovah had "perfected His work" concerning His servant, and assuredly the praise of David's "God and King"
ascended to Heaven with the fragrance of the anointing
oil.

PSALM CXLV.

THEE will I bless, my God and King,
　　Thy praise I will for ever sing,
　　　　2 Each day shall thanks ascend ;
　　Yea, ever will I bless Thy Name :
　　3 Great is Jehovah, great His fame ;
　　　　His greatness knows no end.

4 Age shall to age Thy works unfold ;
　By each Thy wonders shall be told,
　　　Thy mighty power forthshown ;
5 I of Thy majesty will tell,
　My tongue shall on Thy glory dwell,
　　　Thy wondrous works make known.

6 So shall mankind Thy might declare ;
7 With me they shall recall Thy care
    And sing Thy righteousness.
8 Great pity doth Jehovah show ;
  He gracious is, to anger slow,
    Of mercies numberless.

9 To all Jehovah shows His love ;
  His tender mercies from above
    O'er all His works extend.
10 Thy works, Jehovah, Thee shall praise ;
  To Thee Thy saints their songs shall raise,
    Their blessings shall ascend.

11 They in Thy kingdom shall delight ;
  They shall be talking of Thy might,
12   That men Thy power may know ;
13 Thy kingdom shall for ever last,
  And Thy dominion standeth fast
    While endless ages flow.

14 Jehovah holdeth up the weak,
  The bowèd down His love doth seek,
    He raiseth them that fall.
15 All wait on Thee with watchful eyes ;
16 Thy bounteous Hand their wants supplies,
    With plenty filling all.

17 Righteous in every work and way
18 Jehovah is ; to those who pray
    In truth He will be nigh :
19 He will the supplications hear
  Of all His holy Name who fear,
    And save them when they cry.

20 All those who love Him He will keep,
   But all the wicked He will sweep
      From earth with judgment sore.
21 My mouth His praises shall proclaim ;
   O let all creatures bless His Name
      Both now and evermore !

Song lxviii.

" David took the stronghold of Zion."—v. 7.

David was now acknowledged sovereign of the whole
kingdom, but one fortress still held out against him.
Although the lower town of Jerusalem was inhabited by
parts of the tribes of Benjamin and Judah, the citadel of
Zion was in the possession of the Jebusites, a very warlike
portion of the old heathen inhabitants of the country.

Confident in its strength, its occupants declared that
the lame and blind would be sufficient to defend it, and
David, in his anxiety for its capture, offered to make him
who should be the first to scale the walls " captain," or
leader of the army.   This feat was accomplished by his
nephew Joab (1 Chron. xi. 6), and the following may
have been a song of triumph for this glorious conclusion
of the siege.

PSALM XLVII. 1—4.

 ALL ye people, clap your hands,
　　To God with voice of triumph sing ;
2 Jehovah all the earth commands,
　　A terrible and mighty King.

3 The people He to us subdues,
　　Beneath our feet doth nations place :
4 He our inheritance doth choose,
　　The excellence of Jacob's race.

Song lxix.

" David went on, and grew great, and the LORD God of hosts was with him."—v. 10.

At once perceiving the importance of his new acquisition, David determined to make it the capital of his dominions. He fixed his residence in the fort, and commenced enlarging and beautifying the city. For the first time the people of God were in undivided possession of the promised land, and to David was this precious heritage given.

The words of the following beautiful song are so perfectly in unison with the description of prosperity given above that I have chosen it as appropriate to this period.

PSALM LXI. 5—8.

 GOD, Thou hast vouchsafed my vows to
hear,
And given me to claim
The goodly heritage of those who fear
And reverence Thy Name.

6 Thy blessing to the king long life will give,
Which shall as ages last.
7 Let truth, that he before his God may live,
And mercy hold him fast.

8 So I, Thy Name to magnify, will raise
My voice from day to day ;
And daily shall my song resound Thy praise,
That I my vows may pay.

Song lxx.

"And there were yet sons and daughters born to David."—v. 13.

The appropriateness of the following Psalm to the birth of children to David in his new capital is too obvious to need remark.

PSALM CXXVIII.

LEST, surely blest, is he whose heart
    Is to Jehovah near,
Who doth not from His ways depart,
    But walks therein with fear.

2 For thou the labour of thine hands
    Shalt eat, and happy be ;
Yea, thou shalt reap thy fertile lands ;
    It shall be well with thee.

3 Thy wife shall, like a fruitful vine,
    Adorn thy dwelling-place,
Children like olive plants be thine,
    Sons shall thy table grace.

4 His bounteous love their cup shall fill
    Who near Jehovah live ;
Jehovah shall from Zion's hill
    To thee His blessing give.

5 Blest all thy days shall Salem be,
    Within her joy shall dwell ;
6 Thy children's children thou shalt see,
    And peace on Israel.

I CHRONICLES XIII.

Song lxxi.

" Let us bring again the Ark of our God to us."—v. 3.

The order of the narrative after the events already commemorated is a little different in the Books of Samuel and Chronicles, and will be more easily explained by referring to the latter for a few Chapters.

It should, however, first be recalled to mind that just before the death of Eli the Philistines had defeated the Israelites in a great battle and had carried away the Ark of God (1 Sam. iv.). The detention of the Ark among the heathen was usually spoken of by the Hebrews as "The Captivity." During the seven months that it lasted God inflicted fearful judgments upon the captors, on which account their nobles resolved to appease His anger by giving up their dangerous trophy. Placing the Ark on a new cart, they harnessed to it two milch kine whose calves were shut up at home, and they were amazed to behold these animals, contrary to all natural instinct, take the straight road to the land of Judah. The five princes of Philistia witnessed the miracle with awe and wonder, and followed to see the result. We are told that the men of Bethshemesh were reaping their wheat when the Ark appeared in sight, and their surprise and joy seem to be graphically commemorated in Psalm cxxvi. The harvest which had been sown in tears must indeed have been reaped in joy. The Ark was, however,

soon afterwards removed to the house of Abinadab, a
Levite of Kirjath-jearim, where it remained until the
period in David's history at which we have now arrived.

The desire of the king and of all Israel to have this
sacred possession brought to their new capital is alluded
to in the text which I have selected as the heading of
this song, and appears to be compared in the Psalm with
the longing of the dwellers in the thirsty south for the
return of their mountain streams.

PSALM CXXVI.

WHEN our captivity to turn,
    And Israel's bondage to redeem,
  Jehovah deigned, our hearts did burn
      As in a dream.

2 Laughter was heard on every side,
    The heathen wondrous things were taught ;
  " Jehovah mighty things " they cried,
      " For them hath wrought."

3 Yea, wondrous things Jehovah's might
    For our sakes hath vouchsafed to show,
  Whereof with gladness and delight
      Our hearts o'erflow.

4 Jehovah, stretch once more Thine Hand,
    Turn our captivity again,
  As rivers in the southern land
      Return with rain.

5 Who sow in tears in joy shall reap,
6   Who mourning in the furrow leaves
  Good seed, shall not at harvest weep,
      But bring his sheaves.

Song lxxii.

The neglected state of the Ark must have been a cause of deep shame and sorrow to every pious heart in Israel. The disturbed condition of the country from the death of Eli until David was firmly settled on the throne had rendered it impossible to find a suitable resting-place for this most sacred treasure.

Now, however, when the blessing of peace was restored to them, the people of God yearned after their long lost privileges, and hailed with delight the proposal to bring the Ark to Jerusalem. This short song seems to express their joy on this occasion.

PSALM LXXXV. 1—2.

EHOVAH, Thou again hast sought
 With loving grace Thy land,
 And Jacob from his bondage brought,
Redeemed by Thy right Hand.

2 Thy wrath which on Thy people lay,
 The guilt which reigned within,
Thou hast removèd far away,
 And covered all their sin.

L 2

Song lxxiii.

" They carried the Ark of God in a new cart out of the house of Abinadab."—v. 7.

We may suppose that, as soon as David had obtained the ready assent of his subjects to accompany the Ark to Jerusalem in a joyful as well as solemn procession, he prepared a suitable service for the occasion. We cannot now ascertain what songs were composed for it, but I have adopted those that appear to me appropriate to the various incidents of the removal, which was accomplished by two distinct journeys. Ps. lxviii., consisting of four separate Songs, is generally believed to have been used in the course of this double journey, and the first part was probably sung when the procession set out, as it commences with the very words which Moses had employed during the wanderings of the Israelites, whenever the Ark of the Covenant set forward from its temporary resting-place (Numbers x. 35).

I have remarked on the position of "Selah" (at the end of v. 7) in the Introduction, pages xii and xiii.

PSALM LXVIII. 1—6.

LET God arise, and let His foes
        Confounded be ;
  And, scattered by His arm, let those
        That hate Him flee ;
2 As smoke that vanisheth from sight
  By Thee let them be put to flight.

Let sinners fall beneath His eye
  In dire dismay,
Perish, as wax, when fire is nigh,
  Doth melt away ;
3 But glad let all the righteous be ;
Let them rejoice exceedingly.

4 Sing unto God, uplift your song
  His Name to praise,
*Who rides the desert sands along ;
  *His highway raise ;
*Jah is His Name, uplift your voice ;
Jah is His Name, in Him rejoice.

5 A Father to the fatherless,
  The widows' Friend,
God will relieve their sore distress,
  And comfort send ;
Yea, from His holy place will hear,
And save them out of all their fear.

6 He for the desolate and lone
  A household makes ;
He those, who bound in fetters groan,
  From prison takes ;
But those who heed not His command
Shall dwell within a barren land.

Song lxxiv.

" David and all Israel played before God with all their might, and with singing."—v. 8.

There is no recorded event to which Ps. xxxiii. is more appropriate than to the removal of the Ark from the house of Abinadab; for not only do the harp and psaltery to which it alludes coincide with the Bible narrative, but the subject of the song is just what we should expect on that occasion. Opening with a glorious burst of praise of the Creator and Benefactor of the world, it proceeds to extol that discriminating supervision of His creatures of which the return of the Ark was so striking an instance. The counsel of the heathen had by Him been made ineffectual to deprive His chosen people of their sacred treasure, and Jehovah was even then renewing the assurance of His covenant with Israel. Their king would not trust in his armies, but in the knowledge that the Lord was dwelling among them as their Help and Shield.

PSALM XXXIII.

YE that righteous are, rejoice,
  Shouts of joy and gladness raise ;
Praise Jehovah with your voice ;
  Comely for the just is praise.

2 With the harp His praises sing,
  Let the psaltery not be mute ;
Praises to Jehovah bring,
  Praise Him on a ten-stringed lute.

3 Sing to Him an anthem new,
    Skilfully give forth the sound ;
4 For Jehovah's word is true,
    All His works are faithful found.

5 Righteous judgment doth He love,
    Earth is with His goodness bright ;
6 When He spake, the Heavens above
    Sprung with all their hosts to light.

7 He doth gather as an heap
    All the waters of the sea ;
He lays up the ocean deep
    In a mighty treasury.

8 Let the earth fear Him alone ;
    Let in awe the people stand ;
9 For He spake and it was done,
    Fast it stood at His command.

10 Lo, Jehovah's wisdom brings
    All the heathen's schemes to nought ;
He destroys the plots of kings ;
    Vain He makes man's wisest thought.

11 All His counsel standeth fast,
    Fixed for ever to endure ;
All His thoughts for ever last,
    Through all ages firm and sure.

12 Those who on Jehovah rest,
    Making Him their God alone,
Blest are they ; and they are blest
    Whom He chooseth for His own.

13 From His Throne in Heaven on high
    Doth Jehovah see our race ;
14 Those who dwell on earth His eye
    Watcheth from His dwelling-place.

15 By His wisdom He doth mould
    All the hearts of men below ;
All their works He doth behold,
    All their inmost thoughts doth know.

16 Not by greatness of his host
    Doth a king his triumphs gain ;
Mighty men, of strength who boast,
    Seek deliverance in vain.

17 Vain is horse's speed and power
    Life to save on battle-field ;
Vain his strength in danger's hour
    From the foe to prove a shield.

18 Lo, Jehovah's watchful eye
    Rests on them His Name who fear;
They who on their God rely
    Find His mercy ever near.

19 He preserves their soul from death,
    Feeds them with His bounteous Hand,
Still maintains their failing breath,
    E'en when famines waste the land.

20 Waiting doth our soul abide
    Till Jehovah be revealed ;
He will surely help provide,
    He is our Defence and Shield.

21 Trust upon His Name we place,
 Glad in Him our hearts shall be ;
22 O Jehovah, let Thy grace
 Rest on us who hope in Thee.

Song lxxb.

"Uzza put forth his hand to hold the Ark; for the oxen stumbled."—v. 9.

The procession had advanced with demonstrations of joy, such as those recorded in the foregoing Psalms, as far as the threshing-floor of Chidon or Nachon, when it was suddenly overtaken (so says the tradition) by a most terrible thunderstorm. The history informs us that the oxen (probably either through alarm or owing to the slippery state of the road) stumbled, and Uzza, one of the sons of Abinadab and one of the drivers of the cart, took hold of the Ark to save it from falling. This hasty act was the climax of that want of due reverence and conformity to God's directions as to the removal of the Ark which characterized the whole arrangement. In Numbers iv. 15 we read that, when the sons of Aaron had carefully covered the Ark, the sons of Kohath were to bear it, but " they shall not touch any holy thing lest they die." All this had evidently been overlooked, and probably the storm with its attendant catastrophe was the mark of God's displeasure, for Uzza was immediately struck dead, killed, as is supposed, by a flash of lightning. The consternation which ensued made it impossible for the procession to go further. David therefore relinquished for the present his design of bringing the Ark to Jerusalem, and deposited it in the neighbouring house of Obed-edom, there to wait till the anger of the Lord should be appeased. The awful circumstances attending the death of Uzza were possibly in David's memory when he composed the magnificent description of a storm which is found in Psalm xxix.

PSALM XXIX.

*GIVE to Jehovah, ye on high,
　　Ye who in might and power excel,
　Give to Jehovah majesty,
　　Extol His strength, His glory tell.

2 Give to Jehovah glory due,
　　The greatness of His Name confess ;
　Give to Jehovah homage true,
　　*And worship Him in holy dress.

3 Jehovah speaks in Ocean's roar,
　　The God of glory thundereth ;
　The waters, when they lash the shore,
　　Are driven by Jehovah's breath.

4 Jehovah's voice is full of might ;
　　His voice in power is heard on high ;
　Jehovah speaketh from the height ;
　　His voice is full of majesty.

5 Jehovah's voice the cedars breaks,
　　The pride of Lebanon lays low ;
　Jehovah's voice the mountains shakes ;
　　That voice, that mighty voice they know.

6 As a young unicorn doth leap,
　　Springs Lebanon that voice to hear ;
　His place no more may Sirion keep,
　　Trembling to feel Jehovah near.

7 Jehovah's voice the flames of fire
    Doth from the thunder-cloud divide,
8 And when that voice is heard in ire
    The desert shakes on every side.

    Kadesh, thy wilderness doth quake ;
9   The fear-struck hinds bring forth their
            young;
    His voice the forest depths doth shake ;
    His glory in His House is sung.

10 Throned o'er the flood Jehovah reigns,
    A King Whose rule shall never cease ;
11 His might His people's strength maintains,
    His blessing gives His people peace.

Song lxxvi.

" When the Philistines heard that David was anointed king over all
Israel, all the Philistines went up to seek David."—v. 8.

Perhaps the news of David's failure in the attempt to
carry the Ark to his new capital may have inspired the
Philistines with the idea that this was a favourable opportunity for an invasion. They may have imagined that
the God of Israel was opposed to the new king, and
would no longer protect his people. "Where is now
their God?" would be their exulting inquiry. It found a
speedy answer; for David, having asked counsel of the
Lord, met and defeated them at Baal-perazim, and burned
the images which in their flight they had abandoned.
This victory appears to be the subject of Psalm cxv.

PSALM CXV.

David.

NOT unto us the glory be,
　　The praise, Jehovah, be to Thee;
　　O let Thy Name the glory take,
　　Yea, for Thy truth and mercy's sake.
2 O wherefore should the heathen say
"Where now is He to whom they pray?"
3 Our God in highest Heaven doth dwell;
　　And He hath done what pleased Him well.

4 Their gold and silver gods are nought;
  Idols are they which men have wrought;
5 Mouths have they which no speech can find;
  Deaf are their ears; their eyes are blind;
6 Noses that smell not they possess;
  Their throats no language can express;
7 Hands have they—hands that useless prove;
  And feet that have no power to move;
8 Like them are those that have them made;
  Like them are all that trust their aid.

Priest.

9 But thou, O Israel's chosen race,
  Thy trust upon Jehovah place;
  Trust thou in Him; on battle-field
  He is their Helper and their Shield.
10 O Aaron's house, in Him confide;
  Trusting Jehovah still abide;
  He doth His succour to them yield;
  He is their Helper and their Shield.
11 All ye Jehovah's Name who fear,
  To Him with trusting hearts draw near;
  He hath His saving power revealed;
  He is their Helper and their Shield.
12 Jehovah hath us borne in mind;
  Joy in His blessing we shall find;
  He will to Israel blessings send,
  To Aaron's house His grace extend.
13 His blessing upon them shall wait
  Who fear Jehovah, small and great.

14 You and your children shall not cease,
   Blest by Jehovah, to increase.
15 Jehovah, Heaven and Earth Who made,
   His blessing upon you hath laid.

Chorus.

16 The Heavens He makes His dwelling-place,
   But earth He gives to Adam's race.
17 The dead sing not Jehovah's praise,
   Nor those in silence songs upraise ;
18 But we Jehovah will adore.
   Praise ye Jehovah evermore.

Song lxxvii.

" God is gone forth before thee to smite the host of the Philistines."—v. 15.

"The Philistines yet again spread themselves abroad in the valley. Therefore David enquired again of God; and God said unto him, Go not up after them; turn away from them, and come upon them over against the mulberry-trees. And it shall be, when thou shalt hear a sound of going in the tops of the mulberry-trees, that then thou shalt go out to battle."

Such is the context to the verse which I have chosen as a fitting introduction to the following song. What miraculous interposition may have caused the mysterious sound, is not explained. It has been thought that, as the chariots and horsemen of Heaven were revealed to the eye of Elisha (2 Kings vi. 17), so was David permitted to hear the going forth of the celestial army to prove to the enemies of God how terrible are His works and how great is His power. The first part of Psalm lxvi. may refer to the defeat of the Philistines on this occasion.

PSALM LXVI. 1—4.

MAKE to God a joyful noise,
    All ye lands, your voices raise,
2 Sing the honour of His Name,
    Sing, and glorious make His praise.

3 Say to God, "How terrible
    " In Thy mighty works art Thou!
" Through the greatness of Thy power
    " Shall Thy foes submissive bow.

4 " All the earth shall worship Thee,
  " All in song Thy praise proclaim,
 " All before Thee bow the knee,
  " All shall sing unto Thy Name."

Song lxxviii.

" The fame of David went out into all lands ; and the LORD brought the fear of him upon all nations."—v. 17.

Psalm cxliv. is generally admitted to be composite, the original song ending with the refrain at the end of verse 11. Delitzsch suggests that it may have been written in reference to the conquest of Goliath, to which in many respects it is suitable ; but the words in verse 2 " subdueth my people that is under me " are strongly against placing it before David's accession to the throne. It may have been composed in three distinct portions, the second (beginning with " A new song," verse 9, and ending with the second refrain, verse 11,) having been added by David to celebrate a new victory, and the last part appended by him afterwards.

Whatever may have been the period of the composition either of the original song or of the later additions, in its present form it is extremely suitable to the time of victorious peace, described above, whilst the Philistines, though in a measure crushed, still remained to be a source of anxiety.

PSALM CXLIV.

David.

BLEST be Jehovah, blest His Name,
　　My Rock of strength, my Might,
He Who doth teach my hands to war,
　　My fingers train to fight ;

2 He Who my Loving-kindness is,
　　My Fortress, Saviour, Tower,
　My Shield, my Refuge, Who subdues
　　My people to my power.

3 Jehovah, what is man, that Thou
　　Should'st deign on him to look?
　Or what the son of man, that he
　　Be written in Thy book?

Chorus.

4 Man is a thing of vanity,
　　*Yea, even as a breath;
　Like to a shadow are his days
　　That quickly vanisheth.

David.

5 Jehovah, bow Thy Heavens, come down,
　　Descend Thou from the skies;
　Touch Thou the mountains, and behold
　　Their smoke in clouds shall rise.

6 Cast forth Thy lightning; then o'erthrown
　　And scattered they shall lie;
　Shoot out the arrows from Thy bow,
　　And stricken they shall die.

7 Send down Thy judgments from above,
　　Let none before Thee stand;
　O save me from the waterflood,
　　And from the stranger's hand.

Chorus.

8 Whose mouth doth speak of vanity,
  Whose words with lies abound ;
  In whose right hand doth falsehood dwell,
  And wickedness is found.

David.

9 A new and joyful song to Thee
  My voice, O God, shall raise ;
  Upon a ten-stringed psaltèry
  Will I resound Thy praise.

10 His outstretched Arm the victory
   Doth unto kings afford,
   Who doth His servant David's life
   Deliver from the sword.

11 O rescue and deliver me,
   Let none before me stand ;
   Save from the sons of aliens,
   And from the stranger's hand.

Chorus.

Whose mouth doth speak of vanity,
  Whose words with lies abound;
In whose right hand doth falsehood dwell,
  And wickedness is found.

David.

12 That all our sons may in their youth
   Like well-trained plants be grown,
Each daughter like a beautiful
   And polished corner stone.

13 That all our garners may be full,
   With stores of plenty crowned,
In tens of thousands that our sheep
   *May in our fields abound.

14 *That laden be our oxen strong,
   No breach be in our wall,
No sallying forth be from our gates,
   *Nor heard the battle-call.

Chorus.

15 Blest is the people, surely blest,
   To whom such peace is known ;
Blest they whose God Jehovah is,
   Whose God is He alone.

1 CHRONICLES XV.

Song lxxix.

"David made him houses in the city of David, and prepared a place for the Ark of God, and pitched for it a tent."—v. I.

David's increasing greatness only added to the one longing desire which he had cherished from his youth upwards, viz. that he might dwell close to the House of the Lord, and spend much of his time within its courts. No sooner, then, had he obtained a little respite from the attacks of his heathen neighbours than he set about preparing a fit place for the reception of the Ark, determining to make a second attempt to bring it to Jerusalem with every mark of honour and reverence.

We cannot doubt that, while building and embellishing his city, his prevailing thought was of the loving-kindness of his God, and although Psalm xlviii. is not ascribed to David (see Introduction, page xxi), the latter part may express the feelings with which he prepared the Tabernacle and gazed on the rising palaces of Zion.

The word Temple is often used to denote the Sanctuary.

PSALM XLVIII. 9—14.

WITHIN Thy Temple's courts we trod,
　　　And thought upon Thy gracious ways;
10 According to Thy Name, O God,
　　　So is to earth's far ends Thy praise;
　　Beside Thee righteousness doth stand,
　　And justice filleth Thy right Hand.

11   Let Zion's holy mount rejoice,
        And Judah's daughters lift their voice,
      Because Thy judgments fill the land.

12 Round Zion go, about her walk,
        And all her towers and bulwarks tell;
13 Mark them, and be of them your talk,
        Her palaces consider well,
      That all her glory ye may see,
      And show to your posterity.
14   *For such is God, for ever sure,
        Our God for ever to endure,
      He Who our Guide till death will be.

𝕾ong lxxx.

" Sanctify yourselves, ... that ye may bring up the Ark of the
LORD God of Israel unto the place that I have prepared for it.
For because ye did it not at the first, the LORD our God made a
breach upon us, for that we sought Him not after the due order."
—vv. 12, 13.

Three months had passed away since the death of
Uzza, and David heard that God had blessed the house
of Obed-edom on account of its sacred charge.   He
therefore trusted that Jehovah had graciously pardoned
the irreverence which had so greatly aroused His anger,
and would grant success to a second attempt to bring
the Ark to Jerusalem.

Warned, however, by the former failure, he determined
that no carelessness on his part should again mar the
undertaking.   Remembering that none ought to carry
the Ark but the Levites, he called for them with the
priests, and admonished them in the above words with
regard to their holy office.

Psalm lxxxv. may have been compiled with reference
to this occasion from two songs by different authors.
(See Introduction, page xxi.)

Psalm lxxxv.

David.

BROUGHT back is Jacob's bondage now;
    Jehovah, Thou Thy land dost bless;
2 Forgiven is our sin, and Thou
    Hast covered all our wickedness.

3 Thine indignation is no more,
    No longer dost Thou wrath display;
Yea, all Thine anger now is o'er,
    The fierceness of it turned away.

4 O God of our salvation, turn,
    Turn us, and make Thine anger cease;
5 Shall Thy displeasure alway burn?
    Thy wrath from age to age increase?

6 O wilt Thou not new life bestow,
    That we may now rejoice in Thee?
7 Thy mercy, O Jehovah, show,
    And let us Thy salvation see.

(*To Abiathar.*)

8 To hear Jehovah's words I seek;
    What God doth say I fain would learn;
He to His people peace will speak,
    But let them not to sin return.

Abiathar.

9 Salvation to His saints is near,
    That glory this our land may grace;
10 Mercy and truth combined appear,
    And righteousness doth peace embrace.

11 Springing from earth shall truth arise,
    And with its fruits the earth shall crown;
And from the Throne above the skies
    Shall righteousness on man look down.

12 Jehovah shall His goodness show,
    And make our land her fruits provide ;
13 Before Him righteousness shall go,
    *And follow where His footsteps guide.

Song lxxxi.

" So David, and the elders of Israel, and the captains over thousands, went to bring up the Ark of the Covenant of the LORD out of the house of Obed-edom with joy."—v. 25.

All preparations having been made and the procession arranged in its proper order, the Levites raised the Ark upon their shoulders, and the following blessing, corresponding with that appointed in Numbers vi. 24—26, may have been sung.

PSALM LXVII. 1.

GOD to us His mercy show,
    Bless His servants with His grace,
Tokens of His love bestow,
    Cause to shine on us His Face.

Song lxxxii.

" And it came to pass, when God helped the Levites that bare the Ark of the covenant of the LORD, that they offered seven bullocks and seven rams."—v. 26.

We learn from the account in 2 Sam. vi. that they had only proceeded the short distance of about six paces (just sufficient to allow of the blessing being sung), when a halt was made for the above-named sacrifices, after which the march would doubtless be resumed, and the Song which forms the second portion of Psalm lxvii. may have been sung by the whole assembly.

This Song is apparently a fragment, and no name is prefixed to the Psalm.　(See Introduction, page xxi.)

PSALM LXVII. 2—4.

LET Thy way on earth be known,
　　Thy saving health to all men shown ;
3 Their voices let the people raise,
　　Let all the people sing Thy praise.

4 O let the nations joyful be,
　　With gladness let them sing to Thee ;
　　For Thou shalt righteous judgment give,
　　And govern all on earth that live.

Song lxxxiii.

" Thus all Israel brought up the Ark of the covenant of the LORD."—v. 28.

Although some Commentators think that the first part of Psalm xxiv. was not composed for this procession, it seems to me peculiarly appropriate to its arrival at the foot of the hill leading to the city gates.

The Creator of all the earth had vouchsafed to choose Zion for His abode, and, before the ascent of that henceforth holy mountain, the question would reverently be asked, "Who is worthy to go up?" The answer shows how high was the standard of purity required, but those who now approached were truly seeking their God, and might therefore proceed in the full assurance of His blessing and of that gift of righteousness which they desired.

PSALM XXIV. 1—6.

Chorus.

THE earth and all the fulness
    Of earth Jehovah's is ;
The world to Him belongeth,
    The dwellers there are His.

2 By Him it hath been founded,
    And raised above the sea ;
Upon the floods established,
    It stands by His decree.

Single Voice.

3 Who shall ascend the mountain
   Where shines Jehovah's Face?
Or who shall stand rejoicing
   Within His Holy Place?

Another Voice.

4 He that clean hands possesseth
   And heart unstained by spot,
Who vanity ne'er seeketh,
   Who falsely sweareth not.

Chorus.

5 The favour of Jehovah
   That man shall surely bless;
The God of His salvation
   Shall give him righteousness.

6 This is the generation,
   Yea, this the chosen race,
That seek, O God of Jacob,
   With faithful hearts Thy Face.

Song lxxxiv.

" *With shouting, and with sound of the cornet, and with trumpets, and with cymbals, making a noise with psalteries and harps.*"—
v. 28.

Such a song as that which forms the conclusion of Psalm lxviii. must have accompanied these overflowing demonstrations of joy, while " David danced before the Lord with all his might," wearing, instead of his royal robes, the linen ephod which so offended Michal's sense of dignity.

The position of the Selah after verse 32 in the middle of a sentence would alone render it probable that this Song is a fragment of another poem, but there are other reasons for forming this conclusion. (See Introduction, p. xiii.)

PSALM LXVIII. 33—35.

O Him, the Heavens of Heavens Who rides,
    Loud praises sing,
*To Him Who from of old abides
    A glorious King ;
His voice He sendeth from on high
A voice of might and majesty.

34 Praise Israel's Strength, Who in the height
    Hath made His Throne,
35 From out Thy Holy Place Thy might,
    O God, is shown ;
Yea, Israel's God to power hath raised
His chosen people. God be praised.

Song lxxxb.

" The Ark of the Covenant of the LORD came to the city of David." —v. 29.

The following glorious and prophetic Song may have been sung in parts at the gates when the Ark entered the city.

We know that the Ark was sometimes carried to battle with the army; and it is probable that the processional hymn used on its return was always interrupted at the city gates by this dialogue, and was resumed as soon as the Ark and its attendants had passed through them.   This would account for the musical notice (Selah) at the end. (See Introduction, p. xix.)

PSALM XXIV. 7—10.

Single Voice.

PLIFT your heads, ye portals,
    *Uplift, ye ancient gates;
Behold, the King of Glory
    To come within you waits.

Another Voice.

8 Who is this King of Glory?

Chorus.

This title doth belong
To Him in battle mighty,
    Jehovah, great and strong.

Single Voice.

9 Uplift your heads, ye portals,
   *Uplift, ye ancient gates;
Behold, the King of Glory
   To come within you waits.

Another Voice.

10 Who is this King of Glory?
   This title who doth bring?

Chorus.

The Lord of Hosts, Jehovah,
   He is of Glory King.

Song lxxxvi.

" *Michal the daughter of Saul, looking out at a window, saw king
David dancing and playing.*"—v. 29.

Michal appears to have seen the procession when it
halted at David's house, and when probably Psalm xv.
was being sung, for we may imagine that the king, whose
lifelong object it had been to fit himself for the privilege
now so near at hand, had arranged that this Psalm should
come in at the place where its salutary admonition would
most especially apply to himself. It is generally admitted
that Psalm xv. was composed for the removal of the Ark
to Mount Zion, and this is perhaps the strongest argument against the first portion of Psalm xxiv. (see Song
lxxxiii.) forming part of the processional service. The
two songs, however, are suited to different stages of the
journey, and allude to different privileges—Psalm xxiv.
inquiring who is worthy to ascend the holy hill and enter
the Tabernacle, Psalm xv. asking who, yet more blessed,
shall be permitted constantly to dwell therein. The same
qualities are required in both cases, but in the latter they
are more fully dwelt upon.

PSALM XV.

WHO, O Jehovah, shall abide
    Within the Tent that Thou hast blest?
For whom wilt Thou a home provide,
    Upon Thy holy hill a rest?

2 He who a godly life doth lead,
    The man who righteousness doth seek,
He who is pure in thought and deed,
    And from his heart the truth doth speak.

3 Whose tongue doth no man falsely blame,
    To others who no ill hath wrought,
Nor hath to wound his neighbour's fame
    With slander and reproaches sought.

4 He in whose eyes the evil ways
    Of wicked men do vile appear,
Who giveth honour due and praise
    To those Jehovah's Name who fear.

Who, to his neighbour if he swear,
    His covènant will not forsake,
Yea, rather hurt and loss will bear
    Than any solemn promise break.

5 On usury who hath not lent,
    Nor wronged the innocent for gain ;
To him shall saving help be sent,
    Unmoved he ever shall remain.

1 Chronicles XVI.

Song lxxxvii.

" So they brought the Ark of God, and set it in the midst of the tent
that David had pitched for it." —v. 1.

We may now imagine the march resumed. The Ark of
God is at length ascending the hill of Zion after its sad
captivity among the heathen and its long detention from
its destined home, all so suggestive of the past history of
God's chosen people.

The following magnificent hymn may be appropriately
placed in this last stage of the journey.

Psalm LXVIII. 7—19.

GOD, when through the desert Thou
    Didst lead our race,
8 Earth shook, the very heavens did bow
    Before Thy Face;
E'en Sinai's mount was moved with fear,
For God, e'en Israel's God, was near.

9 O God, Thou sendedst from the sky
    A plenteous rain,
Thine heritage, when parched and dry,
    To cheer again.
10 Thine own have dwelt in safety there;
    Thy love did for the poor prepare.

11 *The Lord doth give the word ; to bear
  The tidings far,
 *An host of women's songs declare
  *" We victors are."
12 *Kings with their hosts shall flee, shall flee ;
 Shared in the tent the spoil shall be.

13 Although among the pots ye lay,
  Defiled and sad,
 Ye shall be seen in new array,
  With honour clad,
 As doves their silver wings unfold,
 With feathers bright like burnished gold.

14 *When kings the Almighty doth o'erthrow
  And put to flight,
 *Then is it even as is snow
  In Salmon white.
15 High is of Bashan's mount the crest,
 High is the hill which God hath blest.

16 Why leap ye ? why with envy swell,
  Ye lofty hills ?
 This hill, where God delights to dwell,
  His Presence fills ;
 For ever upon Zion's side
 Jehovah's glory will abide.

17 Thousands of chariots of light
  To God belong ;
 Thousands of Angels, armed for fight,
  Around Him throng ;
 Jehovah is among them found,
 E'en as in Sinai's holy ground.

18 Thou hast gone up and captive made
    *A captive band ;
  *Gifts at Thy footstool men have laid
    From every land ;
Yea, that, although they did rebel,
Jehovah God might with them dwell.

19 Blest be the Lord, our Strength, our Stay ;
    His praise proclaim
  *Who bears our burden day by day ;
    Blest be His Name ;
All power from harm to keep is His,
'Who God of our salvation is.

Song lxxxviii.

"He dealt to every one of Israel, both man and woman, to every one
a loaf of bread, and a good piece of flesh, and a flagon of wine."
—v. 3.

After inaugurating the new Tabernacle with burnt sacrifices and peace-offerings, David, as related above, dis-
pensed to all the people the means of celebrating the
joyful occasion with an abundant feast. This exultant
hymn of praise to the Giver of all good things may have
been sung during the distribution. The whole Psalm was
afterwards a harvest hymn.

PSALM LXVII. 5—7.

ET the people praises sing,
　　*Praise to Thee, O God, address ;
6 Then shall earth her increase bring,
　　Then our God His own shall bless ;
7 God shall bless us ; far and near
　Him the ends of earth shall fear.

Song lxxxix.

" On that day David delivered first this psalm to thank the LORD into the hand of Asaph and his brethren."—v. 7.

I have written this long Psalm (portions of which are found, with a few alterations, in Psalms cv., xcvi., and cvi.) in three different metres, to avoid monotony.

1 CHRONICLES XVI. 8—36.

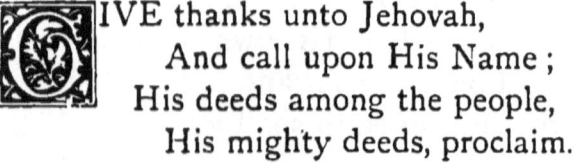IVE thanks unto Jehovah,
    And call upon His Name ;
His deeds among the people,
    His mighty deeds, proclaim.

9 Lift high to Him your voices,
    Sing anthems to His praise,
And let your talk be ever
    Of all His works and ways.

10 Let all who seek Jehovah
    Their tongues in praise employ ;
His Name shall be your glory,
    And fill your hearts with joy.

11 O seek ye then Jehovah,
    And strength from Him implore ;
Seek of His Face the favour,
    O seek it evermore.

12 His mighty works remember,
    The wonders of His hand ;
  Remember every judgment,
    Each law, and each command ;

13 Of Israel His servant
    O ye who are the seed,
  Ye chosen sons of Jacob,
    Whom He vouchsafes to lead.

14 He is our God Jehovah ;
    To earth's far distant ends
  He sendeth forth His judgments,
    His righteousness extends.

15 *His covenant He remembers,
    The word He did ordain
  To thousand generations
    Unbroken to remain —

16 The word He gave to Abrah'm,
    To Isaac which He swore,
17 And hath confirmed to Jacob,
    A law for evermore—

18 The covènant thus spoken,
    " I give this land to thee,
  " This fruitful land of Canaan,
    " Your heritage to be ;"

19 When ye were few in number,
    A small and feeble race,
  And in the land were strangers,
    Without a dwelling-place.

20 From nation on to nation
    When He His people sent,
  From kingdom on to kingdom
    When journeying they went ;

21 He suffered none to wrong them,
    Nor ought from them to take ;
  He even kings reprovèd
    And princes for their sake ;

22 "Against My chosen people
   "Uplift no hostile arm ;
  "Nor touch ye Mine anointed,
   "Nor do my prophets harm."

23 Sing, sing ye praises to Jehovah,
    Sing, all the earth, uplift the voice ;
  Show forth with gladness His salvation ;
    From day to day in Him rejoice.

24 Among the heathen sing His glory,
    To them His majesty declare ;
  Among all nations tell His wonders,
  · His mighty works proclaim ye there.

25 For He is greatly to be praisèd,
    No God like Him is to be feared ;
26 The peoples' gods they are but idols ;
    Jehovah spake—The heavens appeared.

27 Glory and strength are in His Presence,
    Gladness and honour in His Place.
28 Ascribe ye glory to Jehovah
    And strength, all ye of every race.

29 Give ye unto His Name its glory,
  With offèrings His altar crown,
And come before Him ; when ye worship,
  *In holy vestments bow ye down.

30 Fear ye in all the earth before Him ;
  The world itself shall stable be ;
It shall not move from its foundation,
  Fixed firmly there by His decree.

31 O let the heavens be glad and joyful,
  And let the earth rejoice and sing ;
And let them say among the nations
  " Jehovah reigneth—He is King."

32 Let ocean roar, and all its fulness,
  The fields with gladness clad appear ;
33 Sing out, ye trees, Jehovah cometh—
  The Judge of all the earth is near.

34 O give thanks unto Jehovah,
  Give ye thanks, for He is good ;
For His mercy still endureth,
  Firm as it hath ever stood.

35 Say ye, " God of our salvation,
  " Save us, us together bring ;
" From the heathen us deliver,
  " Thanks to Thee and praise to sing."

36 Blessèd ever be Jehovah,
  Let our songs to Him be raised ;
Jacob's God be blessed for ever,
  Israel's God for ever praised.

Song xc.

" He left there before the Ark of the Covenant of the LORD Asaph and his brethren, to minister."—v. 37.

Psalm cxxxiv. may express the mutual farewell blessings of the king and priests when David left the Tabernacle.

PSALM CXXXIV.

David.

LO, bless ye Jehovah,
    Ye servants of His,
By night to stand waiting
    Whose office it is.

2 Your hands lift in worship
    In this holy place,
And bless ye Jehovah,
    While seeking His Face.

Priests.

3 Jehovah, the heavèns
    And earth Who hath made,
Send blessing from Zion
    On thee to be laid.

Song xci.

" All the people departed."—v. 43.

The third part of Psalm lxviii. forms a parallel song to the second, each consisting of thirteen verses ending with a doxology; and as the earlier portion appeared suitable to the march up the hill to the Tabernacle, so does the later part seem applicable to the return down the hill on leaving it.

Before describing the magnificent ceremony which had just taken place, the history of the Israelites is alluded to again, and as the former song foretold the universal blessings which should proceed from Zion, even " for the rebellious," so this one declares that the heathen shall stretch out their hands unto God, and all the kingdoms of the earth sing praises to Him.

PSALM LXVIII. 20—32.

OUR God, the God Who saveth, is
　　The Lord alone;
The Arm that brings from death is His,
　　Jehovah's own.

21 But God shall wound His foemen's head,
Who will not cease in sin to tread.

22 The Lord hath said " From Bashan's land
　　" I will restore;
" E'en from the sea shall My right Hand
　　" Bring back once more;
23 " That thou may'st wash thy foot in blood,
" And that thy dogs may lap the flood."

24 They saw Thee to Thy dwelling go,
       My God and King;
25 First, songs of praise were heard to flow
       From those who sing;
   Then damsels on the timbrels played,
   Where instruments loud music made.

26 O bless ye God amid the throng,
       Lift high your voice;
   E'en to the Lord upraise your song,
       In Him rejoice;
   Join ye, the stream of praise to swell,
   Ye from the fount of Israel.

27 *There Benjamin, the youngest, held
       *The ruler's place;
   *Chiefs and their bands the concourse swelled
       Of Judah's race;
   Zabulon's leaders followed nigh,
   And princes then of Naphtali.

28 Thy God, O Israel, to Thee
       Thy strength hath brought;
   O God, let that established be
       Which Thou hast wrought.
29 *Let kings in Salem tribute pay,
   And on Thine altar offerings lay.

30 *The beast that dwelleth in the reed,
       *Proud Egypt's might,
   *Princes, and people whom they lead,
       Put Thou to flight;
   That they to Thee may tribute bring,
   And humbly make their offering.

31 Princes shall be from Pharoah's lands
    Assembled there ;
And Cush shall soon stretch out his hands
    To God in prayer.
32 Sing unto God, all kingdoms, sing,
   Sing praises to the Lord our King.

Song xcii.

" David returned to bless his house."—v. 43.

The procession appears to have escorted David to his house, and then to have separated, doubtless with one last song of praise. It would be difficult to conceive a more appropriate occasion for the following Song, or a more magnificent conclusion to the services of the day.

The last verse, however, which might seem to allude to the golden shields which David afterwards took from Hadadezer, king of Zobah, may have led the Compiler of Psalm xlvii. to believe that this Song was composed at the time of the removal of the Ark to the Temple of Solomon, when probably the whole of the Psalm was sung together. The uncertainty as to the date of one portion would account for the Psalm having no special ascription. (Introduction, p. xxi.)

PSALM XLVII. 5—9.

GOD with a shout is gone on high,
　　Jehovah with the trumpet's voice;
6 Sing praises God to magnify,
　　Sing praises, in our King rejoice;
7 For God of all the earth is King;
　*His praise with skilful music sing.

8 God o'er the heathen rule doth bear;
　　He sitteth on His holy Throne;
9 Princes of those are gathered there
　　Whom Abrah'm's God hath made His own;
　For lo, the shields of earth are His;
　Greatly our God exalted is.

Song xciii.

"The king sat in his house, and the LORD had given him rest round about from all his enemies."—v. 1.

We may now return to the Second Book of Samuel to continue the history.

After long years of danger and difficulty, followed by excitement and labour in the arrangement of public affairs, David at length had "rest." Not one amongst the many outpourings of his grateful heart which have been handed down to us is so completely in keeping with the verse above quoted as that beautiful Psalm which is universally attributed to the shepherd king, though Commentators differ much with regard to the period of its composition. It appears scarcely necessary to enter into details with regard to my reasons for placing it here, when David was probably reflecting on the many mercies of his past life.

PSALM XXIII.

JEHOVAH'S Self my Shepherd is ;
    I shall not need ;
  2 To pastures green, by waters still,
    He doth me lead.

3 He doth restore my soul ; my Guide
    Himself doth make
Within the paths of righteousness
    For His Name's sake.

4 Yea, though I tread the darksome vale,
    And Death be near,
Although I through the shadows pass,
    I will not fear ;

For Thou art with me ; at my side
    I still have Thee ;
Thy rod, Thy guiding rod, and staff,
    They comfort me.

5 Thou dost a table for me spread
    Before my foes ;
My head with oil Thou dost anoint ;
    My cup o'erflows.

6 Thy lovingkindness all my life
    Shall follow me ;
Jehovah's House for evermore
    My home shall be.

Song xcib.

"And it came to pass that night, that the word of the LORD came unto Nathan."—v. 4.

David's active mind could not long be satisfied without work in the service of his God. In the early part of this Chapter we find him contemplating the erection of a Temple so magnificent as to form a fitting abode for the Ark of God. The prophet Nathan at first encouraged his aspirations, but returned on the following day with a message from the Lord forbidding the undertaking. The king's disappointment, however, was soothed by an assurance of continued favour and a promise that his wishes should be carried out by his son—a promise which also pointed to One far greater than Solomon, of Whose Throne that of David was but the type and shadow.

The first part of Psalm lxxxix., ascribed to Ethan the Ezrahite (one of the leaders of David's choir), appears to be a Song of thankfulness for the glorious promise revealed to Nathan.

PSALM LXXXIX. 1—4.

David.

O sing the mercies of Jehovah
My song shall ever flow ;
My mouth to every generation
Thy faithfulness shall show ;

O 2

2 For " Mercy," I have said, " for ever
   " Shall builded be by Thee ;
  " Thy truth within the very Heavèns
  " Establishèd shall be."

Nathan.

3 For I Myself have with My chosen
  A covènant prepared ;
And have unto My servant David
  With solemn oath declared,

4 "Thy seed I firmly will establish
  " For ever as Mine Own,
  " And build throughout all generations
  " Immovable thy throne."

Song xcb.

" I will be his father, and he shall be my son. If he commit iniquity,
I will chasten him with the rod of men, and with the stripes of
the children of men : but my mercy shall not depart away from
him, as I took it from Saul, whom I put away before thee. And
thine house and thy kingdom shall be established for ever."—
vv. 14—16.

The word of the LORD, communicated to David by
the mouth of Nathan, appears to be recapitulated in vv.
19—37 of Psalm lxxxix., which is ascribed to Ethan the
Ezrahite. Possibly it was repeated to David by the two
High Priests when he went to the Sanctuary for the
purpose of prayer and praise, and when Ethan, who was
a member of the choir, may have been present.

PSALM LXXXIX. 5—37.

David.

THE Heavèns, O Jehovah,
    *Thy wondrousness shall praise ;
Assembled saints their voices
    To laud Thy truth shall raise.

6 In Heavèn with Jehovah
    What name can be compared ?
By whom among the angels
    His majesty be shared ?

7 God in the saints' assembly·
    Is greatly held in fear,
And had by all in reverence
    Around Him who appear.

8 O God of Hosts, Jehovah,
    Who like to Thee is strong?
The faithfulness surrounds Thee
    That doth to Thee belong.

9 Thou rulest in its fury
    The raging of the sea ;
The waves thereof arising
    Are quieted by Thee.

10 Thou hast subduèd Egypt,
    As one that lieth slain ;
O'erthrown by Thee and scattered
    Thine enemies remain.

11 Thine are the heavens above us ;
    Thine is the earth below ;
The world and all its fulness
    Do Thee their Founder know.

12 The North Thou hast created,
    Thine Hand the South did frame,
Tabor and Hermon's mountain
    Are joyful in Thy Name.

13 To Thee all power belongeth,
    Thine Arm doth might command,
Strength in Thine Hand abideth,
    And high is Thy right Hand.

14 Thy Throne is set on judgment,
    On justice is its place ;
And truth and tender mercy
    Shall go before Thy Face.

15 Yea, blessèd is the people
    The joyful sound who know ;
Thy countenance, Jehovah,
    Shall light them as they go.

16 All day Thy Name extolling
    They shall uplift their voice ;
Thy righteousness their glory,
    In Thee they shall rejoice.

17 For Thou their strength art ever,
    The glory of their might ;
Our horns shall be exalted
    With favour in Thy sight.

18 Jehovah is our buckler,
    Who safety doth us bring ;
The Holy One of Israel,
    Jehovah is our King.

Zadok.

19 Thy will to Thy belovèd
    In vision was displayed,
Thou saidst, " Upon the mighty
    " I surely help have laid ;

" Exalted from the people
" My chosen I have led ;
20 " With oil I have anointed
" My servant David's head.

21 " Mine Hand shall him establish,
" And, strengthened by Mine Arm,
22 " The wicked shall not hurt him,
" No foe shall do him harm.

23 " Before him shall be smitten
" All those who bear him hate :
24 " But through My faith and mercy
" His glory shall be great.

25 " His powerful dominion
" Shall reach unto the sea ;
" Extended to the rivers
" His government shall be ;

26 " His cry to Me ascending,
" He thus shall lift his heart,
" ' My God, my Rock, my Father,
" ' Thou my Salvation art.'

27 " Him will I make My firstborn,
" All kings of earth above ;
28 " Ne'er break with him My covenant,
" But keep for him My love.

29 " His seed, by Me established,
" For ever shall endure ;
" And as the days of Heavèn
" His kingdom shall be sure."

Abiathar.

30 " But if his faithless children
        " My holy laws forsake,
    " And walk not in My judgments,
        " And My commandments break,

31 " If they profane My statutes,   ·
        " Forgetful of their God,
32 " My answer shall be scourging,
        " Their punishment the rod."

Zadok.

33 " And yet My lovingkindness
        " From him I will not take ;
34 " The word that I have spoken
        " I surely will not break.

35 " My covènant is certain,
        " My truth shall never fail ;
    " Myself have sworn to David ;
        " That oath shall him avail.

36 " His seed shall dwell for ever,
        " As sun and moon endure ;
37 " And, as a faithful witness
        " In Heaven, his throne be sure."

Song xcvi.

" Therefore now let it please Thee to bless the house of Thy servant, that it may continue for ever before Thee: for Thou, O Lord God, hast spoken it."—v. 29.

In the Bible history which describes the removal of the Ark we see David assuming all the priestly offices; for he not only composed the psalmody and arranged the order of the sacred processions, but, having exchanged his royal robe for a linen ephod, he led the people to the Sanctuary, and there, even in the presence of Abiathar and Zadok, offered the sacrifices and gave the sacerdotal blessing. In all these respects he was a type of that great High Priest for ever, not of Aaron's line but after the order of Melchizedek, spoken of in after-times by Isaiah as coming from Bozrah with garments dyed in blood, a mighty Conqueror, Who appeared to David's prophetic eye as terrible in His wrath, striking down kings, and judging the heathen. It was through that Great Descendant that David's house was to continue for ever before the Lord.

Psalm cx., supposed to have been written about this time, forms a suitable link between the priestly functions, already alluded to, and the wars on which David was about to enter.

PSALM CX.

JEHOVAH spake—To Thee, my Lord,
    He, Jehovah, spake the word,
      " On My right Hand shall be Thy Seat
      " Till Thy foes are 'neath Thy feet."

2 Jehovah shall, from Zion's height,
   Send the sceptre of Thy might ;
When rebels shall against Thee rise,
   Rule Thou 'midst Thine enemies.

3 *Thy people in Thy battle day
   Willingly shall Thee obey,
 *Themselves to offer to Thee glad,
   *All in holy vestments clad.
 *Thy youths are like the dewdrops drawn
   From the womb of morning's dawn.

4 Jehovah's Self hath sworn, and He
   Changeth not ; it sure shall be ;
 " A Priesthood is for ever Thine
   "Of the king of Salem's line ;
 " The endless order Thou shalt hold
   " Of Melchizedek of old."

5 The Lord, Who standeth on Thy right,
   Kings shall in His anger smite ;

6 The Judge of heathens He shall be ;
   They His punishments shall see ;
Of nations He shall wound the head,
   Filling divers lands with dead.

7 From out the brook beside the way
   He shall drink, His thirst to stay,
As onward He His course doth tread ;
   Therefore shall He lift His Head.

2 Samuel VIII.

Song xcvii.

*" David took Metheg-ammah out of the hand of the Philistines.   And
he smote Moab, and measured them with a line, casting them
down to the ground ; even with two lines measured he to put to
death, and with one full line to keep alive."*—vv. 1—2.

Two victories over the Philistines have been already
noticed ; a third war soon followed, which ended in their
complete subjugation.   David's next conquest was the
kingdom of Moab, to which he had sent his family for protection from the pursuit of Saul.   It has been conjectured
that the king had abused his trust and put David's aged
parents to death ; but from the nature of the retribution
recorded above it would seem that the aggression was on
the part of the nation at large, or at least of one portion
of it, on whom David executed signal and bloody vengeance.   It is generally understood that two-thirds of
the Moabites were massacred, but Dr. Chandler, in his
" Life of David," suggests a far more credible interpreta-
tion, founded on comparison with other passages of Scripture.   He supposes that David, having conquered Moab,
ordered a survey of the country, and levelled the
strongest cities with the ground, and that he then measured
out two tracts, one for death, and " the fulness of a line,"
a far larger division, to keep alive, and made the whole
nation tributary.

David may probably allude to his having bathed his
hands in the blood of the Moabites when he figures their
land as the basin wherein he washed.   (See Psalms lx. 8,
and cviii. 9.   Pages 212 and 215.)

Ps. ix. may refer to these wars ; vv. 5, 6, to the taking of Metheg-ammah, viz., Gath and her daughter towns (1 Chron. xviii. 1), and to the casting down of the cities of Moab.   In verse 12 there may possibly be an allusion to the punishment inflicted for the murder of David's family.

PSALM IX.

David to Jehovah.

TO Thee, Jehovah, I will raise
    With all my heart my song ;
    My lips Thy wondrous deeds shall praise,
    My tongue the strain prolong ;
2 In Thee, Most High, I will rejoice,
And praise Thy Name with heart and voice.

3 My foes, turned backward by Thy might,
    Shall at Thy Presence fall ;
4 Thou hast maintained my cause and right,
    As Judge enthroned o'er all
5 The heathen Thou hast put to shame,
And blotted from the earth their name.

Priest to David.

6 The foe now desolate is made,
    For ever overthrown ;
Cities in ruin thou hast laid,
    Their names no more are known.
7 Jehovah ever shall endure ;
His Throne for judgment standeth sure.

8 All nations of the world shall stand
  Before His Judgment Seat ;
Justice and equity His Hand
  Shall to the people mete.
9 Jehovah will a Refuge be,
Whereto the oppressed in grief may flee.

David to Jehovah.

10 And they who know Thy holy Name
   Will put their trust in Thee ;
When from Thy mercy help they claim,
   Thou wilt their Succour be ;
For Thou hast never left to fall
Those who on Thee, Jehovah, call.

To the Congregation.

11 Praise ye Jehovah Who doth dwell
   In Zion's holy place ;
His doings to the people tell ;
   Declare His boundless grace.
12 He, Who for blood doth vengeance take,
Granteth the prayer the poor doth make.

To Jehovah.

13 Have mercy, O Jehovah, see
   My trouble from men's hate,
Thou Who from death doth set me free,
   And lift me from his gate,
14 In Zion's gates to raise my voice,
In Thy salvation to rejoice.

Priest.

15 The heathen are to ruin brought,
　　Sunk in the pit they made ;
　Their foot within the net is caught,
　　Which privily they laid.
16 Jehovah is by judgment known ;
　Sinners by sin are overthrown.

17 The wicked, those who God forget,
　　Shall all be turned to hell.
18 Those in His memory He will set
　　Who now forgotten dwell ;
　The poor who on His promise rest
　Shall find their expectation blest.

All.

19 Arise, Jehovah, in Thy might,
　　And let not man prevail ;
　On heathens let Thy judgments light ;
20　　Let fear their hearts assail ;
　That nations may Thy terrors see,
　And know themselves but men to be.

Song xcviii.

"David smote also Hadadezer, the son of Rehob, king of Zobah, as he went to recover his border at the river Euphrates."—v. 3.

Zobah was a district of Syria, which in the time of Saul had been governed by several chieftains, but was now under the rule of a single sovereign; who invaded a territory which appears to have formed part of David's dominion. David would no doubt repair to the Tabernacle to offer sacrifices and implore the Divine aid before starting on the campaign, and the following Song may have been the blessing of the priest on this occasion.

PSALM XX. 1—3.

JEHOVAH thy petition hear,
　　When troubles compass thee around;
　The Name of Jacob's God be near,
　　To be thy sure Defender found;

2 Send from the Holy Place His aid,
　　And strengthen thee from Zion's height;
3 Remember all thine offerings made,
　　And in Thy sacrifice delight.

Song xcix.

" David took from him a thousand chariots, and seven hundred
horsemen, and twenty thousand footmen."—v. 4.

This brilliant victory was the more remarkable because
there was no cavalry in the army of the Israelites. The
use of horses had been forbidden by Moses, and David
was too conscientious to avail himself even of those
which he had taken in battle, but would trust in
Jehovah's strength alone. This Song of praise may
follow the preceding blessing most appropriately, and
together they reveal the secret of David's success.

PSALM XXI. 1—2.

THE king, exulting in Thy might,
　　Jehovah, greatly shall rejoice,
In Thy salvation shall delight,
　　And lift to Thee his voice.

2 For Thou to him didst favour show,
　　And didst his heart's desire supply,
His lips' request on him bestow,
　　Nor didst his prayer deny.

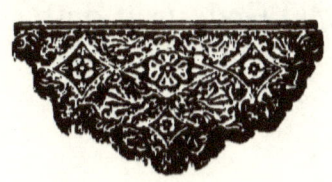

P

Song c.

The triumph of the Israelites was checked by the news that their defeated enemy had been reinforced by a large army of Syrian allies.

The Hebrew title of Ps. lx. does not coincide with the account of any recorded battle (see Introduction, p. xviii.), but the first part was probably composed with reference to one of the series of which an outline is given in this Chapter.

From the triumphant tone which appears in the second portion of the Psalm, as compared with the depression of spirits exhibited in the first part, we may suppose that the first part expresses the alarm caused by an invasion (perhaps that referred to in the text above), and that the other celebrates a victory.

PSALM LX. 1—4.

 GOD, Thou hast us cast aside,
   · Hotly doth Thy displeasure burn ;
Thou hast dispersed us far and wide ;
   Return to us again, return.

2 The trembling land is sore afraid ;
   Thou hast it broken ; it doth quake ;
O heal the breaches Thou hast made,
   Heal them, O God, for it doth shake.

3 Hard things Thou hast Thy people shown,
    Hard things to those Thou callest Thine ;
  Beneath Thy heavy Hand we groan ;
    We drink astonishment as wine.

4 Thy gracious Hand a banner gave
    To them Thy holy Name who fear ;
  O for the truth's sake let it wave
    On battle-field our hearts to cheer.

Song ci.

" David slew of the Syrians two and twenty thousand men."—v. 5.

The second part of Psalm lx., which is a portion of
Psalm cviii., was probably added to the first part in
reference to the result of the battle, in anticipation of
which the first part was written. (See Introduction,
pages xv—xix)

In regard to the figure by which Moab's condition
is described in v. 8, see Preface to Song 97.

PSALM LX. 5—12.

David.

HAT they on whom is set Thy love
From foemen may delivered be,
Save with Thy right Hand from above,
And answer when I call on Thee.

6 God in His Holiness declared ;
My heart shall therefore joyful be ;
The vale of Succoth shall be shared,
And Shechem meted out by me.

7 Now Gilead's hosts by me are led,
And mine is all Manasseh's land ;
*My helmet Ephraim guards my head,
*My sceptre Judah gives command.

Moab my washbowl I have made ;
O'er Edom I my shoe will cast ;
*Philistia, I have might displayed,
*The cry thou raisest long shall last.

9 What captain through the walls will break
　　To humble the strong city's pride ?
Who will the place of leader take ?
　　Who into Edom be my guide ?

Soldiers.

10 *O God, Thou hast not cast away,
　　Nor made us to our foes to yield,
O God, wilt Thou not might display,
　　And lead our armies to the field ?

11 In time of trouble send Thine aid,
　　For vain the help of man is found.
12 Through God our hearts are valiant made ;
　　Our foes He treadeth to the ground.

Song cii.

" David gat him a name when he returned from smiting of the Syrians in the valley of salt, being eighteen thousand men."—v. 13.

Psalm cviii. is generally supposed to refer to this victory. It is the whole Psalm of which the last Song is a fragment. (See Introduction, pages xv and xvi.)

Psalm cviii.

David.

 GOD, a steadfast heart I bring ;
A song to Thee I will upraise,
And with my glory I will sing,
And Thee will praise.

2 Awake, my harp, glad music make,
And thou, my psaltery, tribute pay ;
*My song of gladness shall awake
The dawn of day.

3 Amongst the people I will sing,
Amongst the nations lift my voice,
To Thee, Jehovah, praise will bring,
In Thee rejoice.

4 For great Thy mercy is, Thy love
    Beyond the highest heavens ascends,
And even to the clouds above
    Thy truth extends.

5 Exalt, O God, Thy glorious Name,
    Exalt Thy praise above the sky ;
Thy glory o'er the earth proclaim,
    And set on high.

6 Save Thy beloved in danger's hour,
    Yea, let Thy right Hand set them free ;
O save them by Thy mighty power,
    And answer me.

7 God, where His Presence doth abide,
    Hath spoken ; His decree I hail ;
With joy I Shechem will divide
    And Succoth's vale.

8 Gilead is mine, Manasseh mine ;
    *Defence my helmet Ephraim yields ;
*And as a sceptre Judah's line
    My right hand wields.

9 Moab is made my washbowl base ;
    O'er Edom I will cast my shoe ;
Philistia's sons before my face
    Shall homage do.

10 Who will the strong-built city take ?
    Who will for me its walls o'erthrow ?
Or who will, Edom's pride to break,
    Before me go ?

Soldiers.

11 O God, Thou hast not cast away
       Thy people ; wilt Thou not again
12 Lead forth our hosts ? Thy help display ;
       Man's help is vain.

13 Through God, the God in Whom we trust,
       We, valiant made, no ill shall dread,
    For He it is that in the dust,
       Our foes shall tread.

Song ciii.

"David executed judgment and justice unto all his people."—v. 15.

David probably added the second part of Psalm xix. to the first portion at a time when he was making a diligent study of the Mosaic law in order that he might rule his people justly.

There is a marked difference in the style of composition of the two parts. The earlier exhibits the ardent piety of the young shepherd delighting in the works of the God of all Creation, while the later contains the reflections of the tried servant of Jehovah dwelling on the laws given to His chosen people, and then, as has been before remarked in the preface to the first part (Song ii.), there is a corresponding change in the title by which he designates the Almighty.

PSALM XIX. 7—14.

JEHOVAH'S law is undefiled,
    Restoring souls to sin beguiled ;
    Jehovah's ordinance is sure,
      And His commandment alway pure ;
8 The simple heart it maketh wise,
    And light imparteth to the eyes ;
    The statutes He hath made are right,
    And fill the heart with pure delight.
9 Clean of Jehovah is the fear,
    And everlasting shall appear ;

Holy and righteous is His word ;
In all His judgments truth is heard ;
10 Than finest gold more precious far,
Than honeycomb they sweeter are ;
11 They are Thy servant's guide and guard ;
In keeping them is great reward.

12 By whom are his own errors seen ?
From secret faults O make me clean,
13 And keep me from presumptuous sin,
Lest o'er me it dominion win ;
So shall I still be undefiled,
Nor to the great offence beguiled.
14 O let my words acceptance gain,
And all my thoughts Thy praise obtain ;
My Rock, Jehovah, keep my heart,
O Thou Who my Redeemer art.

Song civ.

" David executed judgment and justice unto all his people."—v. 15.

The last Song explains the source whence David derived that high standard of virtue which in Ps. ci. he expresses his determination to maintain in his court and household. It seems to give weight to the Mussulman tradition that his Ethiopian slave, being asked how he had obtained so much influence with the king, replied, "By always speaking the truth, by always keeping my word, and by never meddling in matters that do not concern me."—Luther called this Psalm David's mirror of a monarch, and it was so greatly esteemed by one of the German princes that he sent a copy of it as a stern rebuke to a minister whom he suspected of dishonesty.

PSALM CI.

MERCY and judgment I will praise ;
    Of them my tongue shall sing ;
Jehovah, I my voice will raise,
    And songs of gladness bring.

2 From wisdom I will ne'er depart :
    When wilt Thou come to me ?
A holy walk and perfect heart
    Within my house shall be.

3 Nought evil shall with me abide,
    Nought vile mine eyes shall grieve ;
The work of them that turn aside
    To me shall never cleave.

4 Far be from me the froward heart,
     I shun the mind impure ;
5 I bid the slandèrer depart,
     Nor will the proud endure.

6 Upon the faithful in the land
     I look, with me to live ;
The upright shall before me stand,
     And service to me give.

7 Whoe'er doth in deceit delight
     With me shall never dwell ;
Nor shall he tarry in my sight
     Who dareth lies to tell.

8 No evil-doer shall remain,
     None rest the land within ;
Jehovah's city shall contain
     None that delight in sin.

Song cv.

" There was a famine in the days of David."—v. 1.

There is no Psalm apparently applicable to the ninth
Chapter, which relates the anxiety of David to show kindness to the family of Saul and his discovery, through
Ziba, of Mephibosheth, the son of Jonathan, on whom he
heaped riches and favours with a liberal hand.

After this there is some difficulty in tracing the course
of the history; but internal evidence is strongly on the
side of those Commentators who place the events recorded
in Chapters xxi. and xxii. next in order to the elevation of
Mephibosheth.

The following Song, written during some long and
grievous chastening, may be applied to the terrible
famine which year after year consumed the people and
grieved the heart of David.

PSALM LXXVII. 4—9.

THOU dost my weary eyelids waking hold ;
So troubled am I that no words I find ;
5 I have considered all the days of old ;
The years of ancient times I call to mind.
6 Throughout the night upon my song I dwell ;
I commune with my heart and search it well.

7 O will the Lord away for ever cast?
   Will He no longer favour to us show?
8 And hath His love away for ever passed,
   His promise failed, His mercy ceased to
   flow?
9 Hath God forgotten to bestow His grace,
   Shut up His love, and hid in wrath His Face?

Song cvi.

" *Rizpah the daughter of Aiah took sackcloth, and spread it for her upon the rock, from the beginning of harvest until water dropped upon them out of heaven, and suffered neither the birds of the air to rest on them by day, nor the beasts of the field by night.*"—v. 10.

We are told that David, having inquired of the Lord as to the cause of the famine referred to in the last Song, was informed that it was sent as a punishment for Saul's slaughter of the Gibeonites. It is not known when this slaughter took place; but it is supposed that the Gibeonites were the inhabitants of the priestly city of Nob, whom Saul slew with the priests on account of Ahimelech's kindness to David. David, in compliance with the demands of the Gibeonites, delivered up to them seven members of the family of Saul, who were " hanged in the hill before the LORD . . . in the beginning of barley harvest." There the dead bodies were guarded by Rizpah, the mother of two of the victims, as recorded above; and the utter desolation expressed in the following cry is touchingly in unison with the account of her watching night and day over her dead.

PSALM LXXXVIII. 1—7.

EHOVAH, God of my salvation, ·
    I day and night have cried to Thee ;
2 O hearken to my supplication,
    To this my cry attentive be ;
3 My soul is full of grief and fear,
    My life unto the grave draws near.

4 For I am counted with the dying,
　　With them who to the pit must go ;
Feeble and faint behold me lying,
　　Like one whose strength is waxen low ;
5 *Left with the dead, and like the slain
Who in the silent grave remain.

Like those forgotten Thou hast made me,
　　Cut off by Thee in death who sleep ;
6 Thou in the lowest pit hast laid me,
　　In darkness, in the silent deep.
Thy wrath lies hard upon my soul,
The waves of sorrow o'er me roll.

Song cvii.

" The bones of Saul and Jonathan his son buried they in the country of Benjamin in Zelah, in the sepulchre of Kish his father."—v. 14.

There can be little doubt but that the destruction of so many members of Saul's family, in order to gratify the Gibeonites, excited great indignation among the partisans of the late dynasty. It was true that David had not acted without consulting the Lord as to what was his duty, and that out of affection for Jonathan he had spared his descendants (one of whom might have become at any time a dangerous claimant of the crown), preferring to sacrifice the far less important children of Rizpah and Michal; yet still it may have been with a view to allay the irritation which had arisen among his subjects that David brought the bones of Saul and Jonathan from Jabesh-Gilead at this time, and gave them an honourable burial in the sepulchre of their family together with the victims of the Gibeonites.

Although the following composite Psalm is not assigned to any particular event, it may perhaps express the sorrow· which David would naturally have felt at this time of general trouble and mourning, and his thankful confidence in God, Who had promised to establish him on the throne.

Psalm lxi.

David.

 GOD, unto my cry attend ;
　Thine ear to my petition lend ;
2 From earth's far ends I cry to Thee
When sorrow hath o'erwhelmèd me.
*O lead me up the Rock too high,
A Rock that higher is than I.
3 My Shelter Thou in time of fear,
My Tower of strength when foes were near,
4 Within Thy Tent I will abide,
Beneath Thy shadowing wings will hide ;
5 For Thou, O God, my vows hast heard,
Thou hast fulfilled Thy promised word,
That I the heritage should claim
Of those that fear Thy holy Name.

Abiathar.

6 To David's life Thy grace shall add
Days unto days, and make him glad ;
7 His throne, before his God secure,
Through countless ages shall endure.
Thy truth prepare, Thy mercy send,
Thine own anointed to defend.

David.

8 So will I sing Thy praise, and pay
My vows to Thee from day to day.

"And after that God was intreated for the land."—v. 14.

David had now done all in his power, first, to appease the anger of Jehovah at a flagrant breach on the part of Saul of a solemn national treaty, secondly, to give satisfaction to the Gibeonites for the wrongs inflicted on their countrymen, and, lastly, to convince the adherents of the late family that he was obeying the will of Jehovah, without any wish to avenge the injuries which he had himself experienced at the hands of Saul. He might, therefore, confidently hope that God would now hear his prayers, and restore peace and prosperity to his kingdom.

PSALM XXXII. 6—7.

FOR this, while still Thou may'st be found,
　　To Thee the godly man shall lift his cry ;
Then surely, when the floods abound,
　　The swelling waves to him shall not
　　come nigh.

7 Thou art my place wherein to hide,
　　Thou shalt preserve me in the time of woe,
And compass me on every side
　　With songs my great deliverance that forth-
　　show.

2 Samuel XXII.

𝔖ong cix.

*" David spake unto the LORD the words of this song in the day that
the LORD had delivered him out of the hand of all his enemies,
and out of the hand of Saul."*—v. 1.

The last Chapter (xxi.), after giving an account of the
famine and of the burial of the bones of Saul and
Jonathan, concludes with a brief narrative of the exploits
of David's valiant captains in the wars with the Philistines.

Chapter xxii. contains perhaps one of the grandest
poems of the greatest of poets, which is almost identical
with Psalm xviii. It appears to consist of two parts,
written at different times but joined by the author himself. In the first part of the Ps., viz. vv. 1—24 (or in
2 Sam. xxii. vv. 1—25), there is a glorious description of
a thunderstorm. It has been thought that the drought,
which caused the three years' famine in the land of
Israel, ended in a violent tempest which, in the
opinion of Bishop Horsley, H. Horne, and others, is
commemorated in Ps. xxix., but to which Ps. xviii.
appears far more applicable, inasmuch as many supplications must have been offered for deliverance from the
drought, and the storm here described was evidently
sent in answer to prayer (see v. 6). There can be no
doubt that in this grand composition David drew on his
recollection of those convulsions of nature which he had

witnessed in his wanderings during Saul's persecution, and that these thoughts would bring forcibly to his mind the merciful deliverances he had experienced.

At v. 25 there is a great alteration in the subject of the poem, and between this point and the conclusion there are several changes of the personal pronouns. It is, therefore, not improbable that the two parts of the Psalm were composed at different times, and that the latter part was intended for two voices.

PSALM XVIII.

THEE will I love, Jehovah, Thee,
    2 My Strength, my Rock, my Shield ;
  Jehovah will my Saviour be
    From foemen in the field ;
In Him I trust in danger's hour ;
He my Salvation is, my Tower.

3 Upon Jehovah I will cry
    Who worthy is of praise ;
My voice in prayer to Him on high
    For succour I will raise ;
So, when mine enemies are near,
I shall be saved ; I will not fear.

4 *The bands of death were on me laid,
    And compassed me around ;
Ungodliness made me afraid,
    Its floods were all unbound ;
5 The sorrows of the grave were there,
  And Death enclosed me in his snare.

6 With sorrow when my heart was stirred,
    I called on God to save ;
Jehovah from His Temple heard,
    My God an answer gave ;
He to my cry for help was near,
It entered even to His ear.

7 When He in His displeasure turned,
    Earth trembled at His look ;
Because His indignation burned,
    The hills' foundations shook ;
When He was wrath, before His Face
Each mountain trembled to its base.

8 Behold from out His nostrils smoke
    In clouds o'ershadowing came ;
Fire from His mouth devouring broke,
    Coals kindled at the flame ;
9 He bowed the Heavens, He left His Seat,
And darkness was beneath His feet.

10 He rode upon the Cherubim,
    On Cherubim did fly ;
The winds their wings to carry Him
    Spread out exultingly ;
11 And, lest His brightness be displayed,
His secret place He darkness made.

Yea, His pavilion there He set ;
    Thick clouds were o'er it spread ;
Around His tent dark waters met,
    Mists were His covering dread ;
12 The clouds from His bright Presence passed,
Hailstones and fire to earth were cast.

13 Jehovah spake—the heavens did rain
    Hailstones with thunder dire ;
The Highest gave His voice—again
    Burst forth the storm and fire :
14 He sent His arrows, and they fled ;
He shot His lightnings—they were dead.

15 The waters' channels were descried,
    The world's foundations shown ;
For, lo, Jehovah's voice did chide
    And make His anger known ;
Forth from His nostrils breath was cast,
Earth quaked and trembled at the blast.

16 When many waters o'er me rose,
    He drew me from the wave ;
17 When round me gathered strong my foes,
    His Arm was near to save ;
For they who bore me cruel hate
Were many, and their strength was great.

18 About me, in my day of woe,
    In anger fierce they lay ;
In vain to hurt me pressed the foe,
    Jehovah was my Stay ;
19 He brought me forth, He set me free,
Jehovah had delight in me.

20 My dealing, righteous in His sight,
    Jehovah did repay,
The cleanness of my hands requite,
    And mark my perfect way ;
21 For I His path did ever take,
    Nor wickedly my God forsake.

22 For all His laws were my delight,   ·
    All my obedience gained,
23 While, uncorrupted in His sight,
    My soul from sin abstained ;
24 Therefore did He with favour bless
    My spotless hands and righteousness.

(*The remainder seems to be intended for two Voices.*)

First Voice.

25 The merciful Thy mercy know ;
    The just Thy justice learn ;
26 Thou to the pure dost pureness show ;
    To rebels Thou art stern ;
27 For Thou wilt save the afflicted soul,
    But haughty looks Thou wilt control.

28 Jehovah, Thou my lamp wilt light,
    My Comforter wilt be ;
    My God shall make my darkness bright,
    My only Guide is He ;
29 A host of men before me fall,
    And by my God I leap a wall.

Second Voice.

30 The way of God is perfect, just ;
    Jehovah's word is tried ;
    A Shield He is to all that trust,
    And in His strength confide ;
31 Who, save Jehovah, God can be ?
    Who is a Rock ? what God but He ?

32 The God that girdeth me with might,
　　And makes my goings straight,
33 My feet like hinds He maketh light,
　　And gives me high estate ;
34 My hands to war He strong doth make,
　　Mine arms a bow of steel to break.

First Voice.

35 In Thy salvation safe I stand,
　　Thy shield my head above,
　　Upholden by Thy strong right Hand,
　　Made mighty by Thy love.
36 Thou, lest my feet therein should slide,
　　Hast made the path before me wide.

Second Voice.

37 So with mine enemies in view
　　I did not turn again,
　　But onward did my foes pursue,
　　Until they all were slain ;
38 Wounded, no more to rise, they die ;
　　Trodden beneath my feet they lie.

First Voice.

39 Girt with Thy strength I fearless go
　　To seek the battle-field ;
　　For Thou didst lay my foemen low,
　　And guard me with Thy shield ;
40 *Thou mad'st mine enemies to flee ;
　　Destroyed are they that hated me.

Second Voice.

41 They cried, but there was no man nigh,
 None could to save avail;
E'en to Jehovah did they cry,
 He answered not their wail;
42 Thus I my foes like clay did grind
Small as the dust before the wind.

First Voice.

43 When many did my power withstand,
 Thou help to me didst send,
And o'er the heathen's distant land
 Hast made my rule extend;
A people whom I have not known
Shall conquered bow before my throne.

44 As soon as they shall hear my name,
 They shall my will obey;
From strangers homage I will claim,
 And make them own my sway;
45 The trembling aliens then shall fade,
And from their coverts be afraid.

Second Voice.

46 Jehovah liveth—I will bless
 The Rock on Whom I lean,
And praise my God Who in distress
 Hath my Salvation been,
47 The God for me that vengeance finds,
And to my yoke the people binds.

First Voice.

48 He saves me from mine enemies,
　　Yea, Thou deliverest me;
　From men who 'gainst me fiercely rise
　　I am preserved by Thee;
49 Jehovah, I my voice will raise
　Among the heathen Thee to praise.

Both Voices.

50 Jehovah will deliverance bring
　　To Him who wears the crown,
　And on His own anointed king
　　Will send His blessing down,
　Yea, evermore bestow His grace,
　On David and on David's race.

2 Samuel X.

Song cx.

*" The children of Ammon sent and hired the Syrians of Beth-rehob,
and the Syrians of Zoba, twenty thousand footmen, and of king
Maacah a thousand men, and of Ish-tob twelve thousand men."
—v. 6.*

We now return to Chapter x., which appears to follow
next in chronological order. We there learn that David
sent an embassy to Hanun, the king of Ammon, to
condole with him on the death of his father, from whom
he (David) had received some kindness not recorded in
the history. Hanun, however, at the instigation of his
courtiers, suspected the ambassadors of being spies, and
treated them with intolerable insults. Fearing the indignation which would naturally be aroused by such conduct, he
hired a powerful army, consisting of Syrians and others,
to aid him in repelling the attack which he anticipated ;
and David may have composed Psalm ii. on hearing of
the gathering together of the united forces.

He probably intended the figurative expressions of the
East, which we find in this Psalm, to apply to himself
only ; but he was doubtless inspired by the Holy Spirit
to utter language which both Jewish and Christian Commentators admit to be far more applicable to the Messiah.

Psalm ii.

WHY fiercely rage the heathen ?
 Why vain attempts devise ?
2 The kings of earth take counsel,
 Rulers for battle rise ;

They plots against Jehovah
   And His anointed lay,
3 " Break we their bands asunder,
   " Cast we their cords away."

4 He Who is throned in Heavèn
   · Shall mock the empty boast ;
Jehovah in derision
   Shall have the rebel host.

5 Then shall He speak in anger,
   And fear upon them bring ;
6 " Yet on My hill of Zion
   " Have I set up My King."

7 'Tis mine to be proclaiming
   Jehovah's firm decree ;
" This day, My Son belovèd,
   " Have I begotten Thee.

8 " Ask, and behold the heathen
   " Thine heritage I make ;
" Ask, and earth's utmost borders
   " For Thy possession take.

9 " Thou shalt with iron sceptre
   " Thy might on them display,
" And dash them all in pieces
   " Like potter's work of clay."

10 *And now, ye kings, learn wisdom ;
   Ye judges, counsel hear ;
11 With trembling serve Jehovah,
   Rejoice with holy fear.

12 *Kiss ye the Son, with pureness
    To Him your homage pay,
Lest, if ye stir His anger,
    Ye perish from the way.

*For, in a little kindled,
    Soon doth His anger burn ;
Thrice blessèd are the people
    That trusting to Him turn.

" Be of good courage, and let us play the men for our people, and for the cities of our God."—v. 12.

To oppose the allies alluded to in the last Song a large army was collected under the command of Joab, who divided it into two bands, one of which he entrusted to his brother Abishai, addressing him in the above encouraging words, well calculated to strengthen the hearts both of the leaders and of the soldiers before whom they were probably spoken.

The following Song is peculiarly in unison with these noble sentiments.

PSALM XLVI. 1—3.

GOD is to us a Refuge,
　　Our Place of Strength is made,
And in the time of trouble
　* A very certain Aid.

2 Our hearts then shall not tremble,
　　*Though Earth should changèd be,
Though mountains be removèd,
　　And carried to the sea ;

3 Although the sea be troublèd
　　And dash against the shore,
Although it shake the mountains,
　　Although its waters roar.

Song cxii.

The result of the battle was a great victory for Israel.
Syrians as well as Ammonites fled before them. Soon,
however, the undaunted Hadarezer, the Syrian king of
Zobah, who had been one of the allies of the Ammonites,
and had more than once already been defeated by David
(2 Sam. viii.), assembled a fresh army headed by the most
renowned general of Syria. This was the news that
caused David to gather all Israel together. We may
well suppose that he addressed them with an assurance
of his perfect trust in the Rock of his Strength, admonish-
ing them that, if they would pour out their hearts before
God and invoke His aid, they would find Him to be
their certain Refuge.

PSALM LXII. 5—8.

WAIT thou, my soul, on God alone ;
    Fixed on my God my trust shall be ;
    God hath to me salvation shown ;
      6 My Rock, my sure Defence is He ;
His Arm hath mine upholder proved,
Therefore I shall not be removed.

7 God my Salvation is, my boast,
    A Rock of Strength in Him I know ;
8 O trust in Him, ye Israel's host,
    In time of joy, in time of woe ;
Pour out your hearts before His Throne ;
God is a Refuge for His own.

Song cxiii.

"And when all the kings that were servants to Hadarezer saw that they were smitten before Israel, they made peace with Israel, and served them."—v. 19.

The sure Strength of Israel did not fail His people in their need. This triumph was even more splendid than the preceding victory; forty thousand horsemen with their captain fell before David's conquering host; the men of seven hundred chariots were also slain, and the chariots themselves were probably captured and burnt as being useless (see Preface to Song xcix.); the leaders of the enemy tendered their submission; and thus for a time at least war was made to cease in the land.

PSALM XLVI. 8—11.

COME, behold the works of God
Making desolations,
9 Staying war throughout the earth,
Giving peace to nations.

He in sunder cuts the spear;
Yea, the bow He breaketh;
Fuel for the burning flame
He the chariot maketh.

10 " Know that I am God; be still;
"All shall homage pay Me;
" Heathens shall exalt My Name;
" All the earth obey Me."

11 On our side Jehovah stands,
 He Who hath all powèr ;
With us is the Lord of Hosts,
 Jacob's God our Towèr.

Song cxib.

" So the Syrians feared to help the children of Ammon any more."—
v. 19.

The last Song may have been an outburst of exultation and ·
gratitude in the remembrance of the burning chariots and
broken spears of the enemy. This calmer hymn of praise
seems more applicable to the conclusion of the campaign, when David reviewed at leisure the terrible dangers
through which his people had been preserved.

PSALM CXXIV.

JEHOVAH was our Helper,
 Now Israel may say,
2 Jehovah was our Helper
 When foes were in array ;

3 Or they had soon consumed us,
 Whose wrath knew no control ;
4 The waters had o'erwhelmed us,
 The stream gone o'er our soul.

5 Yea, o'er us high had risen
 The waves of wrath and pride ;
Our souls had sunk beneath them,
 And perished in the tide.

6 But blessèd be Jehovah,
 Who did His might display,
Through Whom we are not given
 To foemen for a prey.

7 Like bird from snare of fowler,
    Escaped from death are we ;
  Behold, the snare is broken,
    And we are safe and free.

8 Our help is in Jehovah,
    Our hope is in His Name,
  In Him Who made the heavens,
    In Him Who earth did frame.

Song cxb.

" David sent Joab, and his servants with him, and all Israel; and they destroyed the children of Ammon, and besieged Rabbah."—
v. I.

Although the king of Syria and his tributaries had given up all warlike intentions against Israel, David, having probably ascertained that Hanun, king of Ammon, was preparing for a renewed attack, resolved to be before him in the field. Before entering upon the campaign the offerings and sacrifices, with which he had no doubt previously prepared for battle, would be repeated, and the blessing of the Priest would naturally be asked for before each expedition.

Psalm xx. appears to consist of two separate songs, of which the first has already been introduced.—(See Song xcviii.). The second is a much longer song, added to the first by the Compiler, and the whole Psalm, thus composed, seems very suitable to this occasion.

PSALM XX.

Priest.

JEHOVAH hear Thee in the day
      When woes abound ;
The Name of Jacob's God thy Stay
      And Shield be found ;

2 Send from the Holy Place His might
    And thee defend ;
    And from His chosen Zion's height
    Strength to thee lend.

3 Thy gifts may He remember still
    Hallowed by fire ;
4 The counsel of thy mind fulfil,
    Thy heart's desire.

People.

5 For His salvation with our voice
    We God will praise,
    And, while we in His Name rejoice,
    Our banners raise.

Jehovah from His holy hill
    His ear incline ;
Jehovah bless thee, and fulfil
    Each prayer of thine.

David.

6 Jehovah, now I know, from harm
    Will save the king ;
    From out His holy Heaven His Arm
    Shall safety bring.

People.

7 In chariots and horses' might
    While some rely,
    We will remember in the fight
    Our God Most High.

8 They are brought down, and by His Hand
    Subjected yield;
But we are risen, and upright stand
    On battle field.

9 *Save, O Jehovah, save the king,
    Long may he live.
Jehovah, to the prayer we bring
    An answer give.

2 SAMUEL XII.

Song cxbi.

" I have sinned against the LORD."—v. 13.

We pass over in silence the humiliating story recorded in the remainder of the last Chapter. Chapter xii. opens with the well-known parable of Nathan which brought conviction to the sinner's conscience. The bitterness of his repentance is told in Psalm li., which does not require the confirmation of the Hebrew title to affix it without a question to this dark period. To the fall of David we owe that prayer which has been the help and comfort of the penitent in every subsequent age. The latter verses of the Psalm show that a ray of hope had dawned on his heart, and he ventures to pray for a blessing on his people and city, trusting that those sacrifices and burnt offerings, which of themselves could avail nothing, might, when combined with a broken and contrite spirit, be accepted by the Most High.

This appears to me to be a sufficient explanation of the two last verses which Perowne and some other Commentators suppose to have been added at a much later date.

PSALM LI.

O me, O God, Thy mercy show,
Thy lovingkindness let me know,
And pardon for my sins bestow.

2 Wash me, and make me pure and clean,
My guilt as though it had not been,
E'en by Thine eye no longer seen.

3 For I my grievous sins confess,
And day by day my wickedness
My mourning spirit doth oppress.

4 For I have sinned 'gainst Thee alone,
And in Thy sight this evil done ;
Thou art the Just and Righteous One.

5 Behold, my mother's womb within
My members all were formed in sin ;
So early did my guilt begin.

6 But Thou dost inward truth require ;
Thou shalt in secret me inspire
With wisdom such as I desire.

7 Purge me with hyssop ; cleanse Thou me ;
Wash me ; and, purified by Thee,
I whiter than the snow shall be.

8 Gladness and joy make me to hear ;
The bones which Thou hast broken cheer,
That they rejoicing may appear.

9 Upon my sins no longer look ;
Although Thy statutes I forsook,
Blot my transgressions from Thy book.

10 Grant me a spotless heart to win,
A spirit right, renewed within,
And free from every taint of sin.

11 O let me still to Thee be near ;
My soul still let Thy spirit cheer
With holy thoughts and godly fear.

12 Thy saving joy to me restore ;
With Thy free spirit, as of yore,
Uphold me, that I fall no more.

13 Then to transgressors I will preach
The lessons which Thy statutes teach,
Till sinners' hearts conversion reach.

14 O God of my salvation, take
Blood-guiltiness from me, and make
My tongue loud songs of praise to wake.

15 Lord, open Thou my lips in praise ;
My mouth shall then a song upraise,
And show forth all Thy righteous ways.

16 No sacrifice dost Thou demand,
Or I would by Thine altar stand,
And offer it with willing hand.

17 The sacrifice of God implies
A contrite heart that broken lies ;
This, Thou, O God, wilt not despise.

18 From Thee let Zion favour gain ;
Build Salem's walls, her strength maintain,
That there prosperity may reign.

19 They who in righteousness delight
Shall offer then on Zion's height
Burnt offerings pleasing in Thy sight.

Song cxvii.

" The LORD also hath put away thy sin ; thou shalt not die."—v. 13.

God, Who knows the secrets of all hearts, saw that David's repentance was sincere, and commissioned his servant Nathan to reverse the sentence which the king's own lips had pronounced, "The man that hath done this thing shall surely die."

David's gratitude for this mercy seems to be expressed in the following short Song.

PSALM XXXII. 5.

BEFORE Thee all my sins I laid,
    I have not hid my wickedness,
  I said, " Excuse shall none be made,
    " I my transgressions will confess ;"
  And Thou didst hearken to my cry,
  And pardon mine iniquity.

Song cxviii.

"And the LORD struck the child . . . . and it was very sick."—
v. 15.
"David therefore besought God for the child."—v. 16.

Although God had spared the life of his repentant
servant, yet He did not see fit to withhold all chastisement from him, and the child which had been born
unto him, and whom he had probably intended for his
heir, was seized with a mortal sickness.

David had uttered no word in deprecation of his
punishment when it was foretold to him by the prophet
Nathan, but had meekly submitted to his sentence,
because it came from the Lord. He felt that it was
deserved, for his grievous sin had brought dishonour on
his God and the reproach of fools upon himself. Now
however, that the sickness of his child was increasing,
he could no longer refrain from beseeching that the
stroke which had been laid upon him might even yet be
removed.

PSALM XXXIX. 6—11.

MAN only in a shadow walks,
        *Is troubled for a breath ;
    He hoards, but knows not who shall have
    The heaps he gathereth.
7 What wait I for, Jehovah, now ?
    I trust in Thee ; my Hope art Thou.

8 Deliver me from all my sins,
　　Let fools reproach not me ;
9 I silence kept ; no word I spake,
　　For it was done by Thee ;
10 Thy stroke no longer on me lay ;
　　Beneath Thine Hand I waste away.

11 When with rebukes Thou chastenest man,
　　And punishest his sin,
　Thou mak'st his beauty to consume
　　As frets a moth within ;
　His glory surely vanisheth,
　*For all men only are a breath.

Song cxix.

" Then said his servants unto him, What thing is this that thou hast done? thou didst fast and weep for the child, while it was alive; but when the child was dead, thou didst rise and eat bread."—v. 21.

The reply to this question cannot be strictly regarded as a song; but yet it is so full of poetry, beauty, and pathos, and so illustrative of David's character, that this volume would hardly seem to be complete without it. It displays that marvellous combination of tenderness, fortitude, resignation, and faith, which, even in his dark hour of humiliation, makes this erring servant of God the object of our love and admiration.

2 SAMUEL XII. 22—23.

WHILE yet the child alive remained,
    Ere the last hope had passed away,
I wept, yea, I from food refrained;
    For, "Who can tell," my heart would say,
    "If God will gracious be and give
    "An answer that the child may live."

23 But now his spirit hence hath passed,
    Now he is dead—to weep were vain;
Now to what purpose should I fast?
    For can I bring him back again?
    Nay, I shall go to him, but he
    Shall not return again to me.

Song cxx.

" He called his name Solomon ; and the LORD loved him."—v. 24.

The next events related in this Chapter are the birth and naming of that child who was to succeed David on the throne, and the fame of whose wisdom and magnificence was to extend to the ends of the earth, and to last as long as the world should endure.

Psalm cxxvii. bears the title of " A Song of degrees for Solomon," and may have been composed at the time of his birth or circumcision.

PSALM CXXVII.

EXCEPT the house Jehovah buildeth,
　　In vain the builders labour take ;
　Except Jehovah keep the city,
　　In vain doth there the watchman wake;

　2 In vain ye haste to rise up early,
　　In vain your midnight watch ye keep,
　And eat the bread of care and sorrow ;
　　*His loved God blesseth e'en in sleep.

　3 The heritage Jehovah sendeth
　　Is children ; His reward are they :
　4 E'en like the arrows of the mighty,
　　Sons of thy youth shall be thy stay.

　5 Blest he whose quiver thus aboundeth ;
　　No shame upon that man shall wait
　When face to face he foemen meeteth,
　　And speaketh with them in the gate.

Song cxxi.

" He took their king's crown from off his head, the weight whereof was a talent of gold with the precious stones : and it was set on David's head."—v. 30.

One more flickering ray of brightness gilds the path of David, henceforth to be clouded at every turn by the consequences of his sin. The blessing on his arms, implored in Psalm xx. (Song cxv.) before the departure of the expedition against Ammon, had been granted. Rabbah had fallen, and her crown of pure gold had been set on the head of David.

The concluding verse of the Chapter would appear to imply that this triumph was attended with cruelties then commonly practised by those Eastern nations, and it is possible that such may be referred to in vv. 8—10 of the following Psalm. This idea, however, appears incredible when we read in Chap. xvii. 27, that Shobi, the son of Nahash of Rabbah, of the children of Ammon, and brother of the dethroned king, vied with Barzillai in showing kindness to David when a fugitive during Absalom's rebellion. Dr. Chandler considers that a more correct translation of the last verse of 2 Samuel xii. and the parallel passage in 1 Chronicles xx. would imply that David made the captives of Rabbah *to cut with cutting instruments and to work in the mines and brick-kilns ;* and this view is strengthened by the Arabic version, which says that he bound them all with chains, *killing none.* In short, he probably reduced them, as Joshua reduced the Gibeonites in former times, to the lowest state of slavery. I am, therefore, of opinion that vv. 8—10 of Psalm xxi., to

which I have alluded, and which are in the future tense,
only express in a strong figure that God will continue to
bless the arms of David and utterly overthrow his
enemies, as had just been the case in regard to the
people of Rabbah.

Both this Psalm (xxi.) and Psalm xx. appear to consist
of two parts, the first of which has, in each case, been
introduced in 2 Samuel viii. In each case also a longer
song has been added by the Compiler to the first part,
and the whole of the two Psalms, thus formed, seem
respectively very suitable, the one to the commencement,
and the other to the conclusion, of the expedition against
Rabbah.

PSALM XXI.

David.

THE king shall in Thy strength rejoice,
 To Thee, Jehovah, lift his voice,
  In Thy salvation glad ;
2 His heart's desire Thou hast supplied,
 His lips' request hast not denied,
  But him with joy hast clad ;
3 For Thou preventest him with love
 And plenteous blessings from above.

 Him with Thy favour Thou dost grace,
 And on his head a crown dost place,
  A crown of purest gold ;
4 Life which he asked Thy goodness gave,
 And length of days ; him Thou dost save
  And with Thy might uphold ;
 His length of days, in glory passed,
 Shall ever and for ever last.

5 His honour and renown are great :
His majesty and high estate
 On Thy salvation rest ;
Thou on his head shalt worship lay,
And give him majesty and sway ;
6 In Thee he shall be blest ;
Thy countenance his joy shall be,
His heart exceeding glad in Thee.

7 The king doth on his God rely,
And through the grace of the Most High
 He shall not be removed.

People.

8 & 9 Thy right hand shall find out thy foes,
And as a fiery oven make those
 Who have thy haters proved ;
Jehovah these in wrath shall slay,
They shall of fire become the prey.

10 Destroyed by thee shall be their fruit,
Which from the earth thou shalt uproot,
 And from mankind their seed;
11 For evil they against thee plot,
But all their power availeth not
 To carry out the deed.
12 For this they shall be put to flight
When thou dost draw thy bow of might.

All.

13 Jehovah, set Thyself on high,
Exalt Thy glorious majesty,

And in Thy strength arise ;
So will we sing with heart and voice,
And ever in Thy Name rejoice,
Whose glory fills the skies ;
Yea, songs of gladness we will raise,
Thy boundless power and might to praise.

Song cxxii.

" There came a messenger to David, saying, The hearts of the men of Israel are after Absalom."—v. 13.

We have now arrived at a period in which another great change took place in the history of David, and we are again to see him a wanderer and an exile

The Lord, Who had spared his life, saw fit to permit him to be punished by the misery and crimes produced in his family through the indulgence of the same evil passions which had caused his own sin; and his poems show that he fully realized the connexion between his fall and his subsequent troubles.

Passing over the miserable events recorded in 2 Samuel xiii. and xiv., the next Song (Psalm vi.) seems to refer to the day on which David heard of Absalom's rebellion. It has been conjectured that he was prevented by illness from paying his usual attention to public business, and that the general dissatisfaction arising from this and other causes may have suggested to his favourite son, Absalom, the project of dethroning his father. Having by a long course of ostentation and flattery ingratiated himself with the people, Absalom, under a false pretext, obtained leave from the king to retire to Hebron, where he set up the standard of revolt. His adviser was Ahithophel, the king's most intimate friend and trusted counsellor, who was, however, in secret (as may be gathered from the Psalms which are supposed to

apply to him) David's bitter foe. His enmity was probably caused by the wrongs of Bathsheba, for it is
generally thought that Ahithophel was her grandfather.
David was overwhelmed with terror and distress on
receiving the news of the rebellion, and gave directions
for immediate flight.

The night of weeping described in the following Psalm
may not improbably have been that occasioned by the
heart-breaking tidings of this day.

PSALM VI.

EHOVAH, in Thy wrath rebuke no more,
　　Make me no more Thy chastening Hand
　　　to feel ;

2 *I pine away ; on me Thy mercy pour ;
　　My bones are vexed ; O hasten Thou to heal ;

3 My soul is also vexed ; my foes are strong ;
　　But Thou, Jehovah, O how long ! how long !

4 Return, Jehovah, and deliver me ;
　　O for Thy mercy's sake return to save ;

5 In death there no remembrance is of Thee ;
　　Thou art forgotten in the silent grave ;
　　Who from the tomb to Thee shall raise his voice?
　　Who give Thee thanks ? Who there in Thee
　　　rejoice ?

6 O I am weary ; wearily I groan ;
　　All night my couch I water with my tears ;
　　And, while I make my bed to swim, I moan,
　　　Oppressed with doubts, o'erwhelmed with
　　　　anxious fears ;

7 Consumed with grief and sorrow are mine eyes,
　　And waxen old ; for foes against me rise.

8 All ye that evil do, from me away;
   Jehovah sees me weep, He hears my sigh;
9 Jehovah hearkens when to Him I pray;
   Jehovah hears, and will receive my cry.
10 My foes dismayed shall be and vexèd sore,
   Turned backwards and with shame be covered
    o'er.

Song cxxiii.

" The king went forth, and all the people after him, and tarried in a place that was far off."—v. 17.

It was apparently on the morning after David received intelligence of the insurrection that he quitted Jerusalem with all his household except ten concubines. It was a sad as well as an eventful flight, of which nearly every occurrence has been recorded in history, and seems to be alluded to in song. The first halt was at a place called "The Far House," where David may have expressed his strengthened faith in the words which form the first part of Psalm lxii. To these verses the Compiler seems to have added two other songs already applied (see Songs liii. and cxii.), and the whole of the composite Psalm may be appropriately introduced here.

PSALM LXII.

* ONLY in God my soul is still,
    For He hath my Salvation proved ;
2 He is my Rock, my Guard from ill :
    I shall not now be greatly moved.

3 How long will ye with bitter hate
    Devise to cause a man to fall ?
Destruction dire shall be your fate,
    Like tottering fence or broken wall.

4 Only to cast him down they seek ;
    They alway turn from truth aside ;
Though with their mouth they blessings speak,
    Yet curses inwardly they hide.

5 Only in God, my soul, be still,
   He is my Hope, unfailing proved,
6 My Rock, my Guard from every ill,
   My Tower; I shall not now be moved.

7 In God is my salvation, He
   My Glory is, and Righteousness;
Rock of my strength He still will be;
   God is my Refuge in distress.

8 Trust Him at all times; trust His grace;
   Pour out your hearts before His Throne;
Your trust in Him, ye people, place;
   God is our Refuge, God alone.

9 *Only a breath are Adam's race,
   The sons of men are but a lie;
In balance weighed, whate'er their place,
   They lighter are than vanity.

10 From trusting in oppression cease;
   In robbery become not vain;
If riches grow, if wealth increase,
   Set not your heart upon your gain.

11 God once hath spoken; this I heard,
   That power and strength to God belong;
He spake, and twice I heard the word,
   That God is mighty, God is strong.

12 And Thee, O Lord, in Heaven Thy Seat
   Mercy and loving-grace surround;
For Thou to every man dost mete
   According as his work is found.

" I go whither I may."—v. 20.

David and his followers left " The Far House" attended
by his faithful body-guard.   Calling to him Ittai of Gath,
their captain, he bade him return with his companions,
and offer his services to the new king, instead of adhering
to the fortunes of one who, like himself, was now an
exile, and knew not whither he should go.

The bitterness of David's heart at this time may have
been pathetically summed up in

Psalm XXXIX. 12—13.

MY prayer do Thou, Jehovah, hear,
   To this my cry incline Thine ear,
      And to my tears an answer give ;
   For I a stranger am with Thee,
   As were my fathers wont to be,
      And as a sojourner I live.
13 O spare me, strength to me restore,
   Ere hence I go, and be no more.

Song cxxv.

" David went up by the ascent of Mount Olivet, and wept as he went
up."—v. 30.

Ittai was far too loyal and brave a subject to listen to
the proposal of returning, and the whole company passed
over the brook Kidron, weeping and lamenting.   Then
David, with pious and touching words, sent back the Ark
of God, which appears to have accompanied him, under
the care of Zadok and Abiathar and their two sons,
charging them to furnish him with tidings of what was
passing in the city.   After the departure of the Ark the
sorrowful party proceeded on their ascent of Mount
Olivet.   The grief of the fugitives is graphically described
in the history.   The king led the way weeping, and had
his head covered, and went barefoot ; and all the people
covered every man his head, and went up weeping.

How pathetically are these incidents brought to our
minds by the last part of Psalm lxxxix.!

V. 52, being the ascription of praise at the end of the
third Book of the Psalter, does not form part of the
Song.

PSALM LXXXIX. 49—51.

ORD, where are now Thy kindnesses of old ?
  Where is the tender love that Thou did'st
      bear ?
The mercy Thou to David did'st unfold,
  And in Thy faithfulness to him did'st swear ?

50 Lord, the reproaches to remembrance call,
    The foul reproaches on Thy servants laid,
How in my bosom I do bear them all,
    When with their taunts the mighty men up-
        braid ;

51 Wherewith Thine enemies against Thee bring
    Rebukes, Jehovah, and their taunts renew ;
Wherewith the steps of Thine anointed king
    With slanders and reproaches they pursue.

Song cxxvi.

" One told David, saying, Ahithophel is among the conspirators with
Absalom."—v. 31.

This was an unexpected blow to David, and indignation, such as this information would excite, is strongly
expressed in the first part of Ps. lii., which may, therefore,
refer to this occasion, although the whole composite
Psalm, consisting apparently of three separate songs, is
assigned by the Hebrew title to the announcement to
Saul by Doeg of David's visit to Nob. (See Song
xxxiv).

PSALM LII. 1—3.

MIGHTY·man, why dost thou in thy pride
    Boast that thine evil counsels shall avail?
Our God His goodness hath not turned
    aside,
His mercies never fail.

2 Thy tongue destruction alway doth devise,
    And, as a razor sharp, doth mischief seek ;
3 Thou lovest evil more than good, and lies
    Than righteousness to speak.

Song cxxvii.

" David said, O LORD, I pray Thee, turn the counsel of Ahithophel
into foolishness."—v. 31.

Psalm lv. consists of three songs, two of which I have
assigned to other occasions. The terrible denunciations
contained in it, like those of Psalm cix., are generally
looked upon as directed against Ahithophel. Both
Psalms appear to be intended for two singers, one of
whom takes the plaintive, the other the stern expressions ;
but, if the two Psalms are compared, a remarkable contrast will be perceived.

In Ps. lv. a former friend, from whom some injury has
been received, is spoken of pathetically by the plaintive
singer, who may perhaps express the feelings of David
towards Ahithophel before he had learnt the extent of his
treachery, while the other singer (representing one of
David's followers) denounces all the conspirators, and
especially Ahithophel, in much stronger language. In
Psalm cix., however, the parts of the singers are reversed,
for there the enmity of the confederates is but lightly
touched on by the plaintive voice in comparison with the
dreadful imprecations hurled by the other against the
principal traitor, a change of tone which might be expected after David had heard how detestable had been
that counsel of Ahithophel which he had feared.

Psalm lv.

First Voice.

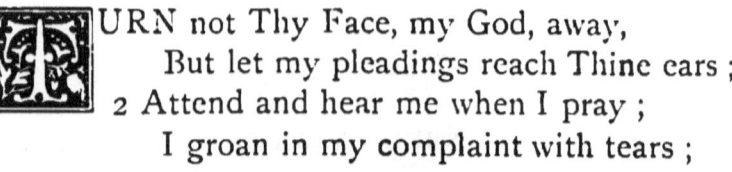URN not Thy Face, my God, away,
But let my pleadings reach Thine ears ;
2 Attend and hear me when I pray ;
I groan in my complaint with tears ;

3 Because the foeman's voice is heard,
Because the wicked me oppress ;
For wrath and hate are in them stirred ;
They cast upon me wickedness.

Second Voice.

4 My heart is sore within my breast ;
Death seems with all its terrors near ;
5 My soul with horror is distressed,
With trembling overwhelmed and fear.

6 "O that I had the wings" (I cried)
"That bear the dove to reach her nest !
7 "For then far off I would abide,
"And in the desert be at rest."

8 I would escape in danger's hour,
And shelter seek from stormy wind ;
And from the raging tempest's power
A place of safety I would find.

First Voice.

9 O let their tongues divided be ;
Jehovah, bring their words to nought ;
For strife it hath been mine to see
And wrong within the city wrought.

10 Both day and night they go around,
    And on the city's walls they meet ;
11 Deceit and wickedness abound,
    Sorrow and woe fill every street.

Second Voice.

12 For it was not an open foe
    That heaped reproaches on my name ;
Then I had borne the heavy blow,
    I had not sunk beneath the shame.

If it mine enemy had been
    That rose against me in his pride,
Then had I sought a place unseen,
    Where I might from him safely hide.

13 But it was thou, my guide of old,
    Mine equal, my familiar friend ;
14 Sweet counsel we were wont to hold,
    God's House together to attend.

First Voice.

15 Let sudden death upon them fall,
    And let them go down quick to hell,
For wickedness pollutes them all,
    And sin is found where'er they dwell.

Second Voice.

16 When unto God my prayers arise,
    Jehovah saves me from my fear ;
17 At evening, morn, and noon, my cries
    S hall loud ascend, and He will hear.

18 He hath redeemed my soul in peace
    When hotly pressed on me the foes ;
He made the shout of battle cease,
    Because against me many rose.

First Voice.

19 This God shall hear, this God shall know,
    Yea, He shall answer speedily ;
God shall afflict and bring them low,
    He from of old enthroned on high.

Because unchanged remains their lot,
    And loss and trouble come not near,
The Name of God they honour not,
    Nay, God Himself they will not fear.

Second Voice.

20 On him his treacherous hands he laid
    With whom he was at peace before,
He broke the covènant he made,
    Nor kept the solemn oath he swore.

21 While burning hate within him glowed,
    Softer than butter were his words ;
More smoothly e'en than oil they flowed,
    Yet were they all as blades of swords.

Both Voices.

22 Thy burden to Jehovah take,
    He shall sustain and strengthen thee ;
The righteous He will ne'er forsake,
    Nor suffer him cast down to be.

23 But sinners Thou, O God, shalt slay ;
  The bloodthirsty deceitful race
Untimely death shall take away ;
  But I in Thee my trust will place.

Song cxxbiii.

" David was come to the top of the mount, where he worshipped God."
v. 32.

It would seem that there was an altar on the summit
of Mount Olivet to which David was perhaps in the
habit of repairing to worship God, as he did on the
present occasion. The Syriac argument of Psalm xxvi.
is " Of David when his friend (Ahithophel) left him,
and he was in exile ;" and this seems the most appropriate place for its introduction.

PSALM XXVI.

LET my cause by Thee be proved,
    Jehovah, I have walked aright ;
*I waver not, nor shall be moved ;
    My trust is in Jehovah's might.

2 Jehovah, try mine inmost breast ;
    *My reins, my heart, O make Thou clean ;
3 I on Thy loving-kindness rest,
    And in Thy truth my walk hath been.

4 I never with the vain have dwelt,
    I hate all those who love deceit,
5 With wicked men I have not dealt,
    And will not evil doers meet.

6 I wash my hands in innocence ;
    So to Thine altar will I go,
7 That I may give Thee thanks from thence,
    And all Thy wondrous doings show.

8 Jehovah, I Thy dwelling-place,
    Thine holy House, have lovèd well,
Which with Thy Presence Thou dost grace,
    And where Thy glory deigns to dwell.

9 My soul with sinners gather not,
    Who wickedness will do for gain ;
10 Cast not with evil men my lot,
    Whose hands the price of blood obtain.

11 But I the paths of righteousness
    In mine integrity will tread ;
Redeem me ; with Thy favour bless,
    And pour down mercy on my head.

12 My foot doth stand on even ground ;
    I, where Thy saints their voices raise,
Among the congregation found,
    Jehovah's holy Name will praise.

Song cxxix.

*" Behold, Hushai the Archite came to meet him with his coat rent,
and earth upon his head."—v. 32.*

The sympathy of this loyal subject was most cheering
to the desponding king; for Hushai was not only dis-
tinguished for his wisdom, but held that high and con-
fidential office in the council which was designated by
the title of "the king's friend." Hoping that he might
be able to defeat the dangerous advice of Ahithophel,
David determined to send him back to Jerusalem for
that purpose.

In the first part of the following Song (Psalm xxviii.)
David may allude to the prayer which he had just offered
at the altar, to which, in vv. 6, 7, he appears to recognize
an answer in the arrival of Hushai.

PSALM XXVIII.

David.

Y Rock, no more Thy voice refrain,
  Jehovah, hear my cry;
 Lest, if Thou silent still remain,
  I be like those that die.

2 O to my prayer attentive be,
  Let it an answer meet,
 When I uplift my hands to Thee,
  Towards Thy Mercy Seat

3 Pluck me not hence with those who seek
    Ungodliness and sin,
Who to their neighbours friendly speak,
    While mischief lurks within.

4 Give them according to their deeds,
    Their wickedness repay,
Nor let what from their hands proceeds
    Unpunished pass away.

Hushai.

5 Because they turn their hearts aside
    From all His works and ways,
Jehovah shall bring down their pride,
    Their horn He shall not raise.

David.

6 Blest be Jehovah ; to my cry
    He doth an answer yield ;
7 Upon Jehovah I rely,
    He is my Strength and Shield.

I trusted Him, He sent His aid,
    In Him I safety found ;
Exultant now my heart is made,
    My songs His praise resound.

Hushai.

8 *His strength is in Jehovah's power,
    Salvation He doth bring ;
He is the Fortress, He the Tower,
    Of His anointed king.

The whole Assembly.

9 O save Thy people, Jacob's seed ;
 With blessing fill their cup ;
Cease not Thine heritage to feed,
 And ever lift them up.

Song CXXX.

" Absalom came into Jerusalem."—v. 37.

Psalm lxix. is supposed by all the old Commentators to refer to the time of David's flight from Absalom, and may express his feelings after the departure of Hushai. His thoughts would then naturally return to the treachery of Ahithophel, the undeserved enmity of many of the rebels, and the ingratitude of part of his own family, to which he may specially allude in ver. 8. The first portion of the Psalm (vv. 1—29) is written in a strain of deep despondency, whilst the last part (vv. 30—36) is exultant. These last verses were probably added by David after his return to Jerusalem, and will be introduced in that part of his history. Its Hebrew title may be taken as a sufficient refutation of the opinion of several modern Commentators that this Psalm is of later date than the age of David ; but the maledictions contained in vv. 22—28 are so inconsistent with David's tender love for Absalom, and his forgiveness of Amasa, whom, on recovering his kingdom, he appointed captain of the host, passing over both Joab and Abishai, that they suggest the possibility of their having been interpolated into this Psalm from some other poem.

PSALM LXIX. 1—29.

SAVE me, O God, in mercy save,
    The floods are come into my soul,
Around me higher swells the wave,
    The waters roll.

2 Here, where no standing place is found,
    I sink into the mire below ;
Deep waters compass me around,
    And floods o'erflow.

3 Weary of cries my throat is dry ;
    With watching long mine eyes are dim ;
While, till my God will hear my cry,
    I wait for Him.

4 More than the hairs upon my head
    Are they who bear me causeless hate ;
They who my guiltless blood would shed
    Are strong and great.

Though I have taken not away,
    Though robbery is to me unknown,
That which is mine I must repay,
    Restore mine own.

5 To Thee my folly is revealed,
    My trespasses before Thee lie ;
O God, my sin is unconcealed
    Beneath Thine eye.

6 O God of Hosts, O Israel's Lord,
    Let none for my sake suffer shame
Who wait on Thee, who trust Thy word,
    And fear Thy Name.

7 For Thy sake shame o'erspreads my face,
    For Thee reproach is on me laid ;
8 My mother's sons, my kindred race,
    Are strangers made.

9 For burning zeal hath me inflamed
    Thine House in honour held to see,
And the rebukes against Thee aimed
    Are fallen on me.

10 I grieved my soul with fasts and tears,
    And that was turnèd to my shame ;
11 I sackcloth wore, and for their jeers
    A mark became.

12 All they who sit within the gate
    Make me their talk, to do me wrong ;
Of drunkards is my sad estate
    Become the song.

13 But I to Thee, Jehovah, cry,
    When Thou dost lend a willing ear ;
In Thy salvation's truth be nigh,
    In mercy hear.

14 Raise from the mire my sinking soul,
    And save me from mine enemies ;
The whelming waterfloods control,
    When fast they rise.

15 Save, when the water overflows,
    Lest swallowed by the deep I be ;
Let not the pit of darkness close
    Her mouth on me.

16 Hear me, Jehovah, when I plead ;
    Thy loving-kindness maketh glad ;
17 Hide not Thy Face ; O hear with speed,
    For I am sad.

18　To me in my distress draw near,
　　　And for my soul a ransom give ;
　　Redeem me from the foes I fear,
　　　　That I may live.

19　Thou knowest my disgrace and shame,
　　　Each foul reproach, each cruel slight ;
　　The foes who at my ruin aim
　　　　Are in Thy sight.

20　My heart is full of heaviness,
　　　Reproaches compass me around ;
　　I looked for comfort in distress,
　　　　But none I found.

21　When crushed with woe they saw me sink,
　　　Bitter was that they brought for meat ;
　　They gave me vinegar to drink,
　　　　And gall to eat.

22　*When they secure appear to be,
　　　A snare and trap their table make ;
23　Cause Thou their eyes no light to see,
　　　　Their limbs to shake.

24　Let Thy displeasure on them wait,
　　　And be Thy wrath upon them sent ;
25　Their dwelling make Thou desolate,
　　　　And void their tent.

26　For persecuting words they speak
　　　Of him whom Thou hast smitten sore ;
　　Thy wounded ones their talk doth seek
　　　　To grieve yet more.

27 Make their offences numberless,
 And add Thou sin unto their sin ;
Let them not share Thy righteousness,
 Nor come therein.

28 Their names do Thou for ever blot
 From out the book of them that live ;
Among the righteous write them not,
 Nor portion give.

29 But I, O God, am poor and sad,
 Sorrow doth heavy on me lie ;
Let Thy salvation make me glad,
 And set me high.

Song cxxxi.

" Let him curse ; for the LORD hath bidden him."—v. 11.

The next incident recorded is the arrival of Ziba with a supply of provisions and the report of his master's conduct which elicited David's hasty transfer of Mephibosheth's property to Ziba. At Bahurim, a short distance further on, the party encountered Shimei, a Benjamite, of the family of Saul. This man, being protected by a deep ravine, threw stones at the king, and cursed him in language so opprobrious that Abishai begged permission to cross over and slay him. David, however, refused, saying that he whose life was in danger from his own son might well bear the curses of a stranger. But neither Shimei's curses nor even Absalom's rebellion appear to have weighed down the heart of the persecuted king so much as the feeling expressed in the text above that they were but instruments in the hands of his offended God.

The following "Psalm of David," which only in a figurative sense describes his own sufferings, whilst it literally applies to Him Who bore our griefs, has been by some Commentators assigned to the period of David's exile, and this climax of woe appears the most fitting place for its introduction.

The latter portion, which refers to sacrifices of thanksgiving for deliverance, was probably composed after the restoration, and I have on that account placed it there.

PSALM XXII. 1—21.

Y God, my God, in this my grief
    O why hast Thou forsaken me?
Why art Thou far from my relief
    When I in anguish cry to Thee?

2 My God, I cry to Thee by day,
    But Thou dost not incline Thine ear;
Nor, when at night to Thee I pray
    And am not silent, dost Thou hear.

3 But Thou art holy, Thou art just;
    *Thee Israel praiseth throned on high;
4 In Thee our fathers put their trust;
    They trusted—Thou to save wast nigh.

5 They cried to Thee when trouble came;
    By Thee was their deliverance wrought;
They trusted in Thy holy Name,
    And were not to confusion brought.

6 But as for me, abhorred by all,
    No man, a very worm, am I;
Scorn and reproaches on me fall,
    Despised by all the passers-by.

7 All they that see me mock my woe,
    Derision in their laugh is heard;
They shoot the lip their scorn to show,
    And shake the head with jeering word—

8 " His trust he on Jehovah laid,
    " That He to save would show His might;
" Now be that might to save displayed,
    " Seeing in him is His delight."

9 But Thou art He that didst me take
From out the womb on Thee to rest,
And Thou did'st hope in me awake
When yet upon my mother's breast.

10 I from the womb was cast on Thee ;
E'en from my birth my God Thou art ;
11 Trouble is near, O leave not me,
For none there is to help impart.

12 Bulls compass me on every side,
Bashan's strong bulls beset my way ;
13 Their gaping mouths are open wide,
As lions roaring for their prey.

14 Poured out like water in my woe
Am I, my bones asunder start ;
Within my body sinking low,
Like wax that melteth, is my heart.

15 My strength is like a potsherd dry,
And to my jaws my tongue doth cleave ;
E'en in the dust of death to lie,
My God, Thou dost Thy servant leave.

16 For many are the dogs unclean
On every side that round me wait ;
A throng of wicked men is seen
Enclosing me with looks of hate.

They pierced my feet, they pierced my hands,
17   Each tortured bone I can descry ;
A staring crowd around me stands
To gaze upon mine agony.

Yea, mine affliction they deride,
    My pain and anguish pitying not ;
18 Behold, my garments they divide,
    And on my vesture cast the lot.

19 But do not Thou far off remain,
    Let not Thy succour be delayed ;
Let me not cry to Thee in vain ;
    My Strength Jehovah, haste to aid.

20 My soul deliver from the grave,
    Yea, from the sword my life defend ;
Mine only one, Jehovah, save,
    Let not the dog my darling rend.

21 O save me from the lion's jaw ;
    *The horns of unicorns are nigh ;
*Save me, for closer yet they draw ;
    *O save me—Thou hast heard my cry.

Song cxxxii.

" It may be that the LORD will look on mine affliction, and that the LORD will requite me good for his cursing this day."—v. 12.

Many Commentators have supposed that Cush, the Benjamite, against whom Psalm vii. is directed by the Hebrew title, is another name for Shimei, no doubt on account of the suitableness of the first portion of the Psalm to his unprovoked malice and enmity, the remainder appearing to refer to all David's enemies.

PSALM VII.

JEHOVAH, O my God, to Thee
  *For shelter do I fly ;
Save me from them that trouble me,
  O be to save me nigh :

2 Lest he my soul in pieces rend,
  And like a lion tear,
While none is near me help to lend,
  None saving help to bear.

3 Jehovah, O my God, if I
  This wickedness have wrought,
If I have done iniquity,
  If I have mischief sought,

4 If evil I did e'er repay
  To him that was my friend
(Yea, rather I unharmed away
  Mine enemy did send),

5 Then let my persecuting foe
    My soul pursue and take,
  Yea, let him lay my glory low,
    My life dishonoured make.

6 Jehovah, in Thy wrath arise
    My foemen's rage to still ;
  Awake, upon mine enemies
    Thy just decree fulfil.

7 *Gather the peoples to Thy feet ;
    *Call the assembly nigh ;
  *And o'er the nations to Thy Seat
    Return again on high.

8 Jehovah judgment shall dispense ;
    Men shall His justice see ;
  According to mine innocence,
    Jehovah, judge Thou me.

9 Let sinners' schemes in ruin lie ;
    Strength to the just impart ;
  For God, the righteous God, doth try
    The very reins and heart.

10 God is my Shield, in Whom I trust,
     Of upright hearts the Stay ;
11 God is a righteous Judge and just,
     Provokèd every day.

12 Unless the sinner will repent,
     He sharpeneth His sword ;
   His bow He hath already bent,
     His arrows wait the word.

U

13 The deadly weapons are arrayed,
　　He hath prepared the dart ;
　The arrow swift is ready made
　　To pierce the oppressor's heart.

14 He mischief hath within his mind
　　Conceived, and brought forth sin ;
15 A pit for others he designed,
　　And he hath fallen therein.

16 His mischief and malicious toil
　　Shall on himself be brought ;
　And on his own head shall recoil
　　The evil he hath wrought.

17 I for Jehovah's righteousness
　　To Him my song will raise,
　The Name of the Most High will bless,
　　And sing Jehovah's praise.

Song cxxxiii.

" The king, and all the people that were with him, came weary, and refreshed themselves."—v. 14.

Leaving the ill conduct of Shimei unpunished, the exiles passed on to the valley of the Jordan, and rested at the ford, or bridge, of the river.   There they refreshed themselves with Ziba's present, and waited for tidings from Jerusalem.

The *Selah* Psalm iv. is a beautiful Song, very suitable for the close of this day of anxiety.   It is evidently a companion Song to Ps. iii. which by its Hebrew title is associated with Absalom's rebellion, and in the first verse there seems to be an allusion to the escape which had just been effected.   The appeal of the king to his misguided and rebellious subjects, the admonition to his faint-hearted friends, and the expressions of joy and trust in the loving protection of his God, are all too evidently appropriate to need further remark.

PSALM IV.

GOD of my righteousness, my petitions hear ;
   *Thou in my straitness hast made room
         for me ;
O let Thy tender mercies now be near,
   *And let my supplications answered be.

2 Ye sons of men, ye who pervert the right,
      How long will ye my glory turn to shame ?
   How long will ye in vanity delight,
      *A lie pursue, and seek an empty name ?

U 2

3 Know that the man in godliness who lives
　　Jehovah for Himself hath set apart ;
　Jehovah hears me and an answer gives,
　　Whene'er to Him in prayer I lift my heart.

4 Stand ye in awe, lest paths of sin ye tread ;
　　Be still, and be each sin to memory brought ;
　Yea, commune with your heart upon your bed ;
　　Search out your spirit, try each secret thought.

5 Offer an acceptable sacrifice,
　　Bring righteousness, the tribute of the just ;
　And, while to Him your supplications rise,
　　Put in Jehovah your unfailing trust.

6 Many there be with faithless hearts that say,
　　" Where shall we find who good to us will
　　　show ?"
　Jehovah, now to us Thy grace display,
　　And of Thy countenance the light bestow.

7 Thou hast caused joy within my heart to spring,
　　Yea, greater joy, more gladness, there is found
　Than when the fields a plenteous harvest bring,
　　And when the stores with corn and wine abound.

8 Now will I lay me down to rest in peace,
　　Now will I close my weary eyes in sleep ;
　For Thou to watch, Jehovah, wilt not cease,
　　Thy care alone doth me in safety keep.

Song cxxxib.

" The counsel of Ahithophel."—v. 23.

Ahithophel's character for wisdom was so fully established that his advice was regarded as oracular; and, vile and hateful as was that given by him to Absalom on their first arrival in Jerusalem, it was certainly fully calculated to attain the object which both had in view, viz. an open and irreconcilable breach between the father and son.

"The counsel of Ahithophel" was probably the cause of the composition of the following Psalm, which contains such terrible maledictions as were on no other occasion elicited from David even by the most deadly attempts on his life or power; indeed his patient endurance of cruel insults had lately been fully proved in the case of Shimei.

Probably the once loved but ungrateful friends, alluded to in vv. 4 and 5, were Amasa and other members of the royal court and family, as well as Ahithophel, to whom the Psalmist then turns (changing from the plural to the singular number) with the torrent of curses alluded to above.

This would be an explanation of the Psalm on the assumption that it is one continuous poem, and I have applied it accordingly. It is, however, possible that verses 6—20, containing the imprecations, may be an interpolation, the subject being complete without them, and the position of the Psalm in the Psalter indicating, perhaps, that such interpolation may have been made during the captivity in Babylon.

In regard to the contrast between this Psalm and Ps. lv., see Song cxxvii.

PSALM CIX.

First Voice.

GOD of my praise, hold not Thy peace ;
2·Deceitful tongues my ruin seek ;
The wicked 'gainst me will not cease
False words with open mouths to speak.

3 Yea, my destruction they have sought,
With words of hate have compassed me,
Without a cause against me fought,
Intent mine overthrow to see.

4 My love doth enmity create,
But I in prayer implore Thine aid ;
5 My love they have returned with hate,
My good with evil have repaid.

Second Voice.

6 Cause him a tyrant's rule to fear ;
Be Satan at his right hand nigh ;
7 Let him when judged his sentence hear,
His prayer become iniquity.

8 Few be his days, cut off by Thee ;
His office let another take ;
9 O let his children orphans be ;
His wife do Thou a widow make.

10 Let all his children begging bread
    *Far from their ruined houses stray ;
11 Let strangers by his toil be fed,
    His goods become the oppressor's prey.

12 Let none to help him stretch the hand,
    None to his orphans favour show ;
13 Root thou his seed from out the land,
    That none his children's name may know.

14 O let Jehovah ne'er forget
    His father's guilt, his mother's sin,
15 Nor from His book efface the debt,
    But from the earth cut off his kin.

16 For mercy he remembered not,
    But pierced the heart oppress'd with woe ;
17 Make Thou the curse he loved his lot,
    The blessing scorned ne'er let him know.

18 He wrapped himself in cursing round,
    As with a garment o'er him laid ;
    Oil in his bones it shall be found,
    As water in his veins be made.

19 E'en like the cloak around him cast,
    Let him by it be covered o'er ;
    And as a girdle holdeth fast,
    So let it gird him evermore.

20 Thus let Jehovah's righteous Hand
    The malice of my foes control,
    And thus reward the wicked band
    Who evil speak against my soul.

First Voice.

21 But thou, O God, the mighty Lord,
    My Helper for Thy Name's sake be ;
Haste Thee deliverance to afford ;
    Good is Thy mercy, save Thou me.

22 For I am poor ; in need I stray ;
    Within me wounded is my heart ;
23 E'en as the locust driven away,
    Yea, like a shadow I depart.

24 My knees through fasting long are weak,
    My body wastes, my flesh is dry ;
25 My foes reproaches 'gainst me speak,
    And shake their heads in mockery.

26 My God Jehovah, near me stand,
    · O be Thy saving mercy shown,
27 That all in this may know Thine Hand,
    That Thou hast done it, Thou alone.

28 Yea, let them curse, but bless Thou still ;
    When they arise with boastful voice,
Their hearts with shame and terror fill,
    But let Thy servant's soul rejoice.

29 Clad with disgrace, with blighted name,
    Be all mine adversaries found ;
And let them clothe themselves with shame,
    As with a mantle wrapped around.

Both Voices.

30 But I a loud and joyful song
   Will to Jehovah's glory raise ;
My mouth amid the assembled throng
   His greatness and His love shall praise.

31 For He beside the poor shall stand,
   When to the judgment he is brought ;
Yea, He shall save him from their hand
   Who to condemn his soul have sought.

Song cxxxb.

" Ahithophel said unto Absalom . . . . I will arise and pursue after
David this night: and I will come upon him while he is weary
and weak-handed, ... and I will smite the king."—vv. 1, 2.

This plan would probably have been successful, had
it not been defeated by the counter influence of Hushai,
who recommended delay until a large army should be
collected, and then privately sent word to the king of all
that had passed.

We may imagine David's indignation at the proposal
of Ahithophel, his once trusted friend, and his stern prophecy that the destruction intended for another should
ere long fall on the traitor's own head.

PSALM LII. 4—5.

DEVOURING words are thy delight,
    Tongue of deceit ;
5 God likewise shall thy sin requite,
    Thy schemes defeat,
Pluck thee away, thy dwelling empty make,
And from the living thy remembrance take.

Song cxxxvi.

" Then David arose, and all the people that were with him, and they passed over Jordan."—v. 22.

The message of Hushai, alluded to with reference to the last Song, was accompanied by an entreaty that the king would cross the river that very night, as the slightest delay might prove fatal. The messengers, Jonathan and Ahimaaz, encountered considerable dangers in executing their mission, and could hardly have reached the encampment till the night was nearly past. After receiving their alarming tidings David at once acted on the advice of Hushai, and before daylight the whole army had crossed over Jordan.

Psalm v. may express David's sentiments as he watched his followers crossing the stream at the first dawn of the morning before the sun had yet risen.

The Hebrew word in the second clause of v. 3, rendered in the English Bible "direct my prayer," was used for laying in order the wood and victim for the sacrifice ; the clause should therefore be translated, " In the morning I will set in order for Thee and watch." Hence Bishop Horsley concludes that this Psalm was an appropriate prayer for the Levite whose duty it was to arrange the altar for the morning sacrifice.

PSALM V.

JEHOVAH, to my words give ear,
  Consider Thou mine every thought ;
 2 My King, my God, my crying hear,
  When unto Thee my prayer is brought.

3 Jehovah, Thou shalt hear my prayer
  When first the dawn of morn I see ;
With morning light I will prepare,
  *In order set, and watch for Thee.

4 For Thou art not a God, full well
  I know, that hath in sin delight,
Neither with Thee shall evil dwell ;
5   Fools shall not tarry in Thy sight.

Thou hatest all whom sins defile ;
6   Destruction liars doth await ;
The bloodthirsty and man of guile,
  On these Jehovah looks with hate.

7 But in Thy boundless mercy I
  Shall in Thy sacred courts appear,
Draw to Thy holy Temple nigh,
  And worship Thee in humble fear.

8 O lead me in Thy righteousness,
  Jehovah, lead me with Thy grace ;
Mine enemies are numberless,
  Make straight Thy way before my face.

9 Their mouth is but a mouth of sin,
  Their throat a grave that open lies ;
Yea, they are wickedness within ;
  •Their tongue doth pour out flatteries.

10 O God, do Thou destroy them all,
  Their countless sins their ruin make,
By their own counsels let them fall,
  For they have dared Thy laws to break.

11 But let all those who trust in Thee
   In shouts of gladness lift their voice,
For Thou wilt their Defender be ;
   Let those who love Thy Name rejoice.

12 To him that righteous paths doth tread,
   Jehovah, Thou wilt blessings send ;
Thy favour Thou wilt round him shed,
   And wilt, as with a shield, defend.

Song cxxxvii.

" By the morning light there lacked not one of them that was not gone over Jordan."—v. 22.

The *Selah* Psalm iii., which is entitled "A Psalm of David, when he fled from Absalom his son," is generally supposed to have been David's prayer on this morning. Beginning with a cry of trouble caused by the growing strength of the insurrection, he turns to thankfulness for the protecting care which had averted the night attack proposed by Ahithophel. This opportunity having been lost, the power of the enemy had been crushed, and the Psalm, therefore, ends with a confident prayer that the blessing of Jehovah may again rest upon His people.

PSALM III.

JEHOVAH, see mine enemies,
　　How fast their numbers grow ;
See how in countless hosts they rise,
　　And seek mine overthrow ;
2 Many there are that say of me,
　"God will to him no Helper be."

3 But Thou my Shield, Jehovah, art,
　　A Covering o'er me spread,
My Glory, Strengthener of my heart,
　　And Lifter of my head.
4 I to Jehovah cried to save ;
　From Zion He an answer gave.

5 I laid me on my bed and slept—
    Again I woke from sleep—
Jehovah me had safely kept ;
    He still is nigh to keep ;
6 I will not fear, although my foes
In tens of thousands round me close.

7 Arise, Jehovah, O my God,
    Stretch forth Thy saving Arm ;
My foes are smitten by Thy rod,
    Crushed is their power to harm.
8 Salvation is Jehovah's own ;
To Israel be Thy blessing shown.

Song cxxxviii.

" When Ahithophel saw that his counsel was not followed, he saddled his ass, and arose, and gat him home to his house, to his city, and put his household in order, and hanged himself."—v. 23.

Ahithophel foresaw the failure of the rebellion when his advice was rejected, and, as he could hope for no mercy at the hands of David, he in despair put an end to his own life.

The last portion of Psalm lii. seems forcibly to express David's righteous exultation, tempered with awe, at the miserable end of a man, high in honour, and great in wisdom, who made not God his strength, but trusted in his wickedness.

PSALM LII. 6—9.

WITH fear the righteous this shall see,
    And o'er him shall rejoice,
Yea, they shall laugh at him exultingly,
    And lift their voice ;

7 " See him who made not God his might,
    " But trust in riches laid,
" The man who wickedness his soul's delight
    " And strength hath made."

8   But I am like an olive-tree
    In God's own House that grows ;
My trust shall alway in the mercy be
    From God that flows.

9 Thy praise I ever will proclaim,
    Who thus Thy might hast shown,
And I will wait upon Thy holy Name,
    Dear to Thine own.

Song cxxxix.

" And (Ahithophel) died, and was buried in the sepulchre of his father."—v. 23.

Psalm xlix. also appears very suitable to the death of Ahithophel, although, as it is a *Selah* Psalm and has not been assigned to David, it is probable that some part of it was supposed by the Compiler not to have been composed by him. (See Introduction, page xxi.)

PSALM XLIX.

* HEARKEN, all ye peoples, hear,
 Dwellers in the world, give ear,
2 Men of low and high estate,
 Poor together with the great ;
3 Wisdom shall my words impart,
 Knowledge dwells within my heart ;
4 To dark words mine ears I bring,
 Parables with harp will sing.
5 Wherefore should I evil fear
 When calamities are near ?
 Malice compasseth my heels,
 Yet my heart no trouble feels.
6 They in riches who confide,
 Making heaps of gold their pride,
7 None to God, that he may live,
 Can his brother's ransom give
8 *(Souls are precious ; for their price
 Never can his wealth suffice),

9 None his brother's life may save,
  None preserve him from the grave ;

10 Nay, he seeth that the wise,
  Like the foolish person, dies ;
  Others shall the wealth receive
  Which both wise and foolish leave.

11 Long they think their homes shall last,
  Through all ages standing fast ;
  Hoping to prolong their fame,
  From themselves their lands they name.

12 Yet in pomp man bideth not ;
  Like the beasts is death his lot ;

13 Folly is in these their ways,
  Yet posterity them praise.

14 *In the world unseen like sheep
  *Death their shepherd shall them keep ;
  O'er them, when that morn they see,
  Shall the just triumphant be.
  Though their form shall waste away
  In the grave, of death the prey,

15 Me my God, His own to make,
  From the grave redeemed shall take.

16 What though one be wealthy made,
  Let thine heart be not afraid ;
  Though his glory should increase,
  Let not this disturb thy peace ;

17 When he lieth still in death,
  When hath ceased his fleeting breath,
  He shall carry nought away,
  Nought of all his vain display.

18 Though a man rejoice in wealth
  While remain his life and health

*(If thou dost successful live,
　Men to thee will honour give),
19 He shall follow them of old
　Who no more shall light behold ;
20 Man in pomp, that knoweth not,
　Hath of beasts that die the lot.

Song cxl.

" Barzillai the Gileadite of Rogelim brought beds, and basons, and earthen vessels, and wheat, and barley, and flour, and parched corn, and beans, and lentiles, and parched pulse, and honey, and butter, and sheep, and cheese of kine, for David, and for the people that were with him."—vv. 27—29.

After crossing the Jordan David occupied the fortress of Mahanaim, where he would soon have been reduced to want but for the liberality of Barzillai and two other great men of the neighbourhood.

If Barzillai were indeed the father of Adriel, mentioned in 2 Sam. xxi. 8, and if, as has been supposed, the famine recorded in that Chapter had already taken place, then five of the victims delivered by David to the vengeance of the Gibeonites had been grandsons of this aged chieftain. In this case the magnanimity of his conduct would be a thousandfold increased, and it could not but have excited the warmest feelings of gratitude in the king, who in Psalm xli. appears to contrast it with the treacherous hatred of Ahithophel. The allusions to sickness probably refer to some illness from which David had been recently suffering, and which may have encouraged Absalom and his followers to rebel.

The last verse is the doxology with which the first Book of the Psalter concludes, and, as it does not properly belong to the Psalm, I have omitted it.

PSALM XLI.

First Voice.

BLEST be he whose thoughtful care
The distressed and needy share,
For Jehovah will bestow
Help on him in time of woe ;
2 He will keep his soul alive
Blest within the land to thrive.

Second Voice.

Thou wilt not to suffer ill
Give him to his foemen's will.

First Voice.

3 When in sickness he doth lie
Then Jehovah will be nigh.

Second Voice.

All his anguish Thou wilt soothe,
Make his bed, his pillow smoothe.

First Voice.

4 Thus I said—" Jehovah, hear,
" O in mercy lend Thine ear,
" Great against Thee is my sin,
" Heal, O heal my soul within."

Second Voice.

5 Those who my destruction seek
  Thus against me evil speak,
  " When shall he to death descend ?
  " When his name and honour end ? "

First Voice.

6 If he come my state to spy,
  All he speaks is vanity ;
  Falsehood in his heart doth dwell ;
  Lies he goeth forth to tell.

Second Voice.

7 All that hate me, whispering low,
  Seek my speedy overthrow ;
  All together counsel take
  How my ruin sure to make,
8 " Sickness to him fast doth cleave,
  " Nought (say they) shall him relieve ;
  " On the bed of death he lies,
  " Never thence shall he arise."

First Voice.

9 Yea, mine own familiar friend,
  Upon whom I did depend,
  Ate my bread his faith to seal,
  Then against me raised his heel.

Second Voice.

10 Look, Jehovah, on my grief,
In Thy mercy send relief;
Raise me up from my distress
To requite their wickedness.

First Voice.

11 This a certain sign is made
Of Thy favour on me laid,
That my fierce and cruel foe
Doth not triumph in my woe.

Both Voices.

12 As for me, Thou art my Stay
In the true and perfect way;
Yea, for evermore Thy grace
Setteth me before Thy Face.

Song cxli.

" Hungry, and weary, and thirsty, in the wilderness."—v. 29.

Some Commentators consider that the following Psalm, which is entitled " A Psalm of David, when he was in the wilderness of Judah," was composed at an earlier period of his history, viz., while he was at enmity with Saul, but the reference in v. 11 to himself as " the king " seems to be a sufficient refutation of this theory, and the feelings of the distressed fugitives on the arrival of the provisions, supplied by Barzillai and his companions, may probably have suggested the allusions in the Psalm to spiritual hunger and thirst and full satisfaction in God.

PSALM LXIII.

GOD, my God Thou ever art ;
  I seek Thee at the break of day ;
For Thee doth thirst my fainting heart,
  To Thee with longing soul I pray
Within this dry and thirsty land,
Where no fresh pools of water stand ;

2 As in Thine House Thou dost unfold
  To me the brightness of Thy light,
I long Thy glory to behold,
  And praise Thy majesty and might,
3 Because to me more precious far
Than life itself Thy mercies are.

4 Thus will I bless Thee while I live,
   And lift my hands to Thee in prayer;
5 To me Thy blessing Thou shalt give,
   And fill my soul with richest fare;
While I with joyful lips proclaim
That great and glorious is Thy Name.

6 Do I not think of Thee by night
   When sleepless on my bed I lie?
And wakeful do I not delight
   To feel that Thou art alway nigh?
7 To me Thy Presence safety brings,
I love the shadow of Thy wings.

8 Upholden by Thy strong right Arm,
   My yearning soul doth follow Thee;
9 But they who seek to do me harm
   O'erwhelmed in Earth's abyss shall be;
10 Yea, let the sword the godless slay,
Their flesh to foxes be a prey.

11 But he who sits on Israel's throne
   With joy in God shall lift his voice;
And all who swear by Him alone
   Shall greatly glory and rejoice;
While they upon whose tongue are lies
Shall perish in their blasphemies.

2 Samuel XVIII.

Song cxlii.

" It is better that thou succour us out of the city."—v. 3.

Absalom, having collected a large army which he placed under the command of his cousin Amasa, crossed the Jordan, and encamped in the land of Gilead. David also at Mahanaim was making preparations for the struggle. He reviewed his troops, proposing to lead them to battle in person. The people, however, would not hear of this; they answered, "Thou shalt not go forth; . . . thou art worth ten thousand of us; . . . it is better that thou succour us out of the city." In what way this succour was to be given is not clear, but we may be quite sure that David would not neglect to ask for God's blessing on their arms.

Psalm xxv. is well adapted to this point in the history. It commences with an entreaty for preservation from enemies, and concludes with a petition that Israel may be delivered out of all his troubles; while in the greater portion of the poem David pours out his soul to God, and gives utterance to thoughts very natural at a time when he was remaining against his will inactive in the fortress.

Psalm xxv.

MY GOD, I lift my soul to Thee;
2   I trust, Jehovah, in Thy Name;
Let not my foes triumphant be,
   And let me not be put to shame.

3 On none of those who on Thee wait
    And seek Thine help let shame be laid,
But let confusion be their fate
    *Who have without a cause betrayed.

4 To me Thy paths, Jehovah, show,
    That I may safe in them abide ;
Make me Thine holy ways to know,
    And still therein my footsteps guide.

5 O lead Thou in Thy truth my heart,
    And teach me, teach me to obey ;
Thou God of my salvation art ;
    On Thee, my God, I wait all day.

6 Thy loving-kindnesses and grace,
    Jehovah, in remembrance hold,
Thy tender mercies to our race,
    For they have ever been of old.

7 My youthful sins remember not,
    Nor let my faults Thy wrath awake ;
In mercy them from memory blot,
    Jehovah, for Thy goodness' sake.

8 Just is Jehovah, gracious, kind,
    To teach them He doth sinners seek,
9 In judgment lead the humble mind,
    His ways He teacheth to the meek.

10 Mercy are all Jehovah's ways,
    And all His paths are truth; they guide
Him who His covènant obeys,
    Those in His statutes who abide.

11 Jehovah, let me mercy win,
    Let not Thy vengeance on me wait ;
For Thy Name's sake forgive my sin,
    O pardon it, for it is great.

12 Who fears Jehovah ? He shall lead
    That man in pathways of His choice;
13 His soul shall dwell at ease; his seed
    Shall in their heritage rejoice.

14 To them Jehovah's Name who fear
    His secret purpose shall be known ;
To them His mercy shall be near,
    To them His covènant be shown.

15 Mine eyes, towards Jehovah set,
    Shall ever fixed and steadfast be;
He plucks my feet from out the net,
    And from the snare will make me free.

16 Turn Thou, nor let Thy mercy cease,
    For I am sad, in loneliness ;
The troubles of my heart increase,
    O bring me out of my distress.

18 Look on my trouble, let Thine eye
    Behold the grief my heart within ;
Forgive Thou mine iniquity,
    And blot out all my grievous sin.

19 Behold my foes, their rage control,
    Many with hate have compassed me ;
20 Keep me, and save from shame my soul,
    For I have put my trust in Thee.

21 Let righteousness on me attend,
    Integrity preserve my heart ;
  On Thee I wait, on Thee depend,
    My trust from Thee shall ne'er depart.

22 Redeem, O God, Thy chosen race,
    To Israel Thy salvation show,
  On Jacob cause to shine Thy Face,
    And save him out of all his woe.

Song cxliii.

" So the people went out into the field against Israel."—v. 6.

It was doubtless with a heavy heart that David waited for news from his faithful soldiers who had gone out to fight against their brethren. Shame as well as sorrow must have filled his mind as he felt that this unnatural civil war might have arisen in a measure as a punishment for his own evil conduct, and he must have looked back regretfully on those days of old when, though an exile as now, he had a light heart and a clear conscience. But the remembrance of past mercies would encourage him to pray earnestly for pardon, deliverance, and guidance, in such strains as those contained in the following (Selah) Psalm, which the Septuagint assigns to this part of David's history.

PSALM CXLIII.

HEAR, O Jehovah, hear my cry,
    To my petitions give Thine ear ;
  O hearken from thy Throne on high,
And all my supplications hear ;
In faithfulness an answer send,
And in Thy righteousness attend.

2 With pity on Thy servant look,
    And into judgment enter not ;
All my transgressions from Thy book,
    Jehovah, in Thy mercy blot;
For in Thy sight, when he is tried,
No living man is justified.

3 For, lo, my persecuting foe
    My life hath smitten to the ground;
  In darkness he hath laid me low,
    As those who in the grave are found ;
4 My soul is bowed by sorrow's weight,
  My heart within is desolate.

5 I call to mind the days of old,
    And muse upon Thy mighty deeds,
  The wonders that Thine Hands unfold,
    Thy goodness which all thought exceeds.
6 For thee I long with outstretched hands,
  As pine for rain the thirsty lands.

7 Hear me, Jehovah, haste to hear ;
    Behold, my spirit waxeth faint ;
  Hide not Thy Face, O still be near
    To hearken to my sad complaint,
  Lest, if Thou hasten not to save,
  I sink untimely to the grave.

8 Cause me Thy tender love to know
    When in the morn from sleep I rise ;
  Cause me within Thy way to go,
    For on Thy strength my soul relies ;
  My Guide within Thy pathway be,
  For I uplift my soul to Thee.

9 Save me, Jehovah, from my foe ;
    O hide me, for to Thee I flee ;
10 Make me Thine holy will to know ;
    Thou art my God, my Teacher be ;
  *In even pathways, straight and wide,
  Let Thy good Spirit be my Guide.

11 O quicken me for Thy Name's sake ;
    Bring forth my soul from its distress ;
12 My foes let ruin overtake,
    And save me in Thy righteousness ;
    Destroy all those who vex my heart,
    For I am Thine, my God Thou art.

Song cxliv.

" The king was much moved, and went up to the chamber over the gate, and wept."—v. 33.

The melancholy story of the death of Absalom by the hand of Joab is too well-known to need repetition. For a time the grief of the father outweighed the triumph of the king, and David could only lift up his voice in the following bitter cry, to omit which would render this attempt to pourtray his character by his own words most incomplete.

2 SAMUEL XVIII. 33.

Y son, my son! O woe is me!
O Absalom, my dearest one!
Would God that I had died for thee,
O Absalom, my son, my son!

Song cxlv.

"Arise, go forth, and speak comfortably unto thy servants." — v. 7.

The first part of Psalm cxxx. (a Song of degrees) may allude to "the depths" of woe from which David was aroused by the expostulations of Joab. The change to expressions of hope and reliance upon God, followed, at the conclusion of the Song, by a charge to Israel to put their trust in Him, seems very appropriate to the comfortable words which the king exerted himself to speak to his people.

PSALM CXXX.

First Voice.

OUT of the lowest depths to Thee,
    Jehovah, do my cries ascend ;
2 Lord, hear my voice, give ear to me,
    And to my mournful prayer attend.

3 If Thou should'st mark iniquities,
    Who in the judgment shall be cleared ?
4 But, Lord, with Thee forgiveness lies,
    That Thou by all men may'st be feared.

Second Voice.

5 I to Jehovah lift mine eye,
        My soul still waiteth for His grace,
    Upon His word do I rely,
        And on His truth my hope I place ;

6 As watchers for the dawning day,
        My longing eyes are waxen dim ;
    Than watchers for the morning ray
        My soul more longing waits for Him.

Both Voices.

7 Let Israel trust Jehovah's love ;
        His mercy in a plenteous stream,
8 His saving mercy from above,
        Shall Israel from his sins redeem.

Song cxlvi.

" Return thou, and all thy servants." —v. 14.

The death of Absalom and the defeat of his army put an end to the enthusiasm with which his charms of person and manner had inspired the nation, and feelings of loyalty to their rightful sovereign revived in all except the jealous and offended tribe of Judah. Wounded by this unkindness on the part of his own " brethren," David sent them an affecting remonstrance, which completely subdued their resentment, and his soul was gladdened by the unanimous invitation quoted above. As in all his affliction one of his greatest trials seems to have been his banishment from the Sanctuary, so one of the first joyful feelings of his heart would be the prospect of returning to it ; and we can imagine no more probable time for the composition of the following " Song of degrees of David," than that at which we have now arrived.

PSALM CXXII.

 WAS glad and joyful
  When I heard the cry,
" Let us seek Jehovah,
  To His House draw nigh."

2 Soon our feet rejoicing
  Salem's gates shall throng ;
3 Salem is a city
  Firmly built and strong.

4 There Jehovah's people
   *By His precept meet ;
There His tribes thanksgivings
   Lay before His feet.

5 There the thrones of judgment
   Set in order stand,
There the house of David
   Governeth the land.

6 Let the peace of Salem
   Ever be your prayer ;
All who love thee, Salem,
   Shall thy blessings share.

7 Peace be in thy city,
   Ever to remain ;
Happiness and plenty
   In thy houses reign.

8 For my dear companions',
   For my brethren's, sake,
I will say, " Within thee
   " Peace her dwelling make."

9 For Jehovah's Temple
   I thy praise will speak ;
For His House most holy
   I thy good will seek.

Song cxlvii.

" So the king returned."—v. 15.

The yearning, which would naturally be increased as
the cherished object of desire was brought nearer within
reach, seems to be beautifully expressed in the *Selah*
Psalm lxxxiv. The Compiler may have thought that ver. 3
referred to the numerous birds which frequented the trees
in the quadrangle of Solomon's Temple, and therefore that
the first portion of the Psalm must have been composed
at a later date. This may account for its not being assigned to David (see Introduction, page xxi.), of whom,
however, it is throughout extremely characteristic.

PSALM LXXXIV. 1—4.

JEHOVAH, Lord of Hosts, Thine House
  How fair and dear to me !
 2 My heart doth long, my soul doth faint
  Jehovah's courts to see ;
My heart and flesh lift up on high
To God, the living God, their cry.

3 The sparrow there hath found a house,
 The swallow built a nest ;
About Thine holy Altar laid
 Her young ones safely rest ;
E'en to Thine Altar doth she cling,
O Lord of Hosts, my God and King.

4 How blest, how surely blest, are they,
    Within Thy courts who dwell,
Who there with joy before Thee serve,
    And of Thy glory tell!
They day and night their voices raise
To sing Thy majesty and praise.

Song cxlviii.

" So the king returned." – v. 15.

The incidents of the return journey (the submission
and pardon of Shimei, the meeting with Barzillai, and the
excuses of Mephibosheth) do not appear to have been
recorded in song like those of the flight. Perhaps
David's thoughts continued to dwell chiefly on his nearer
approach to the Sanctuary, and we may imagine him
pouring out his heart, as he went along, in such strains
as the following.

PSALM LXXXIV. 9—12.

BEHOLD, O God, our Shield,
   And let Thy saving grace
Descend on Thine anointed one ;
   Look down upon his face :
10 For one day in Thy courts to dwell
A thousand days doth far excel.

Yea, I would rather choose
   On thee to humbly wait,
And in Thy holy Temple stand,
   A keeper of the gate,
Than in the tents my home to make
Of wicked men who Thee forsake.

11 For God is Sun and Shield ;
  He grace and glory gives ;
Jehovah no good thing withholds
  From him who godly lives.
12 Jehovah, Lord of Hosts, how blest
  The man whose trust on Thee doth rest !

Song cxlix.

" Then the king went on to Gilgal." —v. 40.

The site of Gilgal cannot now be traced. It appears to have been in the midst of the hot and depressed district which lay between Jericho and the Jordan. To this place the repentant chiefs of Judah accompanied the king, after welcoming him at the river bank on his landing. We may imagine that David in the following Song applied the word " Baca," which signifies " weeping," to this dreary region. It had indeed been a vale of weeping to him in his flight from Absalom, but the blessing of Jehovah had now made it appear like a refreshing well. As the triumphant procession advanced, it grew stronger and stronger in numbers, as well as in the joyful hope of appearing with songs of praise before God in Zion.

PSALM LXXXIV. 5—8.

BLEST is the man whose strength is stayed
        Alone on Thee,
    Whose heart Thy ways hath ever made
        Its joy to be.

6 Who, passing through the weeping vale,
        Makes it a well,
    Where plenteous showers never fail
        The pools to swell.

7 They onward go from strength to strength,
  A joyful band,
Till all before their God at length
  In Zion stand.

8 O God of Hosts, to Thee I cry ;
  Jehovah, hear ;
O God of Jacob, be Thou nigh
  To give Thine ear.

Song cl.

*"Sheba, the son of Bichri, a Benjamite . . . . blew a trumpet, and
said, We have no part in David, neither have we inheritance in
the son of Jesse : every man to his tents, O Israel."*—v. 1.

In the enthusiasm of their newly restored loyalty a
contention arose between the men of Israel and Judah,
assembled at Gilgal, for the leading place in bringing
back the king. Sheba, a Benjamite, and apparently a
powerful adherent of the house of Saul, availed himself of the jealousy of the Northern tribes to sound
the usual cry of rebellion, and to create anew the
miseries of civil war.

To this "man of Belial" David may not improbably
have referred in Ps. xxxvi., in which at the same time he
expresses his firm trust in God's infinite mercy and goodness, whilst in the last verse he perhaps alludes to the
suppression of the late revolt.

PSALM XXXVI.

*THE wicked in his heart doth hear
*Transgression's tempting cries ;
There is of God no holy fear
Before his eyes.

2 *It flatters him before his sight,
      *It blinds his heart within,
   *Nor lets him hate and bring to light
            His grievous sin.

3 Deceit from out his mouth proceeds,
      Upon his lips are lies ;
   No longer righteous are his deeds,
            No longer wise.

4 His heart deviseth on his bed
      How he may mischief do ;
   In ways of good he doth not tread,
            Nor sin eschew.

5 Jehovah, even to the sky
      Thy mercy doth extend ;
   Thy truth above the clouds on high
            Doth far ascend.

6 Thy righteousness unmoved doth stand
      Firm as Thy mountains steep ;
   Great are the judgments of Thine Hand,
            A mighty deep.

   The sons of men beneath Thy care,
      Jehovah, safely rest ;
   Both man and beast Thy bounty share,
            By Thee are blest.

7 O God, how precious is Thy grace !
      Thy love, what joy it brings !
   Their trust the sons of men shall place
            Beneath Thy wings.

8 Thy plenteous stores Thou dost employ
     Their souls to satisfy,
And from the river of Thy joy
          Their drink supply.

9 For, lo, the well of life is Thine,
     Its fountain is with Thee ;
And, when Thy light doth on us shine,
          Light do we see.

10 To them who know Thee still disclose
     Thy love, Thy grace impart,
Thy perfect righteousness to those
          Of upright heart.

11 Let not the foot of pride be strong
     My weakness to assail ;
Nor let the hand that doeth wrong
          O'er me prevail.

12 There are they fallen before mine eyes
     Who work iniquity ;
Cast down are they, no more to rise
          Behold them lie.

Song cli.

" The men of Judah clave unto their king, from Jordan even to Jerusalem."—v. 2.

Escorted by the men of his own tribe, whose loyalty seems to have been strengthened by the disaffection of their rivals, David returned to his capital.

We may imagine the royal poet pouring forth the following beautiful Psalm when his eyes were gladdened by the sight of Zion with its surrounding hills. Recognizing in them an emblem of Jehovah's protecting care of His people, he goes on apparently to invoke a blessing on his faithful followers, whom he describes as the upright, and then to foretell the discomfiture of the rebels.

Psalm cxxv.

THEY whose trust is in Jehovah
    Shall be like our Zion's hill ;
Zion cannot be removèd,
    Firmly it abideth still.

2 Round our Salem stand the mountains,
    So Jehovah round us is,
He from henceforth and for ever
    Guards the people who are His.

3 For the rod of the ungodly
    Shall not rest our lot within,
Lest the righteous be transgressors,
    Putting forth their hands to sin.

4 O Jehovah, to the righteous
   All things good do Thou impart ;
Look with favour on the upright,
   Bless the good and true of heart.

5 Those, to crooked pathways turning,
   Who delight in sin to dwell
*He shall drive away with sinners.
   Peace be on our Israel.

Song clii.

" Joab took Amasa by the beard with the right hand to kiss him. But Amasa took no heed to the sword that was in Joab's hand; so he smote him therewith."—vv. 9, 10.

On his first prospect of restoration to the throne David had sent a message of pardon to Amasa and promised him the command of the army in the room of Joab. To Amasa, therefore, the first order had been given to assemble the men of Judah against Sheba, but for some unknown cause he exceeded the appointed time of three days, and the king, fearing the consequences of this delay, directed Abishai to take the bodyguard and at once pursue the insurgents. Joab, very indignant at his treatment, followed with his band, and, on his meeting with Amasa near the great stone in Gibeon, there ensued a murder even more treacherous than that of Abner related in 2 Samuel iii.

The following fragment may express David's horror of the crime and that dread of the unscrupulous sons of Zeruiah which he had before shown after the death of Abner.

PSALM LV. 19—23.

NVEXED by grief, by change untried,
Unchastened by the rod,
Their hearts are lifted up with pride ;
They fear not God.

20 On him at peace with him he laid
　　　His hand ; the word he spake,
　　The covenant that he had made,
　　　　He dared to break.

21 As butter all his words were smooth,
　　　But war beneath them lay ;
　　Though softer than is oil to soothe,
　　　　Yet swords were they.

22 Thy burden on Jehovah cast,
　　　And He will thee sustain ;
　　By Him the righteous holden fast
　　　　Unmoved remain.

23 But those who walk in falsehood's ways.
　　　O God, destroyed shall be ;
　　These shall not live out half their days ;
　　　　I trust in Thee.

Song cliii.

" *They cut off the head of Sheba the son of Bichri, and cast it out to Joab . . . . And Joab returned to Jerusalem unto the king.*"— v. 22.

His rival being slain, Joab at once reassumed the command of the army and besieged Abel, of which place Sheba had taken possession. Its inhabitants gave a new proof of the prudence for which they had always been celebrated by satisfying the demands of the besiegers in the manner described above. David could not refuse to confirm the conqueror in his post, and the remaining verses of the Chapter enumerate the various appointments in the re-established kingdom.

There can be little doubt that David celebrated this termination of the civil war by a public thanksgiving, and, as has been already said (Song cxxxi.), the concluding part of Ps. xxii. appears to have been composed for that occasion.

The two portions were probably joined together by David at some subsequent period, and the description of the typical feast on the sacrifices, to which the great ones of the land and those ready to perish from want were alike invited, was most appropriately added to the remarkable prophecy of the one great Sacrifice contained in the first part of the Psalm.

PSALM XXII. 22—31.

AMONG my brethren I will raise
My voice to magnify Thy Name,
And in the congregation praise
Thy majesty, Thy might proclaim.

23 All ye Jehovah's Name who fear,
 The praises of His glory tell ;
With praise, ye Jacob's seed, draw near ,
 Fear Him, ye seed of Israel.

24 For He did not the mournful lot
 Of the afflicted one despise ;
From him His Face he turnèd not,
 But bent His ear unto his cries.

25 *From Thee doth come the praise I sing
 When I to all Thy praise display ;
Before His servants gifts I bring,
 And in their sight my vows will pay.

26 Then food shall satisfy the meek ;
 They shall in praises lift their voice ;
Ye who Jehovah's favour seek,
 *For ever let your heart rejoice.

27 Jehovah's Name shall every land
 Remember, and to Him return ;
All kindreds shall before Thee stand,
 To worship Thee all nations learn.

28 For to Jehovah doth belong
 The kingdom, and the power is His ;
He Governor, He Ruler strong,
 He King among the nations is.

29 The great shall eat and on Him call,
 And all who in the dust have lain
Before His Throne shall prostrate fall ;
 For none his own life can sustain.

30 A seed shall serve Him, yea, a seed
    Accounted to the Lord His own ;
31 His righteousness and this His deed
    They shall from age to age make known.

Song cliv.

" And Joab returned to Jerusalem unto the king."—v. 22.

It has been already observed (Song cxxx.) that the latter portion of Ps. lxix. also appears to have formed part of a service of thanksgiving for the re-establishment of peace and order. Peculiarly appropriate to such an occasion would be the blessing in vv. 35, 36, pronounced, in connexion with Zion, on the cities of Judah, the tribe which alone had restored their king to his capital.

PSALM LXIX. 30—36.

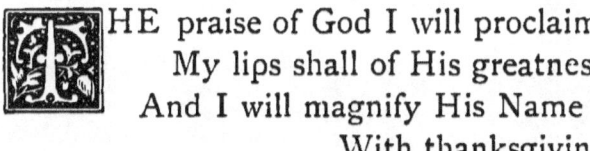

T HE praise of God I will proclaim,
  My lips shall of His greatness sing,
And I will magnify His Name
      With thanksgiving.

31 This better in Jehovah's sight
    Than ox with horns and hoofs shall be,
  Yea, this He will with more delight
      And favour see.

32 This shall the humble and the meek
    Behold, and lift with joy their voice,
  *And let your hearts, ye God who seek,
      In Him rejoice.

33 For to the poor and needy's cries
    Jehovah's ear is alway nigh ;
  His prisoners He doth not despise,
      In bonds who lie.

34 O let the heavens His praises sound,
    The earth and seas their tribute bring,
And all things that therein are found
      His glory sing.

35 For God will Zion's hill sustain,
    And Judah's cities He will bless,
That there His people may remain,
      And them possess.

36 His servant's seed the land shall share
    And for their heritage shall claim ;
And they shall dwell in safety there
      Who love His Name.

1 CHRONICLES XXI.

Song clv.

" The LORD sent pestilence upon Israel : and there fell of Israel
seventy thousand men."—v. 14.

It will now be convenient to turn to the First Book of
Chronicles, where, in Chapter xxi., another melancholy
episode in the life of David is recorded for our instruction. Elated by the increasing wealth and number of
his subjects, he insisted on having a census taken, in
spite of the remonstrances of Joab and the captains of
the host. The pride evinced by this step was punished
by a pestilence, the fearful result of which is related
above.

Psalm lxxxviii. is a wail of misery, such as must have
arisen in many a home in Israel during this calamity.
Heman the Ezrahite, to whom the poem is ascribed, was
probably the person mentioned in 1 Chron. xxv., 5, as
being David's "seer in the words of God, to lift up the
horn."

For my view respecting the component parts of the
Psalm see Introduction, pages xiv. and xv.

PSALM LXXXVIII.

GOD of my salvation, I have cried
    Before Thee night and day ;
2 Thine ear, Jehovah, turn not Thou aside,
    But hearken when I pray.

3 My soul is full of woe, my life draws nigh
  Unto the silent dead ;
4 Counted as those within the tomb am I,
  A man whose strength hath fled,

5 *Cast with the dead away, and like the slain,
  Within the grave who lie,
In Thy remembrance who no more remain,
  Cut off by Thee to die ;

6 Laid in the lowest pit am I by Thee,
  In darkness, in the deep ;
7 Thine indignation lieth hard on me,
  Thy tempests o'er me sweep.

8 Thou puttest mine acquaintance far away
  From me in this my woe ;
Abhorrence of my state their looks display ;
  No more I forth can go.

9 Mine eye doth mourn by reason of my grief ;
  Jehovah, I have prayed
With outstretched hands to Thee to send relief,
  I cries have daily made.

10 Shall all Thy wonders to the dead be shown ?
  Shall they to praise Thee rise ?
11 Shall in the grave Thy love and truth be known ?
  And where destruction lies ?

12 Wilt Thou disclose the wonders of Thine Hand
  Where there is darkness deep ?
Thy righteousness discover in the land
  Where all forgotten sleep ?

13 But, O Jehovah, these my daily cries
    Have unto Thee been made ;
  And in the morning shall my prayer arise,
    And be before Thee laid.

14 Jehovah, why dost Thou cast off my soul ?
    Thy Face from me why hide ?
15 E'en from my youth afflictions round me roll,
    Death hovers by my side.

  My mind is sorely troubled while I see
    Thy terrors to be near ;
16 Thy fierce displeasure goeth over me ;
    I am cut off by fear.

17 Like water did Thy terrors day by day
    Encompass me with dread ;
18 All mine acquaintance Thou hast put away ;
    Lovers and friends have fled.

" *David built there an altar unto the LORD, and offered burnt offer-ings and peace offerings, and called upon the LORD; and he answered him from heaven by fire upon the altar of burnt offer-ing.*

" *And the LORD commanded the angel; and he put up his sword again into the sheath thereof.*"—vv. 26, 27.

The interesting interview between David and Ornan (or Araunah), supposed to be the dethroned Jebusite king of Jerusalem, is too well-known to need description. Beside the threshing-floor of this generous chieftain stood the terrible apparition of the destroying angel, whose sword was sheathed by the command of God, in answer to the sacrifices and prayers of his repentant servant.

PSALM XXXII. 1—4.

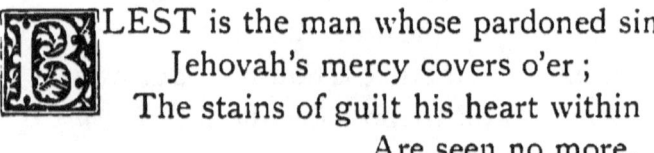

BLEST is the man whose pardoned sin
    Jehovah's mercy covers o'er ;
The stains of guilt his heart within
       Are seen no more.

2 The sentence of iniquity
    Doth on his soul no longer rest ;
No guile there meets Jehovah's eye ;
       That man is blest.

3 Jehovah, when I silence kept,
    And on my bed in sorrow lay,
My bones waxed old as then I wept
       The livelong day.

4 For day and night was heavily
    Upon me laid Thy chastening Hand,
As drought beneath the summer's sky
        Consumes the land.

I CHRONICLES XXII.

Song clvii.

" Then David said, This is the house of the LORD God, and this is
the altar of burnt offering for Israel."—v. 1.

In grateful remembrance of the pardon which had
been there vouchsafed to him, David selected the threshing-floor of Araunah as the site of the Temple, for which
he then began to make preparations. Psalm xxx., of
which the Hebrew title is "A Psalm and Song at the
dedication of the house of David," and which contains
an account of the presumption caused by his prosperity,
its fatal results, his penitence, pardon, and restoration to
joy, appears very appropriate to the circumstances connected with this selection of a site for the House of
God.

PSALM XXX.

THEE, O Jehovah, I will praise,
  For Thou hast set me up on high,
 Nor let my foes in triumph raise
   O'er me their cry.

2 I prayed, and health Thou didst bestow,
  And from the tomb my soul didst save ;
3 Thou keepedst me lest I should go
   Down to the grave.

4 O sing unto Jehovah, sing,
  Ye saints of His, Jehovah bless ;
Remember, as your thanks ye bring,
          His holiness.

5 His wrath doth but a moment last,
  His favour is of life the spring ;
In weeping though the night be past,
          Morn joy shall bring.

6 I said in my prosperity
  " I shall not be removed, Thine Hand,
7 " Jehovah, makes so strong, so high,
          " My hill to stand."

Then Thou from me Thy Face didst hide,
  And I was troubled, sore afraid ;
8 Jehovah, then to Thee I cried,
          To Thee I prayed—

9 " How shall my blood show forth Thy praise
  " When down into the grave I go ?
" Shall dust its thankful voice upraise
          " Thy truth to show ?

10 " Jehovah, hearken to my cry,
  " Vouchsafe Thy mercy to accord,
" Jehovah, in my need be nigh,
          " And help afford."

11 My mourning Thou hast dancing made,
  Thou hast put off my garment sad,
And me in robes of joy arrayed,
          With gladness clad.

12 So that my glory Thee may praise,
    Jehovah, and not silent be :
  I ever thankful songs will raise,
               My God, to Thee.

Song clviii.

" The house that is to be builded for the LORD must be exceeding magnifical, of fame and of glory throughout all countries."—v. 5.

Having been graciously guided in his choice of a site for the House of God, David threw his whole soul into the work of collecting and preparing materials with a pious enthusiasm expressed in the verse quoted above, to which the following Song seems well adapted.

PSALM LXXXVII. 1—3.

HIS foundations firmly rest
On the holy mountain's crest ;
2 Blessing upon Zion's gates
More than on all Jacob waits ;

Israel's dwellings far above,
Zion shares Jehovah's love ;
3 Glorious things are said of Thee,
City where God loves to be.

1 CHRONICLES XXVIII.

Song clix.

*" God said unto me, Thou shalt not build an house for my name,
because thou hast been a man of war, and hast shed blood."*—
v. 3.
" Solomon thy son, he shall build my house."—v. 6.

Some time must have been occupied in collecting
materials for the new Temple. When the magnificent
preparations were completed, David, now "old and full
of days," assembled the great men of Israel, and explained
to them that it had been his desire to build a House for
the Almighty, but that God had been pleased to commit
the privilege of carrying out his purpose to Solomon
rather than to himself.

Commentators differ in regard to the occasion for which
Ps. lxv. was composed. By some it is associated with
the rich harvest which followed the overthrow of Sennacherib's army; but its Hebrew title is, I think, sufficient authority for assigning it to David, and it appears
to me very appropriate to this assembly, which may not
improbably have taken place at a time of unusual plenty,
such as is described in the latter part of the Psalm.

The opening verses mark it as especially suitable to
this occasion. The people of God were waiting with
longing hearts to present their praises to Him in the
Temple, soon to rise in beauty on Mount Zion, in
which all should joyfully assemble; and their king, while
lamenting the obstacles which his past life presented
to his being himself permitted to perform his vow, rejoices in the greater blessedness vouchsafed to his son.

PSALM LXV.

People.

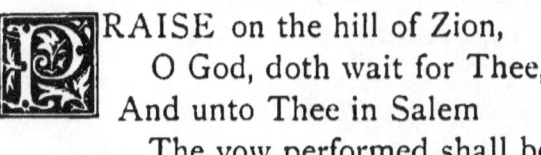RAISE on the hill of Zion,
 O God, doth wait for Thee,
And unto Thee in Salem
 The vow performed shall be.

David.

2 O Thou Whose ears are open
 Whene'er Thy servants pray,
All flesh shall seek Thy footstool,
 Their wants before Thee lay.

3 Iniquities prevailing
 Have strong against me been,
But Thou shalt our transgressions
 Efface and make us clean.

People

4 Blest is the man Thou choosest,
 And causest to draw near,
To make Thy courts his dwelling
 And worship there in fear ;

For of Thy House the goodness
 Shall all our need supply ;
The pleasures of Thy Temple
 Our souls shall satisfy.

5 By fearful things in judgment
 To us on earth who live,
O God of our salvation,
 Wilt Thou an answer give ;

A a 2

The earth's most distant nations
  Put all their trust in Thee,
Protector of the wanderers
  Far off upon the sea.

David.

6 Whose strength sets fast the mountains
  Who girded is with might,
7 Who stills the roar of Ocean,
  Of men the tumult's height.

8 In distant lands Thy tokens
  They see and are afraid ;
From East to West the nations
  By Thee are joyful made.

People.

9 The fount of God o'erflowing
  With riches fills the land,
And thus are plenteous harvests
  Provided by Thine Hand.

10 Thou waterest the ridges,
  Low are the furrows pressed ;
Made soft by plenteous showers
  Earth's springing up is blessed.

11 Thou crown'st the year with goodness ;
  Thy paths drop fatness down ;
12 *Each lonely pasture droppeth ;
  The hills doth gladness crown.

13 With flocks are clothed the meadows ;
  The fields rich harvests bring ;
Corn overspreads the valleys ;
  For joy they shout and sing.

Song clx.

" Give unto Solomon my son a perfect heart, to keep thy command-ments."—v. 19.

After the dedication, in the presence of the great assembly, of the treasures collected for the Temple, David gave an exhortation to Solomon, who was apparently at this time (as well as during the rebellion of Adonijah) publicly proclaimed the successor to the throne, and then offered up the beautiful prayer, a portion of which is quoted above.

Psalm lxxii., entitled "For Solomon," seems to commemorate this occasion. It is placed at the end of the second Book of the Psalter, and concludes with a Doxology; but, as the Doxology was evidently added by the Compiler, according to the usual practice at the termination of each Book, and as the Psalm is complete without it, it is omitted in the following Song.

PSALM LXXII.

 GOD, grant Thine anointed
 Thy judgments to obtain,
The son of Thine anointed
 In righteousness to reign.

2 Then shall he judge Thy people
 With truth and righteousness,
And save the poor with judgment
 From such as would oppress.

3 The mountains to the people
  Shall bring the fruits of peace,
The little hills by justice ;
  For violence shall cease.

4 For he shall judge the people,
  Protect the needy's right,
Shall save the poor man's children,
  And crush oppressors' might.

5 Throughout all generations
  His people Thee shall fear,
While sun in heaven endureth
  And moon doth there appear.

6 He shall be like the raindrops
  Upon the new mown field,
And as the showers, which falling
  Make earth her increase yield.

7 Throughout his days the righteous
  Shall flourish and increase ;
Long as the moon endureth
  Shall be abundant peace.

8 To him shall be dominion
  And rule from sea to sea ;
His kingdom from the river
  To earth's far ends shall be.

9 The dwellers in the desert
  To him shall homage pay ;
And those who rise against him
  He in the dust shall lay.

10 From Tarshish and the islands
    Their kings shall presents bring,
The ruler of Arabia,
    And Ethiopia's king.

11 Yea, kings of every people
    Shall bow before his throne,
All nations do him service,
    And him their ruler own.

12 For he shall save the needy
    That lifteth up his cry;
The poor he shall deliver
    That hath no helper nigh.

13 The needy he shall pity,
    The humble he shall spare,
And save their souls in danger;
    The poor shall be his care.

14 From violence and falsehood
    Their souls he shall redeem;
The blood of those in trouble
    He precious shall esteem.

15 *So shall they live and presents
    Of gold from Sheba bring;
And, praying for him daily,
    His praises they shall sing.

16 Corn waving on the mountains
    Like Lebanon shall stand,
The citizens be countless
    As grass upon the land.

17 His name shall last for ever,
   As lasts the sun his days;
In him shall all be blessèd,
   Him all shall bless and praise.

Song clxi.

"Adonijah the son of Haggith exalted himself, saying, I will be king."—v. 5.

The Book of Kings contains an account of the insurrection of Adonijah, which is not mentioned in the Books of Samuel or Chronicles.

It is uncertain whether this rebellion occurred before or after the great assembly referred to in the last two Songs. Both events must have taken place very shortly before the close of David's life, and I have thought it desirable to conclude the account of the preparations for the Temple, recorded in the Book of Chronicles, before turning to a different subject in another Book.

It would seem that a sickness of David in his old age, either his last fatal illness or one from which he may have recovered, encouraged Adonijah, his eldest surviving son, to attempt to obtain the crown which he well knew that David intended to bequeath to Solomon.

Psalm xxxviii., which is entitled "A Psalm of David, to bring to remembrance," being the mournful complaint of a sick man lamenting over his sins and grieved by the treachery of those who took advantage of his helpless state to rebel against him, may not improbably have been composed at this period.

PSALM XXXVIII.

CEASE, O Jehovah, from Thine anger fierce,
O chasten me no more ;
2 Deeper and deeper do Thine arrows
pierce,
Thine Hand doth press me sore.

3 No soundness hath Thine anger in me left,
No health my flesh within ;
Of rest from pain are all my bones bereft
By reason of my sin.

4 For mine iniquities and sins are great,
And o'er my head they roll ;
E'en as a heavy burden is their weight,
Too heavy for my soul.

5 My putrid wounds my grievous folly show ;
Woes compass me around ;
6 And all day long I sad and mourning go,
Bowed down unto the ground.

7 8 My loins are smitten with a foul disease ;
In pain and grief I moan ;
Worn is my flesh, and feeble are my knees ;
With troubled heart I groan.

9 But my desires Thou, Lord, dost surely know,
Thou hearest all my sighs ;
10 My strength hath failed, my heart doth pant
with woe,
The light hath left mine eyes.

11 Far off my lovers are and friends of old,
    They stand aloof in fear;
  And e'en my nearest kinsmen's hearts are cold,
    Not one will venture near.

12 They too who seek to take my life away
    Lay snares to catch my feet;
  Mine enemies speak evil all the day,
    Imagining deceit. .

13 But I am like one deaf to every sound,
    Like one who doth not hear;
14 Like one with whom are no reproaches found,
    Speechless do I appear.

15 Jehovah, all my trust is in Thy word,
    My hope is fixed on Thee;
  For Thou wilt surely hear, O God my Lord,
    *Wilt hear and speak for me.

16 "O hearken to me, lend Thine ear," I cried,
    "Lest o'er me they rejoice;
  "O hearken, lest, whene'er my footsteps slide,
    "Triumphant be their voice."

17 I alway tread with halting steps and slow,
    While sorrows on me press;
18 I mine iniquities to Thee will show,
    And mourn my wickedness.

19 Behold, all these mine enemies are strong,
    And they with bitter hate
  Who will not rest but strive to do me wrong
    In number now are great.

20 They also ever have against me stood
　　Who good with ill requite,
　Because I follow after what is good
　　And strive to do the right.

21 Jehovah, leave me not ; O God, be nigh
　　Thy succour to impart ;
22 Haste Thee, O Lord, to help me when I cry,
　　Who my Salvation art.

Song clxii.

Behold, Adonijah reigneth; and now, my Lord the king, thou knowest it not."—v. 18.

Solomon was probably the eldest surviving son born after David had been made king over Israel, and was therefore, according to an opinion common in the East, the rightful heir to the throne, and the natural person to act for his father during his sickness. It was, however, not unusual in those days for an elder son, born before his father's accession, to dispute his younger brother's title, and we can hardly be surprised that Adonijah should have felt jealous of the preference given to Solomon. But it was a very different thing for him to tread in the footsteps of his brother Absalom (2 Sam. xv. 1), to assume the ensigns of royalty without his father's sanction, and to proclaim himself king without his knowledge; and his crime would be the more reprehensible if (as was probably the case) he were aware that Solomon had been selected by God Himself as the successor to the throne.

The ease and rapidity with which this insurrection was subdued proved it to be an act no less of madness and folly than of wickedness on the part of Adonijah, such as may have been rebuked in the following Song, which is assigned to Asaph.

PSALM LXXV. 4—10.

 SAID unto the foolish man,
　　Deal not so foolishly ;
And to the wicked thus I cried,
　　Lift not the horn so high ;
5 O lift not up on high your horn,
And speak not proudly words of scorn.

6 Promotion comes not from the East,
　　Nor from the South, nor West ;
7 God is the Judge, and He will do
　　What seemeth to Him best ;
He maketh one in dust to lie,
And sets another up on high.

8 A cup is in Jehovah's Hand,
　　The wine therein is red,
Behold, it is of mixture full,
　　Poured out in anger dread ;
The wicked of the Earth shall drain
The dregs that in that cup remain.

9 But I for ever will declare,
　　And Jacob's God will praise ;
10 I also will smite down the horns
　　Which sinners proudly raise ;
The righteous shall in honour be,
Their horn set up triumphantly.

Song clxiii.

" Now the days of David drew nigh that he should die." —v. 1.

The insurrection of Adonijah was speedily quelled by the prompt measures of David in favour of Solomon ; but the days of the aged king must have been darkened by doubt and suspicion. Psalm xxxix. may perhaps express the thoughts which were uppermost in his mind at this period. Surrounded by many disloyal and rebellious subjects, he may have felt compelled to put a bridle upon his words. lest he should be tempted to speak unadvisedly or with bitterness. To God alone could he pour forth the fulness of his heart, and, aware of his own failing strength, and anxious to see Solomon fairly established as his successor, he would naturally adopt some such prayer as the following, in which he asks for forgiveness of his sins, and entreats that his life may yet a little longer be spared.

PSALM XXXIX.

 SAID, " I will observe my way,
　　" Lest with my tongue I err from right,
　" A bridle on my mouth will lay
　　" While wicked men are in my sight."

2 In silence dumb I long remained,
　My words I laboured to control,
Yea, e'en from good my lips refrained,
　But it was anguish to my soul.

3 My heart within me hotly burned,
　The fire was kindled while I mused;
At length my mouth the bridle spurned,
　And all restraint my tongue refused—

4 "Mine end, Jehovah, make me know,
　" The measure of my days reveal,
"The term of life yet left me show;
　"O that I may my frailty feel!"

5 Lo, Thou hast made my days a span,
　Mine age as nothing before Thee;
*Only a breath is every man:
　*Though firm he stand, a breath is he.

6 Man walketh in a shadow vain,
　*For but a breath is vexed with care;
He labours riches to obtain,
　And knows not who his wealth shall share.

7 And now what wait I for, O Lord?
　My hope in Thee alone doth rest;
8 Cleanse me from sins of deed and word,
　Lest I become of fools the jest.

9 I spake not, for the deed was Thine:
　No more Thy stroke upon me lay;
10 Beneath Thy heavy Hand I pine,
　I am consumed, and waste away.

11 When Thou dost chasten man for sin,
 His beauty is to ruin brought,
As moth a garment frets within ;
 *A breath are all men—surely nought.

12 Jehovah, hearken to my cry,
 Let my petition reach Thine ears ;
Hold not Thy peace when thus I sigh,
 O be not silent to my tears ;

For I a stranger am with Thee,
 As Israel was in days of yore ;
Here I a sojourner must be,
 As all my fathers were before.

13 A little while Thine Hand refrain,
 Until my strength restored hath been ;
Spare me, my vigour to regain,
 Ere I go hence and be not seen.

Song clxib.

" Now these be the last words of David. David the son of Jesse said,
and the man who was raised up on high, the anointed of the God
of Jacob, and the sweet psalmist of Israel, said," —v. 1.

We have now gone through the chief events recorded
in the life of David. Whether he recovered from the illness from which he was suffering at the time of Adonijah's
rebellion is uncertain, as is the exact period in his history
at which that insurrection took place. It seems probable,
however, that he was for a time restored to health and
prosperity, for we are told that he died "in a good old
age, full of days, riches, and honour." (1 Chronicles
xxix. 28.)

Other events in David's history are recorded in the
Second Book of Samuel in Chapters subsequent to that
in which his "last words" are found, and some Commentators suppose that these words were not spoken on his
death-bed. However this may have been, they appear to
sum up in beautiful language the guiding principles and
firm faith of him who was emphatically called, "The
man after God's own heart"

2 SAM. XXIII. 2—7.

BY me Jehovah's Spirit spake,
　　And on my tongue was laid His word;
3 The God of Israel silence brake,
　　The Rock of Israel thus was heard,—
"*The Just One holds the Ruler's rod,
"*He ruleth by the fear of God.

4 " *Jehovah as the morning light,
   " E'en as the glorious sun, doth rise,
 " Yea, as the morning clear and bright,
   " When no dark clouds o'erspread the skies,
 " As tender grass that springs again
 " Blest by clear sunshine after rain."

5 *Truly with God my house shall be
   *E'en thus unstainèd found and pure,
Who hath a covenant made with me,
   Eternal, fixed, in all things sure ;
*All my Salvation Him I know,
*All my desire to Him doth flow.

6 *But Belial's sons shall fade away,
   And rooted up like thorns appear,
7 On whom none dareth hands to lay
   Unfenced by steel and staff of spear ;
These shall by fire be quickly burned
*And in their homes to ruin turned.

I cannot resist the temptation to end this volume with the beautiful remarks of Dean Stanley on these " Last Words of David."

Alluding to the last verse, he says :—" It is a melancholy strain to close a song which begins so full of brightness and joy. But it is a true picture of the chequered life of David, and of the chequered fortunes of the ruler amongst men. It is a true picture of the ' broken lights ' of the human heart, whether in Judea or in England, whether of king or peasant. If there be any part of Scripture which betrays the movements of the human individual soul, it is this precious fragment of David's life. If there be any part which claims for itself, and which gives evidence of, the breathing of the Spirit of God, it is this also. Such a rugged two-edged monument is the fitting memorial of the man who was at once the King and the Prophet, the Penitent and the Saint, of the ancient Church."

INDEX.

THE END.

GILBERT AND RIVINGTON, PRINTERS, ST. JOHN'S SQUARE, LONDON.

A Catalogue of American and Foreign Books Published or Imported by MESSRS. SAMPSON LOW & CO. *can be had on application.*

Crown Buildings, 188, Fleet Street, London,
October, 1878.

𝔄 𝔏𝔦𝔰𝔱 𝔬𝔣 𝔅𝔬𝔬𝔨𝔰

PUBLISHED BY

SAMPSON LOW, MARSTON, SEARLE, & RIVINGTON.

———◆———

ALPHABETICAL LIST.

A CLASSIFIED Educational Catalogue of Works published in Great Britain. Demy 8vo, cloth extra. Second Edition, revised and corrected to Christmas, 1877, 5s.

Abney (Captain W. de W., R.E., F.R.S.) Thebes, and its Five Greater Temples. Forty large Permanent Photographs, with descriptive letter-press. Super-royal 4to, cloth extra, 63s.

About Some Fellows. By an ETON BOY, Author of "A Day of my Life." Cloth limp, square 16mo, 2s. 6d.

Adventures of Captain Mago. A Phœnician's Explorations 1000 years B.C. By LEON CAHUN. Numerous Illustrations. Crown 8vo, cloth extra, gilt, 7s. 6d.

Adventures of a Young Naturalist. By LUCIEN BIART, with 117 beautiful Illustrations on Wood. Edited and adapted by PARKER GILLMORE. Post 8vo, cloth extra, gilt edges, New Edition, 7s. 6d.

Adventures in New Guinea. The Narrative of the Captivity of a French Sailor for Nine Years among the Savages in the Interior. Small post 8vo, with Illustrations and Map, cloth, gilt, 6s.

Africa, and the Brussels Geographical Conference. Translated from the French of EMILE BANNING, by R. H. MAJOR, F.S.A. With Map, crown 8vo, 7s. 6d.

Alcott (Louisa M.) Aunt Jo's Scrap-Bag. Square 16mo, 2s. 6d. (Rose Library, 1s.)

—— *Cupid and Chow-Chow.* Small post 8vo, 3s. 6d.

—— *Little Men : Life at Plumfield with Jo's Boys.* Small post 8vo, cloth, gilt edges, 3s. 6d. (Rose Library, Double vol. 2s.)

—— *Little Women.* 1 vol., cloth, gilt edges, 3s. 6d. (Rose Library, 2 vols., 1s. each.)

A

Alcott (*Louisa M.*) *Old-Fashioned Girl.* Best Edition, small post 8vo, cloth extra, gilt edges, 3*s*. 6*d*. (Rose Library, 2*s*.)

———— *Work and Beginning Again.* A Story of Experience. I vol., small post 8vo, cloth extra, 6*s*. Several Illustrations. (Rose Library, 2 vols., 1*s*. each.)

———— *Shawl Straps.* Small post 8vo, cloth extra, gilt, 3*s*. 6*d*.

———— *Eight Cousins; or, the Aunt Hill.* Small post 8vo, with Illustrations, 3*s*. 6*d*.

———— *The Rose in Bloom.* Small post 8vo, cloth extra, 3*s*. 6*d*.

———— *Silver Pitchers.* Small post 8vo, cloth extra, 3*s*. 6*d*.

———— *Under the Lilacs.* Small post 8vo, cloth extra, 5*s*.

"Miss Alcott's stories are thoroughly healthy, full of racy fun and humour . . . exceedingly entertaining . . . . We can recommend the 'Eight Cousins.'"— *Athenæum.*

Alpine Ascents and Adventures; or, Rock and Snow Sketches. By H. SCHÜTZ WILSON, of the Alpine Club. With Illustrations by WHYMPER and MARCUS STONE. Crown 8vo, 10*s*. 6*d*. 2nd Edition.

Andersen (*Hans Christian*) *Fairy Tales.* With Illustrations in Colours by E. V. B. Royal 4to, cloth, 25*s*.

Andrews (*Dr.*) *Latin-English Lexicon.* 14th Edition. Royal 8vo, 1670 pp., cloth extra, price 18*s*.

Anecdotes of the Queen and Royal Family. Collected and Edited by J. G. HODGINS, with Illustrations. New Edition, 5*s*.

Animals Painted by Themselves. Adapted from the French of Balzac, Georges Sands, &c., with 200 Illustrations by GRANDVILLE. 8vo, cloth extra, gilt, 10*s*. 6*d*.

Art of Reading Aloud (*The*) *in Pulpit, Lecture Room, or Private* Reunions, with a perfect system of Economy of Lung Power on just principles for acquiring ease in Delivery, and a thorough command of the Voice. By G. VANDENHOFF, M.A. Crown 8vo, cloth extra, 6*s*.

Asiatic Turkey: being a Narrative of a Journey from Bombay to the Bosphorus, embracing a ride of over One Thousand Miles, from the head of the Persian Gulf to Antioch on the Mediterranean. By GRATTAN GEARY, Editor of the *Times of India.* 2 vols., crown 8vo, cloth extra, with many Illustrations, and a Route Map.

This Work gives a full and detailed account of the author's adventurous ride of which an epitome appeared in the *Times.*

Atlantic Islands as Resorts of Health and Pleasure. By S. G. W. BENJAMIN, Author of "Contemporary Art in Europe," &c. Royal 8vo, cloth extra, with upwards of 150 Illustrations, 16*s*.

Atmosphere (*The*). *See* FLAMMARION.

Auld Lang Syne. By the Author of "Wreck of the Grosvenor." 2 vols., crown 8vo, 21*s*.

BAKER (*Lieut.-Gen. Valentine, Pasha*). *See* "War in Bulgaria."

Barton Experiment (*The*). By the Author of "Helen's Babies." 1*s.*

THE BAYARD SERIES,

Edited by the late J. HAIN FRISWELL.

Comprising Pleasure Books of Literature produced in the Choicest Style as Companionable Volumes at Home and Abroad.

"We can hardly imagine better books for boys to read or for men to ponder over."—*Times.*

Price 2*s. 6d.* each *Volume, complete in itself, flexible cloth extra, gilt edges, with silk Headbands and Registers.*

The Story of the Chevalier Bayard. By M. DE BERVILLE.

De Joinville's St. Louis, King of France.

The Essays of Abraham Cowley, including all his Prose Works.

Abdallah ; or the Four Leaves. By EDOUARD LABOULLAYE.

Table-Talk and Opinions of Napoleon Buonaparte.

Vathek : An Oriental Romance. By WILLIAM BECKFORD.

The King and the Commons. A Selection of Cavalier and Puritan Songs. Edited by Prof. MORLEY.

Words of Wellington : Maxims and Opinions of the Great Duke.

Dr. Johnson's Rasselas, Prince of Abyssinia. With Notes.

Hazlitt's Round Table. With Biographical Introduction.

The Religio Medici, Hydriotaphia, and the Letter to a Friend. By Sir THOMAS BROWNE, Knt.

Ballad Poetry of the Affections. By ROBERT BUCHANAN.

Coleridge's Christabel, and other Imaginative Poems. With Preface by ALGERNON C. SWINBURNE.

Lord Chesterfield's Letters, Sentences, and Maxims. With Introduction by the Editor, and Essay on Chesterfield by M. DE STE.- BEUVE, of the French Academy.

Essays in Mosaic. By THOS. BALLANTYNE.

My Uncle Toby ; his Story and his Friends. Edited by P. FITZGERALD.

Reflections ; or, Moral Sentences and Maxims of the Duke de la Rochefoucauld.

Socrates : Memoirs for English Readers from Xenophon's Memo- rabilia. By EDW. LEVIEN.

Prince Albert's Golden Precepts.

A Case containing 12 Volumes, price 31s. 6d. ; or the Case separately, price 3s. 6d.

Beauty and the Beast. An Old Tale retold, with Pictures by B. V. B. Demy 4to, cloth extra, novel binding. 10 Illustrations in Colours (in same style as those in the First Edition of "Story without an End "). 12*s. 6d.*

A 2

Beumer's German Copybooks. In six gradations at 4*d.* each.

Biart (Lucien). See "Adventures of a Young Naturalist."
"My Rambles in the New World," "The Two Friends."

Bickersteth's Hymnal Companion to Book of Common Prayer.
The Original Editions, containing 403 Hymns, always kept in Print.

Revised and Enlarged Edition, containing 550 Hymns—

. *The Revised Editions are entirely distinct from, and cannot be used with, the original editions.*

			s.	d.
7A	Medium 32mo, cloth limp		0	8
7B	ditto roan		1	2
7C	ditto morocco or calf		2	6
8A	Super-royal 32mo, cloth limp		1	0
8B	ditto red edges		1	2
8C	ditto roan		2	2
8D	ditto morocco or calf		3	6
9A	Crown 8vo, cloth, red edges		3	0
9B	ditto roan		4	0
9C	ditto morocco or calf		6	0
10A	Crown 8vo, with Introduction and Notes, red edges		4	0
10B	ditto roan		5	0
10C	ditto morocco		7	6
11A	Penny Edition in Wrapper		0	1
11B	ditto cloth		0	2
11C	With Prayer Book, cloth		0	9
11D	ditto roan		1	0
11E	ditto morocco		2	6
11F	ditto persian		1	6
12A	Crown 8vo, with Tunes, cloth, plain edges		4	0
12B	ditto ditto persian, red edges		6	6
12C	ditto ditto limp morocco, gilt edges		7	6
13A	Small 4to, for Organ		8	6
13B	ditto ditto limp russia		21	0
	Chant Book Supplement (Music)		1	6
	Ditto 4to, for Organ		3	6
14A	Tonic Sol-fa Edition		3	6
14B	ditto treble and alto only		1	0
5B	Chants only		1	6
5D	ditto 4to, for Organ		3	6
	The Church Mission Hymn-Book	*per* 100	8	4
	Ditto ditto cloth	*each*	0	4

The "*Hymnal Companion*" *may now be had in special bindings for presentation with and without the Common Prayer Book. A red line edition is ready. Lists on application.*

Bickersteth (Rev. E. H., M.A.) The Reef and other Parables.
1 vol., square 8vo, with numerous very beautiful Engravings, 7*s.* 6*d.*

———— *The Clergyman in his Home.* Small post 8vo, 1*s.*

Bickersteth (Rev. E. H., M.A.) The Master's Home-Call; or, Brief Memorials of Alice Frances Bickersteth. 20th Thousand. 32mo, cloth gilt, 1s.

"They recall in a touching manner a character of which the religious beauty has a warmth and grace almost too tender to be definite."—*The Guardian.*

————— *The Shadow of the Rock.* A Selection of Religious Poetry. 18mo, cloth extra, 2s. 6d.

————— *The Shadowed Home and the Light Beyond.* 7th Edition, crown 8vo, cloth extra, 5s.

Bida. The Authorized Version of the Four Gospels, with the whole of the magnificent Etchings on Steel, after drawings by M. BIDA, in 4 vols., appropriately bound in cloth extra, price 3l. 3s. each.

Also the four volumes in two, bound in the best morocco, by Suttaby, extra gilt edges, 18l. 18s., half-morocco, 12l. 12s.

"Bida's Illustrations of the Gospels of St. Matthew and St. John have already received here and elsewhere a full recognition of their great merits."—*Times.*

Bidwell (C. T.) The Balearic Islands. Illustrations and a Map. Crown 8vo, cloth, 10s. 6d.

————— *The Cost of Living Abroad.* Crown 8vo, 6s.

Black (Wm.) Three Feathers. Small post 8vo, cloth extra, 6s.

————— *Lady Silverdale's Sweetheart, and other Stories.* 1 vol., small post 8vo, 6s.

————— *Kilmeny: a Novel.* Small post 8vo, cloth, 6s.

————— *In Silk Attire.* 3rd Edition, small post 8vo, 6s.

————— *A Daughter of Heth.* 11th Edition, small post 8vo, 6s.

Blackmore (R. D.) Lorna Doone. 10th Edition, cr. 8vo, 6s.

"The reader at times holds his breath, so graphically yet so simply does John Ridd tell his tale."—*Saturday Review.*

————— *Alice Lorraine.* 1 vol., small post 8vo, 6th Edition, 6s.

————— *Clara Vaughan.* Revised Edition, 6s.

————— *Cradock Nowell.* New Edition, 6s.

————— *Cripps the Carrier.* 3rd Edition, small post 8vo, 6s.

Blossoms from the King's Garden : Sermons for Children. By the Rev. C. BOSANQUET. 2nd Edition, small post 8vo, cloth extra, 6s.

Blue Banner (The); or, The Adventures of a Mussulman, a Christian, and a Pagan, in the time of the Crusades and Mongol Conquest. By LEON CAHUN. Translated from the French by W. COLLETT SANDARS. With Seventy-six Wood Engravings. 1 vol., square imperial 16mo, cloth extra, 7s. 6d.

Book of English Elegies. Small post 8vo, cloth extra, 5s.

Book of the Play. By DUTTON COOK. 2 vols., crown 8vo, 24s.

Bradford (Wm.) The Arctic Regions. Illustrated with Photographs, taken on an Art Expedition to Greenland. With Descriptive Narrative by the Artist. In One Volume, royal broadside, 25 inches by 20, beautifully bound in morocco extra, price Twenty-Five Guineas.

Brave Men in Action. By S. J. MACKENNA. Crown 8vo,
480 pp., cloth, 10s. 6d.

Breck (Samuel). *See* "Recollections."

Browning (Mrs. E. B.) The Rhyme of the Duchess May.
Demy 4to, Illustrated with Eight Photographs, after Drawings by
CHARLOTTE M. B. MORRELL. 21s.

Bryant (W. C., assisted by S. H. Gay) A Popular History of
the United States. About 4 vols., to be profusely Illustrated with
Engravings on Steel and Wood, after Designs by the best Artists.
Vol. I., super-royal 8vo, cloth extra, gilt, 42s., is ready.

Burnaby (Capt.) *See* "On Horseback."

Burton (Captain R. F.) Two Trips to Gorilla Land and the
Cataracts of the Congo. By Captain R. F. BURTON. 2 vols, demy
8vo, with numerous Illustrations and Map, cloth extra, 28s.

Butler (W. F.) The Great Lone Land; an Account of the Red
River Expedition, 1869-70, and Subsequent Travels and Adventures
in the Manitoba Country, and a Winter Journey across the Saskatche-
wan Valley to the Rocky Mountains. With Illustrations and Map.
Fifth and Cheaper Edition, crown 8vo, cloth extra, 7s. 6d.

———— *The Wild North Land; the Story of a Winter*
Journey with Dogs across Northern North America. Demy 8vo, cloth,
with numerous Woodcuts and a Map, 4th Edition, 18s. Cr. 8vo, 7s. 6d.

———— *Akim-foo: the History of a Failure.* Demy 8vo, cloth,
2nd Edition, 16s. Also, in crown 8vo, 7s. 6d.

By Land and Ocean; or, The Journal and Letters of a Tour
round the World by a Young Girl, who went *alone* to Victoria, New
Zealand, Sydney, Singapore, China, Japan, and across the Continent
of America home. By F. L. RAINS. Crown 8vo, cloth, 7s. 6d.

CABUL: the Ameer, his Country, and his People. By PHIL
ROBINSON, Special Correspondent of the *Daily Telegraph*, with the
Army of Afghanistan. With a Portrait of Shere Ali, and a Map of
the Seat of the Anglo-Russian Question. 16mo, 1s. Fourth Thousand.

Cadogan (Lady A.) Illustrated Games of Patience. Twenty-
four Diagrams in Colours, with Descriptive Text. Foolscap 4to,
cloth extra, gilt edges, 3rd Edition, 12s. 6d.

Cahun (Leon) Adventures of Captain Mago. *See* "Adventures."

———— *Blue Banner*, which see.

Carbon Process (A Manual of). *See* LIESEGANG.

Ceramic Art. *See* JACQUEMART.

Changed Cross (The), and other Religious Poems. 16mo, 2s. 6d.

Child of the Cavern (The); or, Strange Doings Underground.
By JULES VERNE. Translated by W. H. G. KINGSTON, Author of
"Snow Shoes and Canoes," "Peter the Whaler," "The Three
Midshipmen," &c., &c., &c. Numerous Illustrations. Square crown
8vo, cloth extra, gilt edges, 7s. 6d.

Child's Play, with 16 Coloured Drawings by E. V. B. Printed on thick paper, with tints, 7s. 6d.
—— *New.* By E. V. B. Similar to the above. *See* New.

Chips from many Blocks. By ELIHU BURRITT, Author of "Walks in the Black Country," "From London to Land's End," "Sparks from the Anvil," &c. Demy 8vo, cloth extra, 6s.

Choice Editions of Choice Books. 2s. 6d. each, Illustrated by C. W. COPE, R.A., T. CRESWICK, R.A., E. DUNCAN, BIRKET FOSTER, J. C. HORSLEY, A.R.A., G. HICKS, R. REDGRAVE, R.A., C. STONEHOUSE, F. TAYLER, G. THOMAS, H. J. TOWNSHEND, E. H. WEHNERT, HARRISON WEIR, &c.

Bloomfield's Farmer's Boy.	Milton's L'Allegro.
Campbell's Pleasures of Hope.	Poetry of Nature. Harrison Weir.
Coleridge's Ancient Mariner.	Rogers' (Sam.) Pleasures of Memory.
Goldsmith's Deserted Village.	Shakespeare's Songs and Sonnets.
Goldsmith's Vicar of Wakefield.	Tennyson's May Queen.
Gray's Elegy in a Churchyard.	Elizabethan Poets.
Keat's Eve of St. Agnes.	Wordsworth's Pastoral Poems.

" Such works are a glorious beatification for a poet."—*Athenæum.*

Christian Activity. By ELEANOR C. PRICE. Cloth extra, 6s.

Christmas Story-teller (The). By Old Hands and New Ones. Crown 8vo, cloth extra, gilt edges, Fifty-two Illustrations, 10s. 6d.

Cobbett (William). A Biography. By EDWARD SMITH. 2 vols., crown 8vo, 25s.

Cook (D.) Young Mr. Nightingale. A Novel. 3 vols., 31s. 6d.
—— *The Banns of Marriage.* 2 vols., crown 8vo, 21s.
—— *Book of the Play.* 2 vols., crown 8vo, 24s.
—— *Doubleday's Children.* 3 vols., crown 8vo, 31s. 6d.

Coope (Col. W. Jesser) A Prisoner of War in Russia. By Col. W. JESSER COOPE, Imperial Ottoman Gendarmerie. Crown 8vo, cloth extra, 10s. 6d.

Covert Side Sketches: Thoughts on Hunting, with Different Packs and in Different Countries. By J. NEVITT FITT (H.H. of the *Sporting Gazette,* late of the *Field*). Crown 8vo, cloth extra, 10s. 6d.

Craik (Mrs.) The Adventures of a Brownie. By the Author of "John Halifax, Gentleman." With numerous Illustrations by Miss PATERSON. Square cloth, extra gilt edges, 5s.

Cripps the Carrier. 3rd Edition, 6s. *See* BLACKMORE.

Cruise of H.M.S. " Challenger" (The). By W. J. J. SPRY, R.N. With Route Map and many Illustrations. 6th Edition, demy 8vo, cloth, 18s. Cheap Edition, crown 8vo, small type, some of the Illustrations, 7s. 6d.

"The book before us supplies the information in a manner that leaves little to be desired. 'The Cruise of H.M.S. *Challenger*' is an exceedingly well-written, entertaining, and instructive book."—*United Service Gazette.*
"Agreeably written, full of information, and copiously illustrated." — *Broad Arrow.*

Curious Adventures of a Field Cricket. By Dr. ERNEST
CANDÈZE. Translated by N. D'ANVERS. With numerous fine
Illustrations. Crown 8vo, cloth extra, gilt edges, 7s. 6d.

*D*ANA (R. II.) *Two Years before the Mast and Twenty-Four*
years After. Revised Edition with Notes, 12mo, 6s.

Dana (Jas. D.) Corals and Coral Islands. Numerous Illustrations, Charts, &c. New and Cheaper Edition, with numerous
important Additions and Corrections. Crown 8vo, cloth extra, 8s. 6d.

Daughter (A) of Heth. By W. BLACK. Crown 8vo, 6s.

Day of My Life (A); or, Every Day Experiences at Eton.
By an ETON BOY, Author of "About Some Fellows." 16mo, cloth
extra, 2s. 6d. 6th Thousand.

Dick Sands, the Boy Captain. By JULES VERNE. With
nearly 100 Illustrations, cloth extra, gilt edges, 10s. 6d.

Discoveries of Prince Henry the Navigator, and their Results;
being the Narrative of the Discovery by Sea, within One Century, of
more than Half the World. By RICHARD HENRY MAJOR, F.S.A.
Demy 8vo, with several Woodcuts, 4 Maps, and a Portrait of Prince
Henry in Colours. Cloth extra, 15s.

Dodge (Mrs. M.) Hans Brinker; or, the Silver Skates. An
entirely New Edition, with 59 Full-page and other Woodcuts.
Square crown 8vo, cloth extra, 7s. 6d.; Text only, paper, 1s.

———— *Theophilus and Others.* 1 vol., small post 8vo, cloth
extra, gilt, 3s. 6d.

Dogs of Assize. A Legal Sketch-Book in Black and White.
Containing 6 Drawings by WALTER J. ALLEN. Folio, in wrapper,
6s. 8d.

Doré's Spain. See "Spain."

Dougall's (J. D.) Shooting; its Appliances, Practice, and
Purpose. With Illustrations, cloth extra, 10s. 6d. See "Shooting."

*E*ARLY *History of the Colony of Victoria (The), from its*
Discovery to its Establishment as a Self-Governing Province of the
British Empire. By FRANCIS P. LABILLIERE, Fellow of the Royal
Colonial Institute, &c. 2 vols., crown 8vo, 21s.

Echoes of the Heart. See MOODY.

Elinor Dryden. By Mrs. MACQUOID. Crown 8vo, 6s.

English Catalogue of Books (The). Published during 1863 to
1871 inclusive, comprising also important American Publications.
　　This Volume, occupying over 450 Pages, shows the Titles of
32,000 New Books and New Editions issued during Nine Years, with
the Size, Price, and Publisher's Name, the Lists of Learned Societies,
Printing Clubs, and other Literary Associations, and the Books
issued by them; as also the Publisher's Series and Collections—
altogether forming an indispensable adjunct to the Bookseller's

Establishment, as well as to every Learned and Literary Club and Association. 30*s.*, half-bound.

*** Of the previous Volume, 1835 to 1862, very few remain on sale ; as also of the Index Volume, 1837 to 1857.

English Catalogue of Books (The) Supplements, 1863, 1864, 1865, 3*s.* 6*d.* each ; 1866, 1867, to 1878, 5*s.* each.

Eight Cousins. See ALCOTT.

English Writers, Chapters for Self-Improvement in English Literature. By the Author of "The Gentle Life," 6*s.*

Eton. See "Day of my Life," "Out of School," "About Some Fellows."

Evans (C.) Over the Hills and Far Away. By C. EVANS. One Volume, crown 8vo, cloth extra, 10*s.* 6*d.*

—— *A Strange Friendship.* Crown 8vo, cloth, 5*s.*

FAITH Gartney's Girlhood. By the Author of "The Gayworthy's." Fcap. with Coloured Frontispiece, 3*s.* 6*d.*

Familiar Letters on some Mysteries of Nature. See PHIPSON.

Favourite English Pictures. Containing Sixteen Permanent Autotype Reproductions of important Paintings of Modern British Artists. With letterpress descriptions. Atlas 4to, cloth extra, 2*l.* 2*s*

Fern Paradise (The): A Plea for the Culture of Ferns. By F. G. HEATH. New Edition, entirely Rewritten, Illustrated with eighteen full-page and numerous other Woodcuts, and four permanent Photographs, large post 8vo, handsomely bound in cloth, 12*s.* 6*d.*

Fern World (The). By F. G. HEATH. Illustrated by Twelve Coloured Plates, giving complete Figures (Sixty-four in all) of every Species of British Fern, specially printed from Nature ; by several full-page Engravings ; and a permanent Photograph. Large post 8vo., cloth, gilt edges, 400 pp., 4th Edition, 12*s.* 6*d.*

Few (A) Hints on Proving Wills. Enlarged Edition, 1*s.*

Five Weeks in Greece. By J. F. YOUNG. Crown 8vo, 10*s.* 6*d.*

Flammarion (C.) The Atmosphere. Translated from the French of CAMILLE FLAMMARION. Edited by JAMES GLAISHER, F.R.S., Superintendent of the Magnetical and Meteorological Department of the Royal Observatory at Greenwich. With 10 Chromo-Lithographs and 81 Woodcuts. Royal 8vo, cloth extra, 30*s.*

Flooding of the Sahara (The). An Account of the project for opening direct communication with 38,000,000 people. With a description of North-West Africa and Soudan. By DONALD MACKENZIE. 8vo, cloth extra, with Illustrations, 10*s.* 6*d.*

Footsteps of the Master. See STOWE (Mrs. BEECHER).

Forrest (John) Explorations in Australia. Being Mr. JOHN FORREST'S Personal Account of his Journeys. 1 vol., demy 8vo, cloth, with several Illustrations and 3 Maps, 16*s.*

Franc (Maude Jeane). The following form one Series, small post 8vo, in uniform cloth bindings:—

———— *Emily's Choice.* 5s.

———— *Hall's Vineyard.* 4s.

———— *John's Wife : a Story of Life in South Australia.* 4s.

———— *Marian ; or, the Light of Some One's Home.* 5s.

———— *Silken Cords and Iron Fetters.* 4s.

———— *Vermont Vale.* 5s.

———— *Minnie's Mission.* 4s.

———— *Little Mercy.* 5s.

French Heiress (A) in her own Chateau. Crown 8vo, 12s. 6d.

Funny Foreigners and Eccentric Englishmen. 16 coloured comic Illustrations for Children. Fcap. folio, coloured wrappper, 4s.

GAMES of Patience. See CADOGAN.

Garvagh (Lord) The Pilgrim of Scandinavia. By LORD GARVAGH, B.A., Christ Church, Oxford, and Member of the Alpine Club. 8vo, cloth extra, with Illustrations, 10s. 6d.

Geary (Grattan). See " Asiatic Turkey."

Gentle Life (Queen Edition). 2 vols. in 1, small 4to, 10s. 6d.

THE GENTLE LIFE SERIES.

Price 6s. each ; or in calf extra, price 10s. 6d.

The Gentle Life. Essays in aid of the Formation of Character of Gentlemen and Gentlewomen. 21st Edition.
" Deserves to be printed in letters of gold, and circulated in every house."— *Chambers' Journal.*

About in the World. Essays by the Author of " The Gentle Life."
" It is not easy to open it at any page without finding some handy idea."— *Morning Post.*

Like unto Christ. A New Translation of Thomas à Kempis' " De Imitatione Christi." With a Vignette from an Original Drawing by Sir THOMAS LAWRENCE. 2nd Edition.
" Could not be presented in a more exquisite form, for a more sightly volume was never seen."— *Illustrated London News.*

Familiar Words. An Index Verborum, or Quotation Handbook. Affording an immediate Reference to Phrases and Sentences that have become embedded in the English language. 3rd and enlarged Edition.
" The most extensive dictionary of quotation we have met with."— *Notes and Queries.*

The Gentle Life Series, continued :—

Essays by Montaigne. Edited, Compared, Revised, and Annotated by the Author of "The Gentle Life." With Vignette Portrait. 2nd Edition.

"We should be glad if any words of ours could help to bespeak a large circulation for this handsome attractive book."—*Illustrated Times.*

The Countess of Pembroke's Arcadia. Written by Sir PHILIP SIDNEY. Edited with Notes by Author of "The Gentle Life." 7s. 6a.

"All the best things in the Arcadia are retained intact in Mr. Friswell's edition."—*Examiner.*

The Gentle Life. 2nd Series, 8th Edition.

"There is not a single thought in the volume that does not contribute in some measure to the formation of a true gentleman."—*Daily News.*

Varia : Readings from Rare Books. Reprinted, by permission, from the *Saturday Review, Spectator,* &c.

"The books discussed in this volume are no less valuable than they are rare, and the compiler is entitled to the gratitude of the public."—*Observer.*

The Silent Hour: Essays, Original and Selected. By the Author of "The Gentle Life." 3rd Edition.

"All who possess 'The Gentle Life' should own this volume."—*Standard.*

Half-Length Portraits. Short Studies of Notable Persons. By J. HAIN FRISWELL. Small post 8vo, cloth extra, 6s.

Essays on English Writers, for the Self-improvement of Students in English Literature.

"To all (both men and women) who have neglected to read and study their native literature we would certainly suggest the volume before us as a fitting introduction."—*Examiner.*

Other People's Windows. By J. HAIN FRISWELL. 3rd Edition.

"The chapters are so lively in themselves, so mingled with shrewd views of human nature, so full of illustrative anecdotes, that the reader cannot fail to be amused."—*Morning Post.*

A Man's Thoughts. By J. HAIN FRISWELL.

German Primer. Being an Introduction to First Steps in German. By M. T. PREU. 2s. 6d.

Getting On in the World ; or, Hints on Success in Life. By W. MATHEWS, LL.D. Small post 8vo, cloth, 2s. 6d. ; gilt edges, 3s. 6d.

Gouffé. The Royal Cookery Book. By JULES GOUFFÉ ; translated and adapted for English use by ALPHONSE GOUFFÉ, Head Pastrycook to her Majesty the Queen. Illustrated with large plates printed in colours. 161 Woodcuts, 8vo, cloth extra, gilt edges, 2l. 2s.

—— Domestic Edition, half-bound, 10s. 6d.

"By far the ablest and most complete work on cookery that has ever been submitted to the gastronomical world."—*Pall Mall Gazette.*

—— *The Book of Preserves ; or, Receipts for Preparing and Preserving Meat,* Fish salt and smoked, Terrines, Gelatines, Vegetables, Fruit, Confitures, Syrups, Liqueurs de Famille, Petits Fours, Bonbons, &c., &c. 1 vol., royal 8vo, containing upwards of 500 Receipts and 34 Illustrations, 10s. 6d.

Gouffé. Royal Book of Pastry and Confectionery. By JULES
GOUFFÉ, Chef-de-Cuisine of the Paris Jockey Club. Royal 8vo, Illustrated with 10 Chromo-lithographs and 137 Woodcuts, from Drawings
by E. MONJAT. Cloth extra, gilt edges, 35s.

Gouraud (Mdlle.) Four Gold Pieces. Numerous Illustrations.
Small post 8vo, cloth, 2s. 6d. *See also* Rose Library.

Government of M. Thiers. By JULES SIMON. Translated from
the French. 2 vols., demy 8vo, cloth extra.

Gower (Lord Ronald) Handbook to the Art Galleries, Public
and Private, of Belgium and Holland. 18mo, cloth, 5s.

————— *The Castle Howard Portraits.* 2 vols., folio, cl. extra, 6l. 6s.

Greek Grammar. See WALLER.

Guizot's History of France. Translated by ROBERT BLACK.
Super-royal 8vo, very numerous Full-page and other Illustrations. In
5 vols., cloth extra, gilt, each 24s.
　　"It supplies a want which has long been felt, and ought to be in the hands of all
students of history."—*Times.*
　　"Three-fourths of M. Guizot's great work are now completed, and the 'History
of France,' which was so nobly planned, .has been hitherto no less admirably executed."—*From long Review of Vol. III. in the Times.*
　　"M. Guizot's main merit is this, that, in a style at once clear and vigorous, he
sketches the essential and most characteristic features of the times and personages
described, and seizes upon every salient point which can best illustrate and bring
out to view what is most significant and instructive in the spirit of the age described."
—*Evening Standard*, Sept. 23, 1874.

————— *History of England.* In 3 vols. of about 500 pp. each,
containing 60 to 70 Full-page and other Illustrations, cloth extra, gilt,
24s. each. Vol. III. in the press.
　　"For luxury of typography, plainness of print, and beauty of illustration, these
volumes, of which but one has as yet appeared in English, will hold their own
against any production of an age so luxurious as our own in everything, typography
not excepted."—*Times.*

Guillemin. See "World of Comets."

Guyon (Mde.) Life. By UPHAM. 6th Edition, crown 8vo, 6s.

Guyot (A.) Physical Geography. By ARNOLD GUYOT, Author
of "Earth and Man." In 1 volume, large 4to, 128 pp., numerous
coloured Diagrams, Maps, and Woodcuts, price 10s. 6d.

*H*ABITATIONS *of Man in all Ages. See* LE-DUC.

Hamilton (A. H. A., J.P.) See "Quarter Sessions."

Handbook to the Charities of London. See LOW's.

————————— *Principal Schools of England. See* Practical.

Half-Hours of Blind Man's Holiday ; or, Summer and Winter
Sketches in Black & White. By W. W. FENN. 2 vols., cr. 8vo, 24s.

Half-Length Portraits. Short Studies of Notable Persons.
By J. HAIN FRISWELL. Small post 8vo, cloth extra, 6s.

Hall (W. W.) How to Live Long ; or, 1408 *Health Maxims,*
Physical, Mental, and Moral. By W. W. HALL, A.M., M.D.
Small post 8vo, cloth, 2s. Second Edition.

Hans Brinker; or, the Silver Skates. See DODGE.

Healy (M.) A Summer's Romance. Crown 8vo, cloth, 10s. 6d.

—— *The Home Theatre.* Small post 8vo, 3s. 6d.

Heart of Africa. Three Years' Travels and Adventures in the Unexplored Regions of Central Africa, from 1868 to 1871. By Dr. GEORG SCHWEINFURTH. Translated by ELLEN E. FREWER. With an Introduction by WINWOOD READE. An entirely New Edition, revised and condensed by the Author. Numerous Illustrations, and large Map. 2 vols., crown 8vo, cloth, 15s.

Heath (F. G.). See "Fern World," "Fern Paradise," "Our Woodland Trees."

Heber's (Bishop) Illustrated Edition of Hymns. With upwards of 100 beautiful Engravings. Small 4to, handsomely bound, 7s. 6d. Morocco, 18s. 6d. and 21s. An entirely New Edition.

Hector Servadac. See VERNE. The heroes of this story were carried away through space on the Comet "Gallia," and their adventures are recorded with all Jules Verne's characteristic spirit. With nearly 100 Illustrations, cloth extra, gilt edges, 10s. 6d.

Henderson (A.) Latin Proverbs and Quotations; with Translations and Parallel Passages, and a copious English Index. By ALFRED HENDERSON. Fcap. 4to, 530 pp., 10s. 6d.

History and Handbook of Photography. Translated from the French of GASTON TISSANDIER. Edited by J. THOMSON. Imperial 16mo, over 300 pages, 70 Woodcuts, and Specimens of Prints by the best Permanent Processes, cloth extra, 6s. Second Edition, with an Appendix by the late Mr. HENRY FOX TALBOT, giving an account of his researches.

History of a Crime (The); Deposition of an Eye-witness. By VICTOR HUGO. 4 vols., crown 8vo, 42s.

—— *England.* See GUIZOT.

—— *France.* See GUIZOT.

—— *Russia.* See RAMBAUD.

—— *Merchant Shipping.* See LINDSAY.

—— *United States.* See BRYANT.

—— *Ireland.* By STANDISH O'GRADY. Vol. I. ready, 7s. 6d.

History and Principles of Weaving by Hand and by Power. With several hundred Illustrations. Reprinted with considerable additions from "Engineering," with a chapter on Lace-making Machinery. By ALFRED BARLOW. Royal 8vo, cloth extra, 1l. 5s.

Hitherto. By the Author of "The Gayworthys." New Edition, cloth extra, 3s. 6d. Also, in Rose Library, 2 vols., 2s.

Hofmann (Carl). A Practical Treatise on the Manufacture of Paper in all its Branches. Illustrated by 110 Wood Engravings, and 5 large Folding Plates. In 1 vol., 4to, cloth; about 400 pp., 3l. 13s. 6d.

How to Build a House.   See LE-DUC.

How to Live Long.   See HALL.

Hugo (Victor) "Ninety-Three."   Illustrated.   Crown 8vo, 6s.

—— *Toilers of the Sea.*   Crown 8vo.   Illustrated, 6s. ; fancy
boards, 2s. ; cloth, 2s. 6d. ; On large paper with all the original
Illustrations, 10s. 6d.

—— See " History of a Crime."

Hunting, Shooting, and Fishing; A Sporting Miscellany.
Illustrated.   Crown 8vo, cloth extra, 7s. 6d.

Hymnal Companion to Book of Common Prayer.   See
BICKERSTETH.

ILLUSTRATIONS of China and its People.   By J.
THOMSON, F.R.G.S.   Being 200 permanent Photographs from the
Author's Negatives, with Letterpress Descriptions of the Places and
People represented.   Four Volumes imperial 4to, each 3l. 3s.

In my Indian Garden.   By PHIL. ROBINSON.   With a Preface
by EDWIN ARNOLD, M.A., C.S.I., &c.   Crown 8vo, limp cloth, 3s. 6d.

Irish Bar. Comprising Anecdotes, Bon-Mots, and Biographical Sketches of the Bench and Bar of Ireland.   By J. RODERICK
O'FLANAGAN, Barrister-at-Law.   1 vol., crown 8vo, cloth.

JACQUEMART (A.) History of the Ceramic Art: Descriptive and Analytical Study of the Potteries of all Times and of
all Nations.   By ALBERT JACQUEMART.   200 Woodcuts by H.
Catenacci and J. Jacquemart.   12 Steel-plate Engravings, and 1000
Marks and Monograms.   Translated by Mrs. BURY PALLISER.   In
1 vol., super-royal 8vo, of about 700 pp., cloth extra, gilt edges, 28s.
   "This is one of those few gift-books which, while they can certainly lie on a table
and look beautiful, can also be read through with real pleasure and profit."—*Times.*

KENNEDY'S (Capt. W. R.) Sporting Adventures in the
Pacific.   With Illustrations, demy 8vo, 18s.

—— (*Capt. A. W. M. Clark*).   See " To the Arctic
Regions."

Khedive's Egypt (The); or, The old House of Bondage under
New Masters.   By EDWIN DE LEON, Ex-Agent and Consul-General
in Egypt.   In 1 vol., demy 8vo, cloth extra, Third Edition, 18s.

Kingston (W. H. G.).   See " Snow-Shoes."

—— *Child of the Cavern.*

—— *Two Supercargoes.*

—— *With Axe and Rifle.*

Koldewey (Capt.) The Second North German Polar Expedition
in the Year 1869-70, of the Ships " Germania " and " Hansa," under
command of Captain Koldewey.   Edited and condensed by H. W.
BATES, Esq.   Numerous Woodcuts, Maps, and Chromo-lithographs.
Royal 8vo, cloth extra, 1l. 15s.

*L*ADY *Silverdale's Sweetheart.* 6s. *See* BLACK.

Land of Bolivar (The) ; or, War, Peace, and Adventure in the
Republic of Venezuela. By JAMES MUDIE SPENCE, F.R.G.S.,
F.Z.S. 2 vols., demy 8vo, cloth extra, with numerous Woodcuts and
Maps, 31s. 6d. Second Edition.

Landseer Gallery (The). Containing thirty-six Autotype Reproductions of Engravings from the most important early works of Sir
EDWIN LANDSEER. With a Memoir of the Artist's Life, and
Descriptions of the Plates. Imperial 4to, handsomely bound in cloth,
gilt edges, 2l. 2s.

Le-Duc (V.) How to build a House. By VIOLLET-LE-DUC,
Author of "The Dictionary of Architecture," &c. Numerous Illustrations, Plans, &c. Medium 8vo, cloth, gilt, 12s.

———— *Annals of a Fortress.* Numerous Illustrations and
Diagrams. Demy 8vo, cloth extra, 15s.

———— *The Habitations of Man in all Ages.* By E.
VIOLLET-LE-DUC. Illustrated by 103 Woodcuts. Translated by
BENJAMIN BUCKNALL, Architect. 8vo, cloth extra, 16s.

———— *Lectures on Architecture.* By VIOLLET-LE-DUC.
Translated from the French by BENJAMIN BUCKNALL, Architect. In
2 vols., royal 8vo, 3l. 3s. Also in Parts, 10s. 6d. each.

———— *Mont Blanc: a Treatise on its Geodesical and Geo-*
logical Constitution—its Transformations, and the Old and Modern
state of its Glaciers. By EUGENE VIOLLET-LE-DUC. With 120
Illustrations. Translated by B. BUCKNALL. 1 vol., demy 8vo, 14s.

———— *On Restoration;* with a Notice of his Works by CHARLES
WETHERED. Crown 8vo, with a Portrait on Steel of VIOLLET-LE-
DUC, cloth extra, 2s. 6d.

Lenten Meditations. In Two Series, each complete in itself.
By the Rev. CLAUDE BOSANQUET, Author of "Blossoms from the
King's Garden." 16mo, cloth, First Series, 1s. 6d. ; Second Series, 2s.

Liesegang (Dr. Paul E.) A Manual of the Carbon Process of
Photography, and its use in Making Enlargements, &c. Translated
from the Sixth German Edition by R. B. MARSTON. Demy 8vo, half-
bound, with Illustrations, 4s.

Life and Letters of the Honourable Charles Sumner (The).
2 vols., royal 8vo, cloth. The Letters give full description of London
Society—Lawyers—Judges—Visits to Lords Fitzwilliam, Leicester,
Wharncliffe, Brougham—Association with Sydney Smith, Hallam,
Macaulay, Dean Milman, Rogers, and Talfourd ; also, a full Journal
which Sumner kept in Paris. Second Edition, 36s.

Lindsay (W. S.) History of Merchant Shipping and Ancient
Commerce. Over 150 Illustrations, Maps and Charts. In 4 vols.,
demy 8vo, cloth extra. Vols. 1 and 2, 21s. ; vols. 3 and 4, 24s. each.

Lion Jack: a Story of Perilous Adventures amongst Wild Men
and Beasts. Showing how Menageries are made. By P. T. BARNUM.
With Illustrations. Crown 8vo, cloth extra, price 6s.

Little King; or, the Taming of a Young Russian Count. By
S. BLANDY. Translated from the French. 64 Illustrations. Crown
8vo, cloth extra, gilt, 7s. 6d.

Little Mercy; or, For Better for Worse. By MAUDE JEANNE
FRANC, Author of "Marian," "Vermont Vale," &c., &c. Small
post 8vo, cloth extra, 4s.

Locker (A.) The Village Surgeon. A Fragment of Auto-
biography. By ARTHUR LOCKER. Crown 8vo, cloth, 3s. 6d.

Long (Col. C. Chaillé) Central Africa. Naked Truths of
Naked People : an Account of Expeditions to Lake Victoria Nyanza
and the Mabraka Niam-Niam. Demy 8vo, numerous Illustrations, 18s.

Lord Collingwood: a Biographical Study. By. W. DAVIS.
With Steel Engraving of Lord Collingwood. Crown 8vo, 2s.

Lost Sir Massingberd. New Edition, 16mo, boards, coloured
wrapper, 2s.

Low's German Series—

1. **The Illustrated German Primer.** Being the easiest introduction
   to the study of German for all beginners. 1s.
2. **The Children's own German Book.** A Selection of Amusing
   and Instructive Stories in Prose. Edited by Dr. A. L. MEISSNER,
   Professor of Modern Languages in the Queen's University in
   Ireland. Small post 8vo, cloth, 1s. 6d.
3. **The First German Reader, for Children from Ten to
   Fourteen.** Edited by Dr. A. L. MEISSNER. Small post 8vo,
   cloth, 1s. 6d.
4. **The Second German Reader.** Edited by Dr. A. L. MEISSNER,
   Small post 8vo, cloth, 1s. 6d.

   Buchheim's Deutsche Prosa. Two Volumes, sold separately :—

5. **Schiller's Prosa.** Containing Selections from the Prose Works
   of Schiller, with Notes for English Students. By Dr. BUCHHEIM,
   Professor of the German Language and Literature, King's
   College, London. Small post 8vo, 2s. 6d.
6. **Goethe's Prosa.** Containing Selections from the Prose Works of
   Goethe, with Notes for English Students. By Dr. BUCHHEIM.
   Small post 8vo, 3s. 6d.

Low's Standard Library of Travel and Adventure. Crown 8vo,
bound uniformly in cloth extra, price 7s. 6d.

1. **The Great Lone Land.** By W. F. BUTLER, C.B.
2. **The Wild North Land.** By W. F. BUTLER, C.B.
3. **How I found Livingstone.** By H. M. STANLEY.
4. **The Threshold of the Unknown Region.** By C. R. MARK-
   HAM. (4th Edition, with Additional Chapters, 10s. 6d.)
5. **A Whaling Cruise to Baffin's Bay and the Gulf of Boothia.**
   By A. H. MARKHAM.

Low's Standard Library of Travel and Adventure, continued :—

6. **Campaigning on the Oxus.** By J. A. MacGahan.
7. **Akim-foo: the History of a Failure.** By Major W. F. Butler, C.B.
8. **Ocean to Ocean.** By the Rev. George M. Grant. With Illustrations.
9. **Cruise of the Challenger.** By W. J. J. Spry, R.N.
10. **Schweinfurth's Heart of Africa.** 2 vols., 15s.

Low's Standard Novels. Crown 8vo, 6s. each, cloth extra.

Three Feathers. By William Black.
A Daughter of Heth. 13th Edition. By W. Black. With Frontispiece by F. Walker, A.R.A.
Kilmeny. A Novel. By W. Black.
In Silk Attire. By W. Black.
Lady Silverdale's Sweetheart. By W. Black.
Alice Lorraine. By R. D. Blackmore.
Lorna Doone. By R. D. Blackmore. 8th Edition.
Cradock Nowell. By R. D. Blackmore.
Clara Vaughan. By R. D. Blackmore.
Cripps the Carrier. By R. D. Blackmore.
Innocent. By Mrs. Oliphant. Eight Illustrations.
Work. A Story of Experience. By Louisa M. Alcott. Illustrations. *See also* Rose Library.
Mistress Judith. A Cambridgeshire Story. By C. C. Fraser-Tytler.
Never Again. By Dr. Mayo, Author of "Kaloolah."
Ninety-Three. By Victor Hugo. Numerous Illustrations.
My Wife and I. By Mrs. Beecher Stowe.
Wreck of the Grosvenor. By W. Clark Russell.
Elinor Dryden. By Mrs. Macquoid.

Low's Handbook to the Charities of London for 1877. Edited and revised to July, 1877, by C. Mackeson, F.S.S., Editor of "A Guide to the Churches of London and its Suburbs," &c. 1s.

MACGAHAN (J. A.) Campaigning on the Oxus, and the Fall of Khiva. With Map and numerous Illustrations, 4th Edition, small post 8vo, cloth extra, 7s. 6d.

—— *Under the Northern Lights; or, the Cruise of the* "Pandora" to Peel's Straits, in Search of Sir John Franklin's Papers. With Illustrations by Mr. De Wylde, who accompanied the Expedition. Demy 8vo, cloth extra, 18s.

Macgregor (John) "Rob Roy" on the Baltic. 3rd Edition, small post 8vo, 2s. 6d.

—— *A Thousand Miles in the "Rob Roy" Canoe.* 11th Edition, small post 8vo, 2s. 6d.

—— *Description of the "Rob Roy" Canoe,* with Plans, &c., 1s.

—— *The Voyage Alone in the Yawl "Rob Roy."* New Edition, thoroughly revised, with additions, small post 8vo, 5s.

Mackenzie (D). The Flooding of the Sahara. An Account of
the Project for opening direct communication with 38,000,000 people.
With a Description of North-West Africa and Soudan. By DONALD
MACKENZIE. 8vo, cloth extra, with Illustrations, 10s. 6d.

Macquoid (Mrs.) Elinor Dryden. Crown 8vo, cloth, 6s.

Markham (A. H.) The Cruise of the "Rosario." By A. H.
MARKHAM, R.N. 8vo, cloth extra, with Map and Illustrations.

——— *A Whaling Cruise to Baffin's Bay and the Gulf of
Boothia.* With an Account of the Rescue by his Ship, of the Survivors of the Crew of the "Polaris;" and a Description of Modern
Whale Fishing. 3rd and Cheaper Edition, crown 8vo, 2 Maps and
several Illustrations, cloth extra, 7s. 6d.

Markham (C. R.) The Threshold of the Unknown Region.
Crown 8vo, with Four Maps, 4th Edition, with Additional Chapters,
giving the History of our present Expedition, as far as known, and an
Account of the Cruise of the "Pandora." Cloth extra, 10s. 6d.

*Maury (Commander) Physical Geography of the Sea, and its
Meteorology.* Being a Reconstruction and Enlargement of his former
Work, with Charts and Diagrams. New Edition, crown 8vo, 6s.

*Men of Mark: a Gallery of Contemporary Portraits of the most
Eminent Men of the Day* taken from Life, especially for this publica-
tion, price 1s. 6d. monthly. Vols. I., II., and III. handsomely bound,
cloth, gilt edges, 25s. each.

Mercy Philbrick's Choice. Small post 8vo, 3s. 6d.
    "The story is of a high character, and the play of feeling is very subtilely and
    cleverly wrought out."—*British Quarterly Review.*

Michael Strogoff. 10s. 6d. *See* VERNE.

Mistress Judith. A Cambridgeshire Story. By C. C. FRASER-
TYTLER, Author of "Jasmine Leigh." A New and Cheaper Edition
in 1 vol., small post 8vo, cloth extra, 6s.

Mitford (Miss). See "Our Village."

Mohr (E.) To the Victoria Falls of the Zambesi. By EDWARD
MOHR. Translated by N. D'ANVERS. Numerous Full-page and other
Woodcut Illustrations, four Chromo-lithographs, and Map. Demy 8vo,
cloth extra, 24s.

Mongolia, Travels in. See PREJEVALSKY.

Montaigne's Essays. See Gentle Life Series.

Mont Blanc. See LE-DUC.

Moody (Emma) Echoes of the Heart. A Collection of upwards
of 200 Sacred Poems. 16mo, cloth, gilt edges, price 3s. 6d.

My Brother Jack; or, The Story of Whatd'yecallem. Written
by Himself. From the French of ALPHONSE DAUDET. Illustrated
by P. PHILIPPOTEAUX. Square imperial 16mo, cloth extra, 7s. 6d.
    " He would answer to Hi ! or to any loud cry,
    To What-you-may-call-'em, or What was his name ;
    But especially Thingamy-jig."—*Hunting of the Snark.*

My Rambles in the New World. By LUCIEN BIART, Author of "The Adventures of a Young Naturalist." Translated by MARY DE HAUTEVILLE. Crown 8vo, cloth extra. Numerous Full-page Illustrations, 7s. 6d.

NARES (Sir G. S., K.C.B.) Narrative of a Voyage to the Polar Sea during 1875-76, in H.M.'s Ships "Alert" and "Discovery." By Captain Sir G. S. NARES, R.N., K.C.B., F.R.S. Published by permission of the Lords Commissioners of the Admiralty. With Notes on the Natural History, edited by H. W. FEILDEN, F.G.S., C.M.Z.S., F.R.G.S., Naturalist to the Expedition. Two Volumes, demy 8vo, with numerous Woodcut Illustrations and Photographs, &c. 4th Edition, 2l. 2s.

New Child's Play (A). Sixteen Drawings by E. V. B. Beautifully printed in colours, 4to, cloth extra, 12s. 6d.

New Ireland. By A. M. SULLIVAN, M.P. for Louth. 2 vols., demy 8vo, cloth extra, 30s. One of the main objects which the Author has had in view in writing this work has been to lay before England and the world a faithful history of Ireland, in a series of descriptive sketches of the episodes in Ireland's career during the last quarter of a century. Cheaper Edition, 1 vol., crown 8vo, 8s. 6d.

New Novels.

An Old Story of My Farming Days. By FRITZ REUTER, Author of "In the Year '13." 3 vols., 1l. 11s. 6d.

Cressida. By M. B. THOMAS. 3 vols., 1l. 11s. 6d.

Elizabeth Eden. 3 vols., 1l. 11s. 6d.

The Martyr of Glencree. A Story of the Persecutions in Scotland in the Reign of Charles the Second. By R. SOMERS. 3 vols., 1l. 11s. 6d.

The Cossacks. By COUNT TOLSTOY. Translated from the Russian by EUGENE SCHUYLER, Author of "Turkistan." 2 vols., 1l. 1s.

A Hero of the Pen. 2 vols. By WERNER. Translated by Mrs. S. PHILLIPS. 21s.

The Braes of Yarrow. By C. GIBBON. 3 vols., 1l. 11s. 6d.

Auld Lang Syne. By the Author of "The Wreck of the Grosvenor." 2 vols., 1l. 1s.

A Life's Hazard; or, The Outlaw of Wentworth Waste. By H. ESMOND. 3 vols., 1l. 11s. 6d.

Rare Pale Margaret. 2 vols., 1l. 1s.

A French Heiress. By the Author of "One Only," &c. With Illustrations, 12s. 6d.

New Testament. The Authorized English Version; with various readings from the most celebrated Manuscripts. Cloth flexible, gilt edges, 2s. 6d.; cheaper style, 2s.; or sewed, 1s. 6d.

Noble Words and Noble Deeds. Translated from the French of E. MULLER, by DORA LEIGH. Containing many Full-page Illustrations by PHILIPPOTEAUX. Square imperial 16mo, cloth extra, 7s. 6d.
"This is a book which will delight the young. . . . We cannot imagine a nicer present than this book for children."—*Standard.*
"Is certain to become a favourite with young people."—*Court Journal.*

Notes and Sketches of an Architect taken during a Journey in the North-West of Europe. Translated from the French of FELIX NARJOUX. 214 Full-page and other Illustrations. Demy 8vo, cloth extra, 16s.
"His book is vivacious and sometimes brilliant. It is admirably printed and illustrated."—*British Quarterly Review.*

Notes on Fish and Fishing. By the Rev. J. J. MANLEY, M.A. With Illustrations, crown 8vo, cloth extra, leatherette binding, 10s. 6d.
"We commend the work."—*Field.*
"He has a page for every day in the year, or nearly so, and there is not a dull one amongst them."—*Notes and Queries.*
"A pleasant and attractive volume."—*Graphic.*
"Brightly and pleasantly written."—*John Bull.*

Nursery Playmates (Prince of.) 217 Coloured pictures for Children by eminent Artists. Folio, in coloured boards, 6s.

OCEAN to Ocean: Sandford Fleming's Expedition through Canada in 1872. By the Rev. GEORGE M. GRANT. With Illustrations. Revised and enlarged Edition, crown 8vo, cloth, 7s. 6d.

Old-Fashioned Girl. See ALCOTT.

Oleographs. (Catalogues and price lists on application.)

Oliphant (Mrs.) Innocent. A Tale of Modern Life. By Mrs. OLIPHANT, Author of "The Chronicles of Carlingford," &c., &c. With Eight Full-page Illustrations, small post 8vo, cloth extra, 6s.

On Horseback through Asia Minor. By Capt. FRED BURNABY, Royal Horse Guards, Author of "A Ride to Khiva." 2 vols., 8vo, with three Maps and Portrait of Author, 6th Edition, 38s. This work describes a ride of over 2000 miles through the heart of Asia Minor, and gives an account of five months with Turks, Circassians, Christians, and Devil-worshippers. Cheaper Edition, crown 8vo, 10s. 6d.

On Restoration. See LE-DUC.

On Trek in the Transvaal; or, Over Berg and Veldt in South Africa. By H. A. ROCHE. Crown 8vo, cloth, 10s. 6d. 4th Edition.

Our Little Ones in Heaven. Edited by the Rev. H. ROBBINS. With Frontispiece after Sir JOSHUA REYNOLDS. Fcap., cloth extra, New Edition—the 3rd, with Illustrations, 5s.

Our Village. By MARY RUSSELL MITFORD. Illustrated with Frontispiece Steel Engraving, and 12 full-page and 157 smaller Cuts of Figure Subjects and Scenes, from Drawings by W. H. J. BOOT and C. O. MURRAY. Chiefly from Sketches made by these Artists in the neighbourhood of "Our Village." Crown 4to, cloth extra, gilt edges, 21s.

Our Woodland Trees. By F. G. HEATH. Large post 8vo,
cloth, gilt edges, uniform with "Fern World" and "Fern Paradise,"
by the same Author. 8 Coloured Plates and 20 Woodcuts, 12s. 6d.

Out of School at Eton. Being a collection of Poetry and Prose
Writings. By SOME PRESENT ETONIANS. Foolscap 8vo, cloth, 3s. 6d.

PAINTERS of All Schools. By LOUIS VIARDOT, and other
Writers. 500 pp., super-royal 8vo, 20 Full-page and 70 smaller
Engravings, cloth extra, 25s. A New Edition is being issued in Half-
crown parts, with fifty additional portraits, cloth, gilt edges, 31s. 6d.
"A handsome volume, full of information and sound criticism."—*Times.*
"Almost an encyclopædia of painting. . . . . It may be recommended as a handy
and elegant guide to beginners in the study of the history of art."—*Saturday Review.*

Palliser (Mrs.) A History of Lace, from the Earliest Period.
A New and Revised Edition, with additional cuts and text, upwards
of 100 Illustrations and coloured Designs. 1 vol. 8vo, 1l. 1s.
"One of the most readable books of the season; permanently valuable, always interesting, often amusing, and not inferior in all the essentials of a gift book."—*Times.*

—— *Historic Devices, Badges, and War Cries.* 8vo, 1l. 1s.

—— *The China Collector's Pocket Companion.* With upwards
of 1000 Illustrations of Marks and Monograms. 2nd Edition, with
Additions. Small post 8vo, limp cloth, 5s.
"We scarcely need add that a more trustworthy and convenient handbook does
not exist, and that others besides ourselves will feel grateful to Mrs. Palliser for the
care and skill she has bestowed upon it."—*Academy.*

Petites Leçons de Conversation et de Grammaire: Oral and
Conversational Method; being Little Lessons introducing the most
Useful Topics of Daily Conversation, upon an entirely new principle,
&c. By F. JULIEN, French Master at King Edward the Sixth's
Grammar School, Birmingham. Author of "The Student's French
Examiner," which see.

Phelps (Miss) Gates Ajar. 32mo, 6d.

—— *Men, Women, and Ghosts.* 12mo, sewed, 1s. 6d.; cl., 2s.

—— *Hedged In.* 12mo, sewed, 1s. 6d.; cloth, 2s.

—— *Silent Partner.* 5s.

—— *Trotty's Wedding Tour.* Small post 8vo, 3s. 6d.

—— *What to Wear.* Fcap. 8vo, fancy boards, 1s.

Phillips (L.) Dictionary of Biographical Reference. 8vo,
1l. 11s. 6d.

Phipson (Dr. T. L.) Familiar Letters on some Mysteries of
Nature and Discoveries in Science. Crown 8vo, cloth extra, 7s. 6d.

Photography (History and Handbook of). See TISSANDIER.

Picture Gallery of British Art (The). 38 Permanent Photographs after the most celebrated English Painters. With Descriptive
Letterpress. Vols. 1 to 5, cloth extra, 18s. each. Vol. 6 for 1877,
commencing New Series, demy folio, 31s. 6d. Monthly Parts, 1s. 6d.

Pike (N.) Sub-Tropical Rambles in the Land of the Aphanapteryx. In 1 vol., demy 8vo, 18s. Profusely Illustrated from the Author's own Sketches. Also with Maps and Meteorological Charts.

Placita Anglo-Normannica. The Procedure and Constitution of the Anglo-Norman Courts (WILLIAM I.—RICHARD I.), as shown by Contemporaneous Records; all the Reports of the Litigation of the period, as recorded in the Chronicles and Histories of the time, being gleaned and literally transcribed. With Explanatory Notes, &c. By M. M. BIGELOW. Demy 8vo, cloth, 14s.

Plutarch's Lives. An Entirely New and Library Edition. Edited by A. H. CLOUGH, Esq. 5 vols., 8vo, 2l. 10s.; half-morocco, gilt top, 3l. Also in 1 vol., royal 8vo, 800 pp., cloth extra, 18s.; half-bound, 21s.

—— *Morals.* Uniform with Clough's Edition of "Lives of Plutarch." Edited by Professor GOODWIN. 5 vols., 8vo, 3l. 3s.

Poe (E. A.) The Works of. 4 vols., 2l. 2s.

Poems of the Inner Life. A New Edition, Revised, with many additional Poems, inserted by permission of the Authors. Small post 8vo, cloth, 5s.

Poganuc People: their Loves and Lives. By Mrs. BEECHER STOWE. Crown 8vo, cloth, 10s. 6d.

Polar Expeditions. See KOLDEWEY, MARKHAM, MACGAHAN and NARES.

Pottery: how it is Made, its Shape and Decoration. Practical Instructions for Painting on Porcelain and all kinds of Pottery with vitrifiable and common Oil Colours. With a full Bibliography of Standard Works upon the Ceramic Art. By G. WARD NICHOLS. 42 Illustrations, crown 8vo, red edges, 6s.

Practical (A) Handbook to the Principal Schools of England. By C. E. PASCOE. Showing the cost of living at the Great Schools, Scholarships, &c., &c. New Edition corrected to 1878, crown 8vo, cloth extra, 3s. 6d.
"This is an exceedingly useful work, and one that was much wanted."— *Examiner.*

Prejevalsky (N. M.) Travels in Mongolia. By N. M. PREJE-VALSKY, Lieutenant-Colonel, Russian Staff. Translated by E. DELMAR MORGAN, F.R.G.S., and Annotated by Colonel YULE, C.B. 2 vols., demy 8vo, cloth extra, numerous Illustrations and Maps, 2l. 2s.

—— *From Kulja, across the Tian Shan to Lob-Nor.* Translated by E. DELMAR MORGAN, F.R.G.S. With Notes and Introduction by SIR DOUGLAS FORSYTH, K.C.S.I. 1 vol., demy 8vo, with a Map.

Price (Sir Rose, Bart.). See "Two Americas."

Prince Ritto; or, The Four-leaved Shamrock. By FANNY W. CURREY. With 10 Full-page Fac-simile Reproductions of Original Drawings by HELEN O'HARA. Demy 4to, cloth extra, gilt, 10s. 6d.

Prisoner of War in Russia. *See* COOPE.

Publishers' Circular (The), and General Record of British and Foreign Literature. Published on the 1st and 15th of every Month.

QUARTER Sessions, from Queen Elizabeth to Queen Anne : Illustrations of Local Government and History. Drawn from Original Records (chiefly of the County of Devon). By A. H. A. HAMILTON. Crown 8vo, cloth, 10s. 6d.

RALSTON (W. R. S.) Early Russian History. Four Lectures delivered at Oxford by W. R. S. RALSTON, M.A. Crown 8vo, cloth extra, 5s.

Rambaud (Alfred). *History of Russia, from its Origin to the* Year 1877. With Six Maps. Translated by Mrs. L. B. LANG. 2 vols. demy 8vo, cloth extra.

Recollections of Samuel Breck, the American Pepys. With Passages from his Note-Books (1771—1862). Crown 8vo, cloth, 10s. 6d. "The book is admirable."—*Standard.*

Recollections of Writers. By CHARLES and MARY COWDEN CLARKE. Authors of "The Concordance to Shakespeare," &c. ; with Letters of CHARLES LAMB, LEIGH HUNT, DOUGLAS JERROLD, and CHARLES DICKENS ; and a Preface by MARY COWDEN CLARKE. Crown 8vo, cloth, 10s. 6d.

Reynard the Fox. The Prose Translation by the late THOMAS ROSCOE. With about 100 exquisite Illustrations on Wood, after designs by A. J. ELWES. Imperial 16mo, cloth extra, 7s. 6d.

Robinson (Phil.). *See* "In my Indian Garden."

Roche (Mrs. H.). *See* "On Trek in the Transvaal."

Rochefoucauld's Reflections. Bayard Series, 2s. 6d.

Rogers (S.) Pleasures of Memory. *See* "Choice Editions of Choice Books." 2s. 6d.

Rohlfs (Dr. G.) Adventures in Morocco, and Journeys through the Oases of Draa and Tafilet. By Dr. G. ROHLFS. Demy 8vo, Map, and Portrait of the Author, 12s.

Rose in Bloom. *See* ALCOTT.

Rose Library (The). Popular Literature of all countries. Each volume, 1s. ; cloth, 2s. 6d. Many of the Volumes are Illustrated—
  1. **Sea-Gull Rock.** By JULES SANDEAU. Illustrated.
  2. **Little Women.** By LOUISA M. ALCOTT.
  3. **Little Women Wedded.** Forming a Sequel to "Little Women."
  4. **The House on Wheels.** By MADAME DE STOLZ. Illustrated.
  5. **Little Men.** By LOUISA M. ALCOTT. Dble. vol., 2s. ; cloth, 3s. 6d.

Rose Library (*The*), *continued* :—

6. **The Old-Fashioned Girl.** By LOUISA M. ALCOTT. Double vol., 2*s.* ; cloth, 3*s.* 6*d.*
7. **The Mistress of the Manse.** By J. G. HOLLAND.
8. **Timothy Titcomb's Letters to Young People, Single and Married.**
9. **Undine, and the Two Captains.** By Baron DE LA MOTTE FOUQUÉ. A New Translation by F. E. BUNNETT. Illustrated.
10. **Draxy Miller's Dowry, and the Elder's Wife.** By SAXE HOLM.
11. **The Four Gold Pieces.** By Madame GOURAUD. Numerous Illustrations.
12. **Work.** A Story of Experience. First Portion. By LOUISA M. ALCOTT.
13. **Beginning Again.** Being a Continuation of "Work." By LOUISA M. ALCOTT.
14. **Picciola; or, the Prison Flower.** By X. B. SAINTINE. Numerous Graphic Illustrations.
15. **Robert's Holidays.** Illustrated.
16. **The Two Children of St. Domingo.** Numerous Illustrations.
17. **Aunt Jo's Scrap Bag.**
18. **Stowe (Mrs. H. B.) The Pearl of Orr's Island.**
19. —— **The Minister's Wooing.**
20. —— **Betty's Bright Idea.**
21. —— **The Ghost in the Mill.**
22. —— **Captain Kidd's Money.**
23. —— **We and our Neighbours.** Double vol., 2*s.*
24. —— **My Wife and I.** Double vol., 2*s.* ; cloth, gilt, 3*s.* 6*d.*
25. **Hans Brinker; or, the Silver Skates.**
26. **Lowell's My Study Window.**
27. **Holmes (O. W.) The Guardian Angel.**
28. **Warner (C. D.) My Summer in a Garden.**
29. **Hitherto.** By the Author of "The Gayworthys." 2 vols., 1*s.* each.
30. **Helen's Babies.** By their Latest Victim.
31. **The Barton Experiment.** By the Author of "Helen's Babies."
32. **Dred.** By Mrs. BEECHER STOWE. Double vol., 2*s.* Cloth, gilt, 3*s.* 6*d.*
33. **Warner (C. D.) In the Wilderness.**
34. **Six to One.** A Seaside Story.

Russell (*W. H., LL.D.*) *The Tour of the Prince of Wales in* India, and his Visits to the Courts of Greece, Egypt, Spain, and Portugal. By W. H. RUSSELL, LL.D., who accompanied the Prince throughout his journey ; fully Illustrated by SYDNEY P. HALL, M.A., the Prince's Private Artist, with his Royal Highness's special permission to use the Sketches made during the Tour. Super-royal 8vo, cloth extra, gilt edges, 52*s.* 6*d.*; Large Paper Edition, 84*s.*

SANCTA *Christina: a Story of the First Century.* By ELEANOR E. ORLEBAR. With a Preface by the Bishop of Winchester. Small post 8vo, cloth extra, 5*s.*

Schweinfurth (Dr. G.) Heart of Africa. Which see.

—— *Artes Africanæ.* Illustrations and Description of Productions of the Natural Arts of Central African Tribes. With 26 Lithographed Plates, imperial 4to, boards, 28s.

Scientific Memoirs: being Experimental Contributions to a Knowledge of Radiant Energy. By JOHN WILLIAM DRAPER, M.D., LL.D., Author of "A Treatise on Human Physiology," &c. With a fine Steel Engraved Portrait of the Author. Demy 8vo, cloth extra, 473 pages, 14s.

Sea-Gull Rock. By JULES SANDEAU, of the French Academy. Royal 16mo, with 79 Illustrations, cloth extra, gilt edges, 7s. 6d. Cheaper Edition, cloth gilt, 2s. 6d. *See also* Rose Library.

Seonee: Sporting in the Satpura Range of Central India, and in the Valley of the Nerbudda. By R. A. STERNDALE, F.R.G.S. 8vo, with numerous Illustrations, 21s.

Shakespeare (The Boudoir). Edited by HENRY CUNDELL Carefully bracketted for reading aloud; freed from all objectionable matter, and altogether free from notes. Price 2s. 6d. each volume, cloth extra, gilt edges. Contents :—Vol I., Cymbeline—Merchant of Venice. Each play separately, paper cover, 1s. Vol. II., As You Like It—King Lear—Much Ado about Nothing. Vol. III., Romeo and Juliet—Twelfth Night—King John. The latter six plays separately, paper cover, 9d.

Shooting: its Appliances, Practice, and Purpose. By JAMES DALZIEL DOUGALL, F.S.A., F.Z.A. Author of "Scottish Field Sports," &c. Crown 8vo, cloth extra, 10s. 6d.

"The book is admirable in every way. . . . . We wish it every success."—*Globe.*
"A very complete treatise. . . . . Likely to take high rank as an authority on shooting."—*Daily News.*

Silent Hour (The). *See* Gentle Life Series.

Silver Pitchers. *See* ALCOTT.

Simon (Jules). *See* "Government of M. Thiers."

Six Hundred Robinson Crusoes; or, The Voyage of the Golden Fleece. A true Story for old and young. By GILBERT MORTIMER. Illustrated. Post 8vo, cloth extra, 5s.

Six to One. A Seaside Story. 16mo, boards, 1s.

Sketches from an Artist's Portfolio. By SYDNEY P. HALL. About 60 Fac-similes of his Sketches during Travels in various parts of Europe. Folio, cloth extra, 3l. 3s.
"A portfolio which any one might be glad to call their own."—*Times.*

Sleepy Sketches; or, How we Live, and How we Do Not Live. From Bombay. 1 vol., small post 8vo, cloth, 6s.
"Well-written and amusing sketches of Indian society."—*Morning Post.*

Smith (G.) Assyrian Explorations and Discoveries. By the late GEORGE SMITH. Illustrated by Photographs and Woodcuts. Demy 8vo, 6th Edition, 18s.

Smith (*G.*) *The Chaldean Account of Genesis.* Containing the Description of the Creation, the Fall of Man, the Deluge, the Tower of Babel, the Times of the Patriarchs, and Nimrod; Babylonian Fables, and Legends of the Gods; from the Cuneiform Inscriptions. By the late G. SMITH, of the Department of Oriental Antiquities, British Museum. With many Illustrations. Demy 8vo, cloth extra, 5th Edition, 16s.

Snow-Shoes and Canoes; or, the Adventures of a Fur-Hunter in the Hudson's Bay Territory. By W. H. G. KINGSTON. 2nd Edition. With numerous Illustrations. Square crown 8vo, cloth extra, gilt, 7s. 6d.

South Australia: its History, Resources, and Productions. Edited by W. HARCUS, J.P., with 66 full-page Woodcut Illustrations from Photographs taken in the Colony, and 2 Maps. Demy 8vo, 21s.

Spain. Illustrated by GUSTAVE DORÉ. Text by the BARON CH. D'AVILLIER. Containing over 240 Wood Engravings by DORÉ, half of them being Full-page size. Imperial 4to, elaborately bound in cloth, extra gilt edges, 3l. 3s.

Stanley (*H. M.*) *How I Found Livingstone.* Crown 8vo, cloth extra, 7s. 6d. ; large Paper Edition, 10s. 6d.

—————— *"My Kalulu," Prince, King, and Slave.* A Story from Central Africa. Crown 8vo, about 430 pp., with numerous graphic Illustrations, after Original Designs by the Author. Cloth, 7s. 6d.

—————— *Coomassie and Magdala.* A Story of Two British Campaigns in Africa. Demy 8vo, with Maps and Illustrations, 16s.

—————— *Through the Dark Continent,* which see.

St. Nicholas for 1878. The First Number of the New Series commenced November 1st, 1877, and contains a New Story by LOUISA M. ALCOTT, entitled "Under the Lilacs." 1s. Monthly.

Story without an End. From the German of Carové, by the late Mrs. SARAH T. AUSTIN. Crown 4to, with 15 Exquisite Drawings by E. V. B., printed in Colours in Fac-simile of the original Water Colours; and numerous other Illustrations. New Edition, 7s. 6d.

—————— square 4to, with Illustrations by HARVEY. 2s. 6d.

Stowe (*Mrs. Beecher*) *Dred.* Cheap Edition, boards, 2s. Cloth, gilt edges, 3s. 6d.

—————— *Footsteps of the Master.* With Illustrations and red borders. Small post 8vo, cloth extra, 6s.

—————— *Geography,* with 60 Illustrations. Square cloth, 4s. 6d.

—————— *Little Foxes.* Cheap Edition, 1s.; Library Edition, 4s. 6d.

—————— *Betty's Bright Idea.* 1s.

Stowe (Mrs. Beecher) My Wife and I ; or, Harry Henderson's History. Small post 8vo, cloth extra, 6s.*

———— *Minister's Wooing,* 5s.; Copyright Series, 1s. 6d.; cl., 2s.*

———— *Old Town Folk.* 6s.: Cheap Edition, 2s. 6d.

———— *Old Town Fireside Stories.* Cloth extra, 3s. 6d.

———— *Our Folks at Poganuc.* 10s. 6d.

———— *We and our Neighbours.* 1 vol., small post 8vo, 6s. Sequel to "My Wife and I."*

———— *Pink and White Tyranny.* Small post 8vo, 3s. 6d. ; Cheap Edition, 1s. 6d. and 2s.

———— *Queer Little People.* 1s.; cloth, 2s.

———— *Chimney Corner.* 1s. ; cloth, 1s. 6d.

———— *The Pearl of Orr's Island.* Crown 8vo, 5s.*

———— *Little Pussey Willow.* Fcap., 2s.

———— *Woman in Sacred History.* Illustrated with 15 Chromolithographs and about 200 pages of Letterpress. Demy 4to, cloth extra, gilt edges, 25s.

Street Life in London. By J. THOMSON, F.R.G.S., and ADOLPHE SMITH. One volume, 4to, containing 40 Permanent Photographs of Scenes of London Street Life, with Descriptive Letterpress, 25s.

Student's French Examiner. By F. JULIEN, Author of " Petites Leçons de Conversation et de Grammaire." Square crown 8vo, cloth extra, 2s.

Studies from Nature. 24 Photographs, with Descriptive Letterpress. By STEVEN THOMPSON. Imperial 4to, 35s.

Sub-Tropical Rambles. *See* PIKE (N).

Sullivan (A.M., M.P.). *See* " New Ireland."

Summer Holiday in Scandinavia (A). By E. L. L. ARNOLD. Crown 8vo, cloth extra, 10s. 6d.

Sumner (Hon. Charles). *See* Life and Letters.

Surgeon's Handbook on the Treatment of Wounded in War. By Dr. FRIEDRICH ESMARCH, Professor of Surgery in the University of Kiel, and Surgeon-General to the Prussian Army. Translated by H. H. CLUTTON, B.A., Cantab, F.R.C.S. Numerous Coloured Plates and Illustrations, 8vo, strongly bound in flexible leather, 1l. 8s.

TAUCHNITZ'S English Editions of German Authors. Each volume, cloth flexible, 2s. ; or sewed, 1s. 6d. (Catalogues post free on application.)

* *See also* Rose Library.

Tauchnitz (B.) German and English Dictionary. Paper, 1s. cloth, 1s. 6d. ; roan, 2s.

———— *French and English.* Paper, 1s. 6d. ; cloth, 2s ; roan, 2s. 6d.

———— *Italian and English.* Paper, 1s. 6d. ; cloth, 2s. ; roan, 2s. 6d.

———— *Spanish and English.* Paper, 1s. 6d. ; cloth, 2s. ; roan, 2s. 6d.

———— *New Testament.* Cloth, 2s. ; gilt, 2s. 6d.

The Telephone. An Account of the Phenomena of Electricity, Magnetism, and Sound, as Involved in its Action ; with Directions for Making a Speaking Telephone. By Prof. A. E. DOLBEAR, Author of "The Art of Projecting," &c. Second Edition, with an Appendix Descriptive of Prof. BELL's Present Instrument. 130 pp., with 19 Illustrations, 1s.

Tennyson's May Queen. Choicely Illustrated from designs by the Hon. Mrs. BOYLE. Crown 8vo (*See* Choice Series), 2s. 6d.

Textbook (A) of Harmony. For the Use of Schools and Students. By the late CHARLES EDWARD HORSLEY. Revised for the Press by WESTLEY RICHARDS and W. H. CALCOTT. Small post 8vo, cloth extra, 3s. 6d.

Thebes, and its Five Greater Temples. See ABNEY.

Thomson (J.) The Straits of Malacca, Indo-China, and China ; or, Ten Years' Travels, Adventures, and Residence Abroad. By J. THOMSON, F.R.G.S., Author of "Illustrations of China and its People." Upwards of 60 Woodcuts. Demy 8vo, cloth extra, 21s.

Thorne (E.) The Queen of the Colonies ; or, Queensland as I saw it. 1 vol., with Map, 6s.

Through the Dark Continent : The Sources of the Nile ; Around the Great Lakes, and down the Congo. By HENRY M. STANLEY. 2 vols., demy 8vo, containing 150 Full-page and other Illustrations, 2 Portraits of the Author, and 10 Maps, 42s. Sixth Thousand.

———— *Map to the above.* Size 34 by 56 inches, showing, on a large scale, Stanley's recent Great Discoveries in Central Africa. The First Map in which the Congo was ever correctly traced. Mounted, in case, 1l. 1s.

"One of the greatest geographical discoveries of the age."—*Spectator.*
"Mr. Stanley has penetrated the very heart of the mystery. . . . He has opened up a perfectly virgin region, never before, so far as known, visited by a white man."—*Times.*

To the Arctic Regions and Back in Six Weeks. By Captain A. W. M. CLARK KENNEDY (late of the Coldstream Guards). With Illustrations and Maps. 8vo, cloth, 15s.

Tour of the Prince of Wales in India. See RUSSELL.

Trollope (A.) Harry Heathcote of Gangoil. A Story of Bush
Life in Australia. With Graphic Illustrations. Small post, cloth, 5*s.*

Turkistan. Notes of a Journey in the Russian Provinces of
Central Asia and the Khanates of Bokhara and Kokand. By EUGENE
SCHUYLER, Secretary to the American Legation, St. Petersburg.
Numerous Illustrations. 2 vols, 8vo, cloth extra, 5th Edition, 2*l.* 2*s.*

Two Americas; being an Account of Sport and Travel, with
Notes on Men and Manners in North and South America. By Sir
ROSE PRICE, Bart. 1 vol., demy 8vo, with Illustrations, cloth
extra, 2nd Edition, 18*s.*

Two Friends. By LUCIEN BIART, Author of "Adventures of
a Young Naturalist," "My Rambles in the New World," &c. Small
post 8vo, numerous Illustrations, 7*s.* 6*d.*

Two Supercargoes (The) ; or, Adventures in Savage Africa.
By W. H. G. KINGSTON. Square imperial 16mo, cloth extra, 7*s.* 6*d.*
Numerous Full-page Illustrations.

VANDENHOFF (George, M.A.). See "Art of Reading
Aloud."

—— *Clerical Assistant.* Fcap., 3*s.* 6*d.*

—— *Ladies' Reader (The).* Fcap., 5*s.*

Verne's (Jules) Works. Translated from the French, with
from 50 to 100 Illustrations. Each cloth extra, gilt edges—

Large post 8vo, price 10*s.* 6*d. each—*

1. **Fur Country.**
2. **Twenty Thousand Leagues under the Sea.**
3. **From the Earth to the Moon, and a Trip round It.**
4. **Michael Strogoff, the Courier of the Czar.**
5. **Hector Servadac.**
6. **Dick Sands, the Boy Captain.**

Imperial 16*mo, price* 7*s.* 6*d. each—*

1. **Five Weeks in a Balloon.**
2. **Adventures of Three Englishmen and Three Russians in
   South Africa.**
3. **Around the World in Eighty Days.**
4. **A Floating City, and the Blockade Runners.**
5. **Dr. Ox's Experiment, Master Zacharius, A Drama in the
   Air, A Winter amid the Ice, &c.**
6. **The Survivors of the "Chancellor."**
7. **Dropped from the Clouds.** } The **Mysterious Island.** 3 vols.,
8. **Abandoned.**   22*s.* 6*d.* One volume, with some of the
9. **Secret of the Island.**   Illustrations, cloth, gilt edges, 10*s.* 6*d.*
10. **The Child of the Cavern.**

Verne's (Jules) Works, continued :—

The following Cheaper Editions are issued with a few of the Illustrations, in paper wrapper, price 1s. ; cloth gilt, 2s. each.

1. Adventures of Three Englishmen and Three Russians in South Africa.
2. Five Weeks in a Balloon.
3. A Floating City.
4. The Blockade Runners.
5. From the Earth to the Moon.
6. Around the Moon.
7. Twenty Thousand Leagues under the Sea. Vol. I.
8. ——— Vol. II. The two parts in one, cloth, gilt, 3s. 6d.
9. Around the World in Eighty Days.
10. Dr. Ox's Experiment, and Master Zacharius.
11. Martin Paz, the Indian Patriot.
12. A Winter amid the Ice.
13. The Fur Country. Vol. I.
14. ——— Vol. II. Both parts in one, cloth gilt, 3s. 6d.
15. Survivors of the "Chancellor." Vol. I.
16. ——— Vol. II. Both volumes in one, cloth, gilt edges, 3s. 6d.

Viardot (Louis). See "Painters of all Schools."

WALLER (Rev. C. H.) The Names on the Gates of Pearl, and other Studies. By the Rev. C. H. WALLER, M.A. Crown 8vo, cloth extra, 6s.

·——— *A Grammar and Analytical Vocabulary of the Words in* the Greek Testament. Compiled from Brüder's Concordance. For the use of Divinity Students and Greek Testament Classes. By the Rev. C. H. WALLER, M.A., late Scholar of University College, Oxford, Tutor of the London College of Divinity, St. John's Hall, Highbury. Part I., The Grammar. Small post 8vo, cloth, 2s. 6d. Part II. The Vocabulary, 2s. 6d.

——— *Adoption and the Covenant.* Some Thoughts on Confirmation. Super-royal 16mo, cloth limp, 2s. 6d.

War in Bulgaria : a Narrative of Personal Experiences. By LIEUTENANT-GENERAL VALENTINE BAKER PASHA. Together with a Description and Plan of the Works constructed by him for the Defence of Constantinople. Also Maps and Plans of Battles. 2 vols., demy 8vo, cloth extra, 2l. 2s.

Warner (C. D.) My Summer in a Garden. Rose Library, 1s.

——— *Back-log Studies.* Boards, 1s. 6d. ; cloth, 2s.

——— *In the Wilderness.* Rose Library, 1s.

——— *Mummies and Moslems.* 8vo, cloth, 12s.

Weaving. *See* " History and Principles."

Westropp (H. M.) A Manual of Precious Stones and Antique Gems. By HODDER M. WESTROPP, Author of " The Traveller's Art Companion," " Pre-Historic Phases," &c. Numerous Illustrations. Small post 8vo, cloth extra, 6s.

Whitney (Mrs. A. D. T.) The Gayworthys. Cloth, 3s. 6d.

———— *Faith Gartney.* Small post 8vo, 3s. 6d. Cheaper Editions, 1s. 6d. and 2s.

———— *Real Folks.* 12mo, crown, 3s. 6d.

———— *Hitherto.* Small post 8vo, 3s. 6d. and 2s. 6d.

———— *Sights and Insights.* 3 vols., crown 8vo, 31s. 6d.

———— *Summer in Leslie Goldthwaite's Life.* Cloth, 3s. 6d.

———— *The Other Girls.* Small post 8vo, cloth extra, 3s. 6d.

———— *We Girls.* Small post 8vo, 3s. 6d.; Cheap Edition, 1s. 6d. and 2s.

Wikoff (H.) The Four Civilizations of the World. An Historical Retrospect. Crown 8vo, cloth, 12s.

Wills, A Few Hints on Proving, without Professional Assistance. By a PROBATE COURT OFFICIAL. 5th Edition, revised with Forms of Wills, Residuary Accounts, &c. Fcap. 8vo, cloth limp, 1s.

Wilson (H. Schültz). *See* " Alpine Ascents and Adventures."

With Axe and Rifle on the Western Prairies. By W. H. G. KINGSTON. With numerous Illustrations, square crown 8vo, cloth extra, gilt, 7s. 6d.

Woolsey (C. D., LL.D.) Introduction to the Study of Inter-national Law; designed as an Aid in Teaching and in Historical Studies. Reprinted from the last American Edition, and at a much lower price. Crown 8vo, cloth extra, 8s. 6d.

Words of Wellington: Maxims and Opinions, Sentences and Reflections of the Great Duke, gathered from his Despatches, Letters, and Speeches (Bayard Series). 2s. 6d.

World of Comets. By A. GUILLEMIN, Author of " The Heavens." Translated and edited by JAMES GLAISHER, F.R.S. 1 vol., super-royal 8vo, with numerous Woodcut Illustrations, and 3 Chromo-lithographs, cloth extra, 31s. 6d.

" The mass of information collected in the volume is immense, and the treatment of the subject is so purely popular, that none need be deterred from a perusal of it."—*British Quarterly Review.*

Wreck of the Grosvenor. By W. CLARK RUSSELL. 6s. Third and Cheaper Edition.

XENOPHON'S Anabasis; or, Expedition of Cyrus. A Literal Translation, chiefly from the Text of Dindorff, by GEORGE B. WHEELER. Books I to III. Crown 8vo, boards, 2s.

—— *Books I. to VII.* Boards, 3s. 6d.

YOUNG (J. F.) Five Weeks in Greece. Crown 8vo, 10s. 6d.

London:

SAMPSON LOW, MARSTON, SEARLE, & RIVINGTON,

CROWN BUILDINGS, 188, FLEET STREET.